Praise for

HEAVY HITTER SELLING

"*Heavy Hitter Selling* isn't another sales process book. Any sales professional worth his salt has surveyed and mastered the sales process classics. *Heavy Hitter Selling* examines the more subtle but critical human factors during technology selling. *Heavy Hitter Selling* can make the most experienced sales rep more cognizant of managing the human aspects of the technology sale and expose junior reps to an experience in the human technology sales interactions that normally take a career to master. I've seen it work in action."

John Schroeder, President, Rainfinity

"Many of us believe that we are effective speakers and skilled listeners. Reading this book will cause you to challenge these beliefs and help you actually become a master communicator. *Heavy Hitter Selling* provides valuable insight into a very challenging topic and does it in a compelling way."

Edwin C. Winder, Chairman,
President, and CEO, Tradec

"This book is full of practical advice that anyone who is trying to penetrate the high-tech industry should read."

Dr. Ichak Adizes, Founder and CEO, Adizes Institute
Author of Corporate Lifecycles: How and Why
Corporations Grow and Die and What to Do about It

"I really enjoyed reading the book! An unusual way of looking at sales through perfecting the communications process. I agree, relationships and rapport lead to revenue."

Dr. Shuki Bruck, Gordon Moore Professor of Computation
and Neural Systems and Electrical Engineering,
California Institute of Technology

"*Heavy Hitter Selling* goes beyond the standard selling methodologies and instead focuses on those intangibles that separate the outstanding salesperson from the mediocre. In an ever-increasing economy of 'tough sells,' this book can make the difference to a struggling salesperson."

Rich Williamson, Vice President, Red Hat, Inc.

"Sales is a competitive world and there can be only one winner. This book gives the reader an unfair advantage!"

Jon Hanson, Vice President, Sales, Apriso

"Companies, like the individuals that represent them, speak a distinct language, have unique personalities, and look to serve different motivations. As such, the principles delivered in *Heavy Hitter Selling* are just as applicable to the successful creation of strategic alliances as they are to closing sales with customers."

Chris Rose, Vice President, Business Development, Upshot

"Having trained with Dr. Erickson and after reading this book, I am convinced that Dr. Erickson would have been proud."

Dr. Constantine Callas, Founder and Chairman, Medata

"I have experienced firsthand Steve Martin's success as a sales leader. It is rare to see someone translate his accomplishments into a well-written book with clear principles and a methodology that others can easily understand. It is a book you prefer your competitors not to have."

Ofir Kedar, Founder and Past CEO, SQRIBE Technologies, Former Chairman, Brio Software

HEAVY HITTER SELLING

How Successful High-Technology Salespeople Use Language and Intuition to Persuade Customers to Buy

Steve W. Martin

SAND HILL PUBLISHING

RANCHO SANTA MARGARITA, CALIFORNIA

P. O. Box 80190
Rancho Santa Margarita, CA 92688
(949) 635-0153
E-mail: info@heavyhitterselling.com
Web site: heavyhitterselling.com

Individual Sales. This book can be ordered directly from Sand Hill Publishing
at the address above or from heavyhitterselling.com.

Quantity Sales. Special discounts are available on quantity purchases by corporations,
associations, and others. For details, contact the Special Sales Department at
sales@heavyhitterselling.com.

Printed in the United States of America

ISBN 0-9721822-0-9

Cover Design: Catherine L. Hunt
Interior Design & Production: Beverly Butterfield, Girl of the West Productions
Editorial Services: PeopleSpeak
Indexing: Rachel Rice

07 06 05 04 03 02   10 9 8 7 6 5 4 3 2 1

To Mary, my beloved wife and best friend.

To my three wonderful children—

Brooke, Michael, and Emily—

this is what Dad does for a living.

Acknowledgments

EVEN GIVEN today's challenging times, I consider myself very fortunate to have been involved in high technology for the past twenty years. I don't believe there is another industry that is composed of people who are as talented, intelligent, and enterprising. I would like to thank all my friends and colleagues that I have worked with over the years, as well as another very important group of people, the thousands of customers who have taught me so much about human nature.

This book would not have been possible had it not been for some exceptional people. Thanks to all the salespeople whom I have had the privilege to lead and learn from. You're the best. A special thanks to Ted "Moon" Mullen, Peter Riccio, and Teresa Fitzgerald, who provided constant encouragement during the nearly two years it took to complete this project. Many thanks to Sharon Goldinger for her extraordinary help. A belated thank-you to Dr. Callas, whose genius is only matched by his generosity. Finally, thank you to my wife, Mary, for always encouraging me to pursue my dreams.

> I do not mean that I am already as God wants me to be.
> I have not yet reached that goal. But I continue trying to
> reach it and to make it mine . . . But there is one thing
> I always do. I forget the things that are past. I try as hard as
> I can to reach the goal that is before me.
> —PHILIPPIANS 3:12–13

Contents

Introduction   ix

1   The Heavy Hitter   1

2   How People Communicate   15

3   How People Are "Wired"   45

4   How People Think   79

5   Finding the Truth   101

6   Choosing Your Battles   137

7   Building Customer Rapport   163

8   The Complete Hitter   187

9   Finding Your Coach   215

10   The Deeper Meaning of Language   259

11   Intuitive Persuasion   279

Epilogue   297

Notes   301

Bibliography   303

Glossary   305

Index   311

About the Author   321

Introduction

Words, of course, are the most powerful drug
known to mankind.

—RUDYARD KIPLING

UNKNOWINGLY, I BEGAN writing this book while I was preparing
for an upcoming board meeting. Our company would soon be
launching a new product targeted at an entirely different technology
market. I began analyzing our existing sales methodology and identifying all the changes we would need to make across every aspect of
the sales department. We would have to change how we prospected
to generate leads, how the sales teams presented our solution, and the
processes surrounding the evaluation of our product. We would need
to train our salespeople to sell to an entirely different target audience.
I was trying to answer the fundamental question I was sure to be
asked by the president, board of directors, and outside investors,
"How are we going to sell our new product?"

If you ask a salesperson in a company, "How do you sell your
product?" you will most likely get a less-than-accurate answer, if any
answer at all. The salesperson may recite an oversimplification of the
sales process, such as "We get a lead. We meet with the members of
the potential customer's team to determine if our product fits. They
evaluate our product, and if they like it, they buy it."

By providing this superficial answer, the salesperson is not trying
to be evasive or condescending. Rather, to try to explain all the com-
plexities and the intricacies of the sales process would be an exhaust-
ing, time-consuming project. Frankly, they may not even know the

real answer because most successful salespeople are simply doing what comes naturally.

However, not all high-technology salespeople are successful. Given the same sales tools, level of education, and propensity to work, why do some salespeople succeed where others fail? Is one better suited to sell the product because of his or her technical background? Is one more charming or luckier? Or is one able to utilize past sales cycle experiences and adapt them to the current sales environment?

In addition, the world of the high-technology salesperson has changed dramatically in the past two years. Long gone are the days of "order taking" or closing deals without much effort in a superheated business market. Following a decade of unprecedented technology expenditures by corporations migrating to open systems, implementing client-server applications, building Web sites, and ensuring that the transition to the year 2000 went smoothly, capital spending is at a fraction of its previous level.

This situation has only been compounded by a downturn in the overall economy and the terrorist attacks. With so little money available, information technology projects must be continually justified and are constantly being reprioritized. These issues are reflected in the protracted length of today's selection process and the intense scrutiny vendors face daily. Unfortunately, most salespeople have sold only during prosperous times and lack the skills necessary to sell in tough times such as these.

Throughout this book, we'll examine what successful high-technology salespeople do and explain their unique ability to acquire information about a customer and discern a deeper level of meaning from what the customer has said. They possess an insight that enables them to develop the optimum account strategy by comparing what they've learned from previous wins and losses with the current situation.

Four major attributes separate successful salespeople from unsuccessful ones. Successful salespeople

- Are skillful builders of personal relationships. At the foundation of all sales is a relationship between people. Great salespeople have an innate talent to build these relationships by creating rapport. Their presence has an appeal that makes a customer feel at ease. The customer enjoys their company. They build personal alliances based upon understanding individual wants and needs. The customer trusts them.

- Are masters of language. They are accomplished communicators who know what to say and, equally important, how to say it. Through their mastery of language, they are able to convey and decipher deep underlying messages that less successful salespeople miss. While using the same language as most salespeople, they have developed an uncanny ability to persuade nonbelievers.

- Are sales cycle experts. The sales cycle is the formalized information exchange between a customer and a salesperson. It consists of a series of steps that are designed to gather information about the customer and present information about the salesperson's solution. While a company has identified these steps for the sales force, successful salespeople enhance this process by drawing upon past sales experiences. They use this reservoir of experience to manage and control their deals. As a result, they close more business.

- Have highly developed intuition. Successful salespeople are continually cataloguing their successes and failures. They store patterns of individual and company behavior and link them to the sales process. From this base of intuitive knowledge they are able to create and execute account strategies. They also use a unique form of highly developed intuition to ensure their message is acted upon by the customer. Through their intuition, they are able to integrate their spoken words with the sales situation based upon their experiences with different types of people and past sales cycles.

HEAVY HITTERS

A successful salesperson is commonly referred to as a "Heavy Hitter." Heavy Hitters have an extraordinarily developed intuition, or deeper level of understanding, about the deals they will close. This understanding is somewhat equivalent to the ability to predict the future or analogous to reading minds. Heavy Hitters have a "feel" for their deals. They can "see" which deals will close this quarter and they can accurately forecast future deals. They not only listen to a customer but also speak the customer's language. This book is about understanding and modeling the Heavy Hitter's behavior. Based upon my personal experience teaching these concepts to salespeople, I believe that almost all salespeople can become Heavy Hitters if they study the concepts presented in this book and put them to use.

From this point on, I will refer to a successful salesperson as a "Heavy Hitter." And, for the sake of simplicity, I will alternate the pronouns "he" and "she" from chapter to chapter.

The goal of this book is to help you learn how to apply the principles of intangible human behavior to the high-technology sales cycle. The behavior is considered intangible because it can't be seen. However, to Heavy Hitters it is quite real. The principles are presented through practical models that can be implemented by anyone. However, you must be willing to take the time to understand and apply the concepts of *Heavy Hitter Selling*.

Chapter 1 outlines what Heavy Hitters are and how to achieve their level of success. Starting in chapter 2, we will examine the layers of communication that occur in every conversation between Heavy Hitters and their customers. We will also reveal the structure of dialogue exchanges between a Heavy Hitter and a customer.

When I use the term "customer" throughout the book, I specifically mean someone a Heavy Hitter is trying to sell something to. This includes suspects who have yet to be introduced to the Hitter's solution, prospects in the process of evaluation, as well as existing customers who may buy again.

In chapter 3, we will introduce the fundamentals of neurolinguistics, and we will build upon that foundation to examine how the brain and the entire body work in conjunction with language. This is how people are "wired" to communicate. The brain's organization and its impact on the communication process is described in chapter 4. How language, brain, and body work in combination will be further scrutinized in chapter 5. We'll analyze the sales cycle in chapter 6 to examine how Heavy Hitters choose their battles, or select the deals they will work. In chapter 7, we will study the different processes Heavy Hitters use to create rapport with their customers. How Heavy Hitters interact with one of their most important customers, their sales manager, will be the focus of chapter 8. We will also review what motivates Heavy Hitters to achieve. In chapter 9, we will explain how Heavy Hitters find a coach and build a deep relationship with him or her. Chapter 10 reveals an additional dimension of meaning and structure within language that can be used to change skeptics into believers. Finally, in chapter 11, we will detail the Heavy Hitters' unique intuitive skills of persuasion.

SOME PERSONAL HISTORY

At this point, you might be curious about my background and what areas of knowledge have been combined to create *Heavy Hitter Selling*. From working with computers when I was a teenager, I became acutely aware of the preciseness of language and the importance of modeling. In my early twenties I was introduced to the concepts of neurolinguistics, the study of how the brain uses and interprets language. Since then, I have spent nearly twenty years in high-technology sales.

During my career, while serving in positions ranging from salesperson to vice president, I calculate that I have been directly responsible for over a quarter of a billion dollars in sales. Of equal importance to my practical experience are my natural curiosity about and fascination with people. I enjoy understanding what makes them "tick." While I am not a doctor of psychological behavior, I feel I am an expert on individual behavior during the sales cycle.

I was introduced to computer systems in the late '70s. At that time, a high-quality personal computer cost about $10,000 ($25,000 in today's dollars), and the Control Program/Microprocessors, or CP/M, operating system was just as well known as the operating system from a small company called Microsoft. Regardless of the operating system, the screen was black with a green or yellow command line.

While I was attending school, I worked part-time in the stockroom for a medical billing review company. The stockroom was adjacent to the computer room. The computer room was a white, glass-enclosed room with raised floors. Inside were several rows of large computers with banks of 400-megabyte disk drives that both looked and shook like washing machines. Everything about this room captivated me: the sterile white environment, the frigid air-conditioned atmosphere, the rows of blinking machines, and the rhythmic beat of the printers. Even though it had a secure entry and access was limited to a handful of people, I tried to spend as much time as possible there. To accomplish this, I became friends with several of the programmers and system operators.

In addition, I would sneak into the separate research and development lab late at night when I knew one of my programmer pals would be there. The lab had several cutting-edge computers of the time. However, it was the private domain of the company's founder. After he caught me there late one night, instead of being fired, I was transferred into the computer department as a system operator. For the next four years, I literally spent every hour when I was not in school in that building, learning what I could about computers.

I became knowledgeable about the fundamentals of how computers work. I learned the importance of the structure of language and how to build a "model." Models are the descriptions and representations of how a system works. Understand a model and you can recreate a system. Models enable repeatable, predictable experiences.

Computers also taught me about the preciseness of language. After becoming versed in the workings of operating systems, I began programming. I wrote and sold several programs that enabled me to have the luxury of owning a computer (I actually bought three). Programming requires great discipline, and I began to realize the importance of maintaining logic along with the construction of words. Order is just as critical as precision. Because a program has layers of complexity, I also began to recognize the interrelation among two or three separate concurrent streams of logic. In other words, I began to train myself to maintain multiple states of thought at the same time.

When I transitioned into sales, I quickly realized that the language my customers used was directly related to their behavior. I could build models to create successful relationships based upon customers' language, personalities, and thought processes. In addition, I was able to track and catalogue the different types of verbal and nonverbal communication my customers used. Without any prior sales experience, I became the top salesperson at my software company for the following four years. I went on to be a perennial top sales producer at a billion-dollar software company before being promoted into management to imprint my "selling model" on other salespeople within the organization.

USING THIS BOOK

While this book is primarily targeted at people involved in sales, the concepts and fundamentals are applicable to anyone who works directly with customers. This includes presales engineers, inside salespeople, sales managers, and consultants, as well as those in business development and technical support. In addition, it is suggested reading for people in marketing and product management and for management teams of high-technology organizations. All of these people need to understand their customers' language. This book is also for any person who wants to understand the art of sales.

This book is a textbook as well as a reference book. I encourage you to write in it while you are reading. Have a pencil handy to make notations. Underline key concepts and important terms to help you remember their significance. This book is intended to be a continual resource. Throughout this book, real-world case studies are presented to illustrate the practical application of these concepts. These examples, known as "cultural transmissions," are true and based on my personal experience. A cultural transmission is the method of learning a behavioral technique by emulating a successful practitioner.

In addition to the concepts of neurolinguistics, I will also use various established psychological theories to explain the behavior of the Heavy Hitter and the customer, theories that I have adopted and use as a framework to explain the specific behavior I have observed.

While I was serving as vice president of sales, the chairman of my company once told me, "I don't understand what you do. To me sales seems like magic." This was understandable given his highly technical, nonsales background. Take your time reading this book, complete all the exercises honestly, and you will find it is great fun and very rewarding to be able to create your own "magic."

1

The Heavy Hitter

After hundreds of hours of intensive research and a rigorous product evaluation, the day had arrived for the customer to publicly announce which product the company would purchase. The customer opened the meeting in a solemn voice, causing the salesperson's heart to skip a beat. "Well, I guess you know why we asked you to come in today," she said. Then her expression suddenly changed to a happy grin. "We have submitted our recommendation to management to purchase your product!" The salesperson exhaled a sigh of relief and laughter filled the room. In the festive atmosphere that followed, congratulations and many thanks were exchanged between these new friends.

Established sales training methodologies, such as Target Account Selling, Strategic Selling, and Consultative Selling, have merit and are well worth studying. However, they are mainly focused on the logical steps of guiding the sales cycle process, such as prospecting, qualification, and closing techniques, with limited attention given to the less-perceptible aspects of the sales process. None of these methodologies explain how to create what is truly at the heart of all sales: how to build relationships between people, how salespeople develop intuition to ensure they are executing the best account strategy, and how to say the "right" words at the "right" time to persuade customers to buy.

Each of these programs assumes salespeople are already capable of building rapport and have an aptitude for establishing trust, that salespeople possess highly developed communication techniques, are proficient in determining what information is important, and can discern when someone is misleading them.

These methodologies do not explain or fully take into account the human characteristics of the people who actually make the purchase decision. They concentrate on the logical and procedural aspects of the sales cycle. In short, they offer frameworks that are limited to the "tangible" processes of the sales cycle. These may include the basic questions a salesperson commits to rote memory, such as, "What is your budget?" and "What is your time frame?" Or the programs may emphasize the financial justification of a salesperson's solution. They explain how to create a return-on-investment (ROI) model in order to show customers how much money they will save by selecting a product.

However, there is an entirely intangible human side to the sales process. And, it is the mastery of the intangible, intuitive human element of the sales process that separates Heavy Hitters from other salespeople.

The art of mastering the intangible side of the sales process can be found in the field of neurolinguistics, the study of how the human brain uses and interprets language. I first began studying this field when I was working at the medical billing company. Dr. Constantine Callas, the owner, introduced me to the works of Dr. Milton Erickson. A leading originator and practitioner of psychiatric hypnosis, Dr. Erickson had an uncanny ability to help people with severe medical problems. Both psychiatrists and neurolinguists have studied his language strategies for changing patient behavior. Dr. Callas had trained under Dr. Erickson and had successfully utilized Dr. Erickson's techniques in his own practice. Learning the Ericksonian approach to neurolinguistics dramatically changed my life.

I have been practicing neurolinguistics for over twenty years. During this time, I have extended the concepts Dr. Erickson used, as well as created many entirely new paradigms. Most importantly, I have specifically applied all of these concepts and paradigms to the high-technology sales process.

Before he died in 1980, Dr. Erickson published hundreds of professional articles. Within the medical community, he was both respected and considered controversial. His works and teachings have been painstakingly analyzed, documented, and recorded. He wanted the world to understand the formal methodologies he used to communicate with his patients. These methodologies are also directly applicable to communicating with potential customers. The following passage by Dr. Erickson is from *Advanced Techniques of Hypnosis and Therapy: Selected Papers of Milton H. Erickson, M.D.*[1]

> I had a polio attack when I was seventeen years old and I lay in bed without a sense of body awareness. I couldn't even tell the position of my arms or legs in bed. So I spent hours trying to locate my hand or foot or toes by a sense of feeling, and I became acutely aware of what movements were.
>
> People use little telltale movements, those adjustive movements that are so revealing if one can notice them. So much communication is in our bodily movements, not in our speech. So much is communicated by the way a person speaks. My tone deafness has forced me to pay attention to inflections in the voice. This means I'm less distracted by the content of what people say. Many patterns of behavior are reflected in the way a person says something rather than in what he says.

Most people recognize someone's spoken words as the most significant element of communication. However, the language a person uses is composed of both verbal and nonverbal communication. Through the use of this "whole" language, we express our needs, wants, desires, and experiences to the outside world. The verbal and nonverbal language you use is a complete representation of your personality and yourself.

As I began to read more about Dr. Erickson's work, I gained an entirely new understanding of how language is directly related to predicting human behavior. I observed that if you understood how a person used language, you could build a model of expected behavior.

I also became acutely interested in hypnosis. Normally, you communicate with people's conscious minds. You rely on their conscious minds to forward your message to their subconscious minds. The subconscious mind is where information is validated and decisions are ultimately made. Hypnosis enables a person to bypass this forwarding process and communicate directly with the subconscious mind.

HYPNOSIS

People have different perceptions about hypnosis. Some think of a swinging pocket watch and a soft voice repeating, "You are getting sleepy." Others think of a stage hypnotist making unsuspecting subjects perform embarrassing acts for laughs. Every day, newspaper advertisements stress the benefits of using hypnosis to help provide the will power to lose weight or stop smoking. Meanwhile, some people strongly believe that hypnosis does not exist. To some extent, each of these observations is correct.

In fact, each and every communication between people has hypnotic qualities, but in varying degrees. Some conversations have a lot of hypnotic qualities and others almost none. Therefore, if you are staring intensely at an object while being told you are getting tired, you will probably accept the suggestion since your eyes will become fatigued. This communication interaction has multiple dimensions—the physical aspect of your eyes getting tired coupled with the verbal suggestion being given. Conversely, if you are having a brief conversation with a colleague at the copy machine, the discussion is more likely to be more superficial (or one-dimensional) and lack hypnotic qualities.

Hypnosis is about influencing another person's behavior with suggestions that correspond to their values and beliefs; it is not about making someone fall asleep or dance the "funky chicken" on a stage in front of strangers. Dr. Erickson also thought of it as "Intellectual learning by the unconscious."[2] In reality, Heavy Hitters are hypnotists who use hypnosis all the time, in every conversation. Therefore, one could argue it is just a normal part of their conversation and doesn't really exist. It's merely an additional dimension of language.

Heavy Hitters hypnotize their customers with a fantasy. The fantasy is that their product will make customers' lives easier and less expensive or enable the customers to make more money. Although Heavy Hitters are competing against similar fantasies being told by competitors, their message reigns supreme, and their product is accepted by their customers as being superior.

Heavy Hitters want to influence potential customers to buy their solution. They accomplish this through their natural ability to communicate with customers and make them feel at ease. By analyzing and modeling their communication strategy and tactics, we can learn how they persuade customers to buy. However, this requires understanding how each individual uses his or her own unique language to communicate.

Intuitively, Heavy Hitters have learned the fundamentals of neurolinguistics, and they apply the concepts naturally and automatically. Somehow, they know that if they speak in a certain way, in a particular style, a customer will respond positively. They also recognize that the style they use changes from customer to customer naturally. This skill set can be learned by thoroughly understanding the mechanics of how people use language to think and how the brain works in conjunction with the entire body to communicate.

A BREED APART

Salespeople are a different breed of people in society. Stereotypes about their gregariousness, tenacious drive, and money-based motivation show how the rest of the world (including their own companies) view them. While Heavy Hitters may share these characteristics, they have additional superior qualities that separate them from their peers. Clearly, they understand that one of their key responsibilities is building and managing relationships.

They have to manage a tremendous number of relationships externally with customers and partners and internally within their companies. To accomplish this, they have developed an extraordinary ability to communicate and influence people while making them feel safe and comfortable.

Building relationships requires rapport. Building rapport requires the complex process of human communication, so we will examine the different layers of communication that occur in every conversation between Heavy Hitters and customers.

Members of another exotic profession share some of the same qualities as salespeople—professional poker players. Like sales, their profession is about strategy, knowing human nature, and winning. Poker players have acquired an uncanny ability to read their opponents' unintentional mannerisms and predict the cards they are holding. Meanwhile, professional poker players are masters of their own emotions who are as comfortable matching the pot on a bluff as they are when they hold four aces.

Poker players know that any novice can have a lucky streak. However, it's the serious players who make money in the long run. They study the game and constantly seek to improve their skills. Seasoned gamblers have encountered every card combination. They always remember which cards have been dealt and measure their bets carefully in accordance with their odds of winning. They select their strategy based upon the latest information; in this case, it is the last card dealt facing up.

THE IMPORTANCE OF RAPPORT

Heavy Hitters know that the value of information depends upon its accuracy, timeliness, and confidentiality. So, how do they get privileged intelligence about the deal they're working on? By building a deep relationship with someone within the customer's organization. This is one of the fundamental premises of the high-technology sales cycle. For many years, the term "coach" has been used by all types of salespeople, selling every conceivable product, to define the person who provides this data.

Literally, all high-tech sales involve being "coached" through the evaluation process. Why would someone coach one salesperson versus another? To establish a relationship with a coach, Heavy Hitters build different types of rapport with a customer. At the foundation is a special relationship, a personal rapport between two individuals. Although powerful, this personal rapport is meaningless unless technical rapport is present. Technical rapport is achieved when a product's features satisfy the customer's requirements. Finally, there must be a business rapport between the two companies to consummate the deal.

Heavy Hitters' secret to survival is being able to qualify an opportunity. Every company has competitors. Today's enemy may seem to be the company that is twice your size and invading your market space. It could also be the little company with an exciting new product. But the real enemy is time.

Heavy Hitters manage their time by qualifying people. They are trying to find one fundamental truth, "Will I win the deal?" They will use their intuition to validate every piece of information in order to find the answer to this question as soon as possible. Most importantly, once they determine they can win a deal, they are able to persuade the customer to choose their product. Persuasion is a key distinguisher between Heavy Hitters and other salespeople.

Qualifying a deal is a complex process. The qualification occurs most simply at the technical level. Does the product fit the customer's technical environment? Does it solve the customer's technical problem? This type of qualification is a fairly straightforward process. However, qualifying the business and political environments requires intuition.

Heavy Hitters have developed an intense intuition. They uncover important information by analyzing their prospect's words, actions, and behavior. They know when they are being told the truth. Anyone can acquire this skill by understanding how language, the brain, and the body work in combination. Interestingly, they don't always say the same thing. Being able to decipher truthful communication is critical to Heavy Hitters' success. Just as poker players know when an opponent is bluffing, Heavy Hitters have the ability to "read" each of the individuals involved in a deal.

Heavy Hitters intimately understand that selling is a process as well as a specific result. The sales process starts with the creation of a relationship between people who understand each other's needs. Heavy Hitters are always trying to determine what a customer wants and to create an environment that encourages the customer to be receptive to their message. They will decide where they should spend their time and where they shouldn't waste resources.

During the early '90s, the term "win-win relationship" was being used everywhere to explain how to successfully negotiate your position while still enabling the other party to achieve its goal. However, the concept of win-win relationships does not go far enough in characterizing human relationships. Relationships are created when people share the same activities or when they are motivated to achieve the same goals. Goals can be defined into very personal prioritized desires, called "benefactions," where a personal benefit is gained from taking an action. Heavy Hitters strive to understand the benefactions of each member of the selection team, the people who will decide whether or not to buy the Hitter's product.

At the foundation of Heavy Hitters' success are credibility and integrity. Heavy Hitters know their environment will influence their behavior and their behavior will influence the environment. A president of a company once rationalized, "If the truth is better served by a lie, then it's okay to lie." This attitude is wrong. When fundamental benefactions do not match or when one party takes advantage of another, buyer's remorse and resentment will break up the current relationship and ruin all potential future partnerships. Heavy Hitters exhibit a morally sound code of conduct in all their dealings with customers.

Heavy Hitters know they probably will be selling products for several different companies during the next ten years. They understand that technical innovation is moving at an unimaginable, accelerated rate. This, in turn, is compressing the life cycles of companies and their products, which succeed or fail in a shortened time frame. Heavy Hitters can return to a company they have previously sold to and be perceived as credible. With that being said, the key asset Heavy Hitters bring to their next job is not the contacts in their PalmPilots or laptops. The main reason for hiring an established Heavy Hitter is that he or she has demonstrated success at building and managing relationships, and this process can be repeated infinitely, resulting in consistent sales performance.

HIGH-TECHNOLOGY SALES

The primary goal of a sales organization is to deliver revenue to the company by winning business. This goal is accomplished mainly by adding new customers or by creating new opportunities with existing customers. In every company, each department has its own customers.

For example, marketing defines a product for engineering, engineering builds a product for sales, and accounting provides the funds for marketing. With the exception of the sales department and support-related functions, each department's customers are mainly internal to the company, both physically and culturally. The sales department is unique. Its focus is on external customers, geographic and cultural outsiders to the organization. Just as gamblers traveling from town to town must be aware of the local laws and customs, salespeople who journey from customer to customer must adapt their behavior to each customer's particular environment.

The nature of high-technology sales is that the deals are large, the decision process is complex, and great personal rewards are possible for individuals who can close deals. But what exactly is a "high-technology" sale? It has three major characteristics. Obviously, the first characteristic is that the product is based on technology. If you are involved in the computer hardware, software, Internet, medical equipment, or telecommunications industries, you are selling a high-tech product.

Today, almost every salesperson is selling a high-technology product. Cars have global positioning systems, boats are completely computerized, and airplanes always utilize leading-edge technology. If you are selling any product with complicated electronics or sophisticated machinery, you are involved in high-technology sales. This includes anything from drilling equipment to a telephone system.

The second characteristic is the complex nature of the sales cycle. It is a process that involves multiple people, or multiple groups of people, who in varying degrees make the purchase decision. The decision is made over a period of time that is typically measured in weeks or months.

Finally, the size of the deals is large. A deal can be either one large single purchase or a steady stream of future revenue. These sales may involve material items such as computers and equipment or the creation of new ideas, license agreements, and partnerships.

The concepts and principles of this book apply to a wide range of sales segments that share these characteristics. They also apply to any product that is typically evaluated and purchased by a committee. This may vary from the purchase of a building or selection of an advertising firm to the acquisition of a company. However, all the nomenclature and examples in this book are based upon my personal experience, which happens to be in the computer industry.

The high-technology sales organization is typically a mentor-based environment. Inexperienced salespeople don't know what they haven't seen for themselves. Usually, it's through the "school of hard knocks" that they gain their experience. Unfortunately, this takes time. By emulating how Heavy Hitters view the sales cycle, this time frame can be shortened, and the predictability of results can be improved.

In a typical sales organization, role modeling occurs very informally and irregularly. However, through nonstructured interactions, salespeople learn tactics to help close deals. All organizations include both good and bad salespeople. Obviously, we want to model the successful ones. We want to understand how they have mastered rapport, language, and the sales cycle and developed their intuition. Equally important, we want to understand what doesn't work and shouldn't be modeled.

Professional baseball players who continually make mistakes are demoted to teams in the minor leagues. These obscure teams play in small towns across America. In the slang of baseball, the players are called "bush leaguers." High-tech sales also has its share of bush leaguers, who make the following common mistakes:

1. They talk too much on a sales call and don't listen to the customer enough.

2. They present the same pitch in the same way to every customer.

3. They don't know their customer or product well enough to drive account strategy.

4. They assume information they don't know, thereby taking the wrong action.

5. They fidget with many accounts and don't focus on the winnable ones.

6. They don't put themselves in the position of being their own customer.

7. They don't take the time to continuously analyze their performance.

8. They don't understand how to martial their resources or use their manager.

9. They set unrealistic customer expectations or make commitments that their product or company can't fulfill.

10. They expect to win the deal without a coach or think they have a coach when they don't.

Most importantly, bush leaguers don't consistently close business. Compared to Hitters, their wins take longer, require more resources, and are less predictable. Bush leaguers need to model Heavy Hitters most of all.

If this is a weekday and you happen to be reading this book on an airplane, chances are the majority of the passengers on your flight are salespeople on their way to customer meetings. You have to wonder how many will be successful and how many of these trips are unnecessary. Travel is one of the largest sales-related expenses in any high-technology company. Inexperienced salespeople are infamous for "chasing bad deals," or pursuing business they can't win. The opportunity expense of doing this is just as big. Spending time on deals you can't win means you are not spending time on deals you can.

Just as Heavy Hitters will only spend their time on winnable deals, they will only be part of a winnable sales environment. They know that their manager plays a key role in their success. The manager is responsible for the infrastructure that supports their efforts. Heavy Hitters also manage their managers. In other words, they understand their manager's style and act accordingly.

The concept of the sales force has changed dramatically during the past decade. The days of command-and-control military-style sales organizations are over. Heavy Hitters want to be part of an interactive sales democracy. They want their opinions heard and their recommendations acted upon. Most of all, they want to make an impact.

CONCLUSION

Heavy Hitters understand how to build personal relationships and have mastered the art of communication and persuasion. They have accumulated a reservoir of experience working with customers during the sales process and possess a highly developed intuition that drives their choice of strategy and persuades a customer to buy.

If you are in sales, you make your living by talking. If you were a pilot, you would attend years of flight training school and many hours of simulator training before you were allowed in the cockpit of a jumbo jet. If you were a lawyer, you would intensely study law for several years and have to pass your state's bar exam to ensure your proficiency. If you are in sales, you need to understand the use and interpretation of language. You need to understand the process of communication and how it determines the level of rapport that is established between people. You must be able to adapt your use of language to a customer's thought process and personality. Language can be directly linked to a person's behavior. It can be deciphered to predict future behavior and truthfulness or used proactively to influence a person's thinking or opinions.

Different assumptions can be made about why you are reading this book. You may be relatively new to sales and want to improve your base level of knowledge. You may already be an experienced salesperson seeking to expand your sales skills with additional techniques. Or you may work completely outside of sales and desire to discover what the field is all about. Regardless of your motivation, you can summarize almost everything regarding sales in a single sentence: Sales is all about speaking the language of the customer.

2

How People Communicate

After some initial introductions, the sales presentation was about
to start. The sales rep was visibly nervous and with good reason.
He was speaking to the biggest potential customer in his company's history, seeking the opportunity to install his software on
325 different servers. He presented the company's background
and product suite as he had done many times before.

Bart, the manager in charge of all of the servers and the key
decision maker for this project, sat with his arms and legs crossed
and leaned back in his chair. He seemed disinterested. The atmosphere was tense and no questions were asked. Following the sales
rep's presentation, the system engineer began an interactive
demonstration of the product. Bart moved his left hand and held
it by his ear. The system engineer continued the presentation. A
few minutes later, Bart put his left hand on his chin and leaned
forward slightly. Soon, he put both arms on the table and was
finally engaged in the demonstration.

Asales call is a scheduled communication event. However, each
party participating in this event has different goals. Heavy Hitters' main goal is to gain continued access to the prospect. They will
accomplish this by explaining their product's features and the merits
of their company and demonstrating the quality of its people as represented by the sales team on the call. If the team members' performance meets with the customer's approval, they will be given the

chance to have additional meetings or granted the privilege of study-ing the customer's operation. They may be given the opportunity to install an evaluation copy of their product. If each step is successful, the customer may grant them the highest level of continued access, making a sale. A Heavy Hitter is a suitor, trying to court a customer into forming a long-term relationship, akin to a marriage.

The customer has a different set of goals. Relationships are expensive and involve investments of valuable time. Customers have to spend time to determine whether a product's characteristics are as they have been represented. They have to spend time evaluating other suitors to determine whether they are picking the best possible part-ner to solve their company's business problem. They will have to spend time learning to use the new products they select, implementing them, and most likely, debugging or fixing product problems.

These relationships also cost money. The customers will have to acquire the technology and pay ongoing maintenance fees to keep the technology current. They may have to pay for professional ser-vices or hire additional staff to help implement a solution. And they may need to buy additional technology in order to make the solu-tion work.

Heavy Hitters create relationships between companies based upon the process of communication between people. This process is very complex. However, since we are communicating all the time, we may underestimate the complexity of communication and take the process for granted. We tend to ignore the subtleties and, for the most part, become preoccupied with our side of a conversation. To com-prehend the complexity of the entire process, it is helpful to exam-ine a much simpler model of communication. By comparing how computers speak to one another with how people communicate with each other, we can begin to understand the multiple dimensions of information that are constantly being transmitted.

Computers connect to one another via established standards. Standards are required because the various computer manufacturers use a diverse set of operating systems (DOS, Unix, NT, and so on). This standard is called the seven-layer Open Systems Interconnection model (OSI model). Within the model, layers of functionality are needed to have one computer "talk" with another. At the bottom layer (layer 1) is the physical cable that connects the two machines. This is the least complex layer. The top layer (layer 7) is the application layer. You can think of this as the invisible protocol used by an application to identify itself, and it is far more technically complex than the cable at the bottom layer.

Below is a diagram of the seven-layer model with each of the layers identified. It really isn't important to understand the function of each layer. Rather, what is important to know is that once these layers are in place, information can be sent from one machine, and the exact information will be received and deciphered by another machine. In addition, it is important to recognize that the layers are built on top of each other, like the floors of a building.

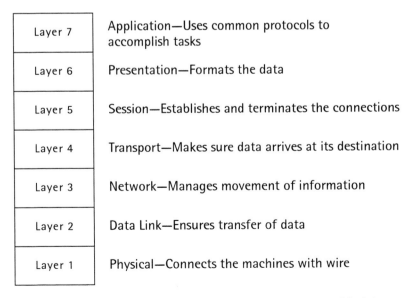

Layer 7	Application—Uses common protocols to accomplish tasks
Layer 6	Presentation—Formats the data
Layer 5	Session—Establishes and terminates the connections
Layer 4	Transport—Makes sure data arrives at its destination
Layer 3	Network—Manages movement of information
Layer 2	Data Link—Ensures transfer of data
Layer 1	Physical—Connects the machines with wire

Figure 2.1 The Seven-Layer Computer Communication Model

The human communication process is much more complex and much more efficient. Unlike computers, we are able to bypass layers of communication. We can abbreviate thoughts while still preserving the original message. Humans also have the flexibility to send the same message structure with distinctly different meanings. Take the following example:

- Mary, could you please send the report.

- Mary, could you *please* send the report.

- MARY, COULD YOU PLEASE SEND THE REPORT.

All these sentences use the same words but result in very different interpretations. When Mary reads the first sentence, she will feel a low sense of urgency and receive no indication of any unhappiness that the report has not been sent. The other sentences imply a different sense of urgency and even discontent that the report hasn't been sent.

People, like computers, also have layers of communication. However, these layers are much more flexible and can be combined in many different ways. Layers can be entirely eliminated or they can be fused together to form entirely new meanings. The layers of the human communication model are shown below.

Unlike the layers in the computer model, which are structured like a building with multiple floors, the human communication model layers are more like piano keys. All the keys may be pressed at one time or only certain keys may be pressed. Different sounds, or meanings, are created by pressing particular keys together in patterns or repetitions. Piano keys may be depressed forcefully or softly, just as communication may be explicit or subtle. The combination of keys may result in a soothing melody or just noise. In order to understand their role in the communication process, let's examine these layers in more detail.

Phonetic	The enunciation of the words you are speaking
Content	The actual words spoken
Purpose	The reason or point you are communicating
Representational System	The system used to interpret and present those words
Internal Dialogue	The never-ending dialogue inside your mind
Physical	The impact the words you are receiving or sending have on your body

Figure 2.2 The Human Communication Model

PHONETIC LAYER

The phonetic layer is the enunciation of the actual words we have strung together in the form of a sentence. This layer can alter the meaning of the sentence to convey a completely new and/or sometimes opposite meaning. For example, let's say I tell my wife, "Your hair looks great," but my voice trails off at the end of the sentence. She would immediately be concerned that her hair does not look good. This incongruence would then cause her to ask what I actually meant. Incongruence can be thought of as "truth in communication." If I say to her, "Your hair looks great!" and emphasize the word "great," my sentence is aligned (congruent) with the content of the words. Here's an example of how a Heavy Hitter determines if the enunciation of certain words are incongruent with the actual words being spoken.

We had just finished a grueling two-hour sales presentation. The customer had installed our major competitor's product, albeit not altogether successfully. The company had yet to fully implement the competitor's software across all the systems it had originally intended to. The installation process was overly complex, and the software was not perceived to be stable on the systems where they had it installed.

Bob, the leader of the project, had been through a great deal of pain and frustration during the past ten months. We had been invited to present our solution and gave a compelling case why our product was technically superior to the competitor's. Bob listened intently to all of our arguments and vigorously questioned each presenter.

The lynchpin of our account strategy was to get the project team to evaluate our product so it could physically compare our ease of installation and configuration against the incumbent's product. Following the formal presentation, we closed the meeting by asking Bob to evaluate our product in his company's lab environment. He bowed his head slightly, looked down to the right, and said, "We'll find some time to schedule a lab test." Instead of saying the sentence with excitement and conviction, he said it with a sullen tone and a lack of enthusiasm, bordering on disappointment.

We instinctively knew Bob never would schedule the lab time. Sensing this, we unsuccessfully tried to gain a commitment on a date to start the lab test. Although Bob didn't come right out and say it, we knew the deal was lost.

CONTENT LAYER

How did we know we'd lost the deal? Because when Bob said he would "find some time to schedule a lab test," the content layer (the actual words being used) contradicted, or was incongruent with, the phonetic layer. The content layer is what most people think of and listen to when they are having a discussion. However, people usually assume the content words they are using have the same meaning to everyone.

Suppose I go to a fast-food restaurant and order a cheeseburger. Regardless of the way I enunciate the word "cheeseburger," whether enthusiastically, soberly, or abruptly, I will still be served a cheeseburger. The phonetic layer has little impact on the content of my message. I could drive up to the drive-through window and yell, "Cheeseburger!!!" and the server would know what I want. In this example, "cheeseburger" has a specific meaning. A cheeseburger specifically has a bun, cheese, and a beef patty.

Now suppose I decide to go to a pizza parlor. When I am asked for my order, I say, "Pizza." The server will give me a blank stare. Do I want a deep-dish, regular, or thin crust? Do I want toppings? Unless the restaurant only has one pizza on the menu, "pizza" is a general word. A general word requires the use of additional words for the message to be received accurately. These additional words, called "operators," are used in conjunction with the general word to change the meaning.

When I introduced the concept of ordering a pizza, the first picture to enter your mind may have been a thin-crust cheese pizza. This would have been your own specific interpretation of the word "pizza." Let's say I was imagining biting into a deep-dish pepperoni pizza. This would have been my specific meaning of the word "pizza." Obviously, they are not quite the same.

General Word: Pizza

First-level operator	Regular, deep-dish, or thin crust
Second-level operator	Pepperoni, mushroom, olives, etc.
Third-level operator	Large, medium, or small

Figure 2.3 Examples of General Word with Operators

Unless I add more operators to the word "pizza," the server won't know what type of pizza I really want. Also, in this case I can place the operators in any order and still have my message be correctly understood. I could order by saying "I'll have a large, deep-dish, pepperoni and olive" or "I'll have a pepperoni and olive, deep-dish, large." They both mean the same thing. However, sometimes the order of the operators can change the meaning. Going to the lumberyard and ordering a six-foot-long two-by-four board is very different from asking for a board that is a four-foot-long two-by-six.

Since the interpretation of a general word's meaning is up to the receiver of the message, such words have been used by psychics, fortunetellers, and astrologers for centuries. Look at the following examples with the general words in italics. Try to determine if any of these apply specifically to you and whether the astrological sign is yours.

- Astrological sign: Members of this sign are admired for their *generosity* and *sensitive* nature. They often make excellent businesspeople or salespeople because of their *honesty, skill,* and *genuine* communication.

- Psychic hotline: Someone you know is having *troubles.*

- Fortune cookie: You will soon receive *good news* from a *faraway place.*

What happened? When you were reading these sentences, you most likely added your own operators to gain some personal meaning. As you read about the astrological sign, did you think it was your sign? Nearly everyone wants to be admired for his or her generosity and honesty. You may have even thought of a specific person (spouse, child, or friend) or an event (giving a donation) to validate the idea that you are generous and honest.

The psychic understands that everyone knows someone who is having troubles. "Troubles" could be anything ranging from a flat tire to a life-threatening disease. The fortune cookie leaves you to interpret what "soon" means. Is it hours, days, or months? What is considered "good" news? How far is the faraway place? Basically, it is impossible to prove these statements to be false since they apply to almost situation!

So why are pizza, horoscopes, and fortune cookies important to Heavy Hitters? They show that general words used by themselves are, in fact, meaningless. If you tell a customer your solution is "fast and reliable," what have you communicated? It's through the use of operators that specific meanings are added and meaningful communication is completed. If you tell a customer your solution is "fast and reliable, will print two hundred pages per minute, and has a 99.99 percent uptime rate," you have communicated something meaningful.

Let's take another look at how computers communicate. Once again, here's the seven-layer communication model for computers. Each layer is further defined with an additional operator. The use of the additional operator enhances or completely changes the meaning

	General	Operator
Layer 7	Application	E-Mail
Layer 6	Presentation	POP/SMPT
Layer 5	Session	POP/25
Layer 4	Transport	TCP
Layer 3	Network	IP
Layer 2	Data Link	Ethernet
Layer 1	Physical	Coaxial Cable

Figure 2.4 The Seven-Layer Computer Communication Model with Sample Operators

of the general word. For example, although coaxial and fiberoptic are two types of cables, they are very different. Each has different uses and capabilities, and they can't be used interchangeably.

It's important to recognize the difference between general and specific words. In high-tech sales, general words are used predominantly to describe and market product advantages. Probably three of the most regularly used terms are "performance," "reliability," and "scalability." The phrases below were taken from the Web site home pages of three prominent high-technology companies.

- "ABC Software enables organizations to exceed performance and reliability expectations."

- "DEF Hardware combines power and scalability to meet your e-business needs."

- "XYZ Solutions automatically and intelligently delivers the best possible Internet performance and availability."

Other popular general terms include "flexibility," "transparency," "manageability," "powerful," and "price performance." Little meaning can be derived from these product claims unless operators are added. Here's the point: Heavy Hitters always validate the general claims about their products with specific features or specific examples to give credence and meaning to their statements.

Using Operators

The following example shows how operators can be used to add a tangible meaning to generic marketing claims. It is more important to understand the structure of the language in these examples than the technical terms being used. In this scenario, the Heavy Hitter is presenting a product to a group of network engineers who work for a major financial institution in a large city. This example provides the basic thought process and technique the Heavy Hitter uses to drive his point home to a customer. He is building a business case for selecting his product.

"We offer superior performance because our architecture is based upon virtual processes, and that is more efficient than our competitor's architecture, which uses a single-machine address." The Heavy Hitter always presents his arguments with operators. The general word "performance" is being operated on by the descriptor "architecture based upon virtual processes." The term "more efficient" is being operated on by the phrase "uses a single-machine address." The purpose of this statement is to differentiate the Hitter's architecture from his competitor's.

"While the single-machine address solution redundantly broadcasts all messages, our solution sends specific information packets to the applicable computer. This results in less traffic and faster performance of the network." After introducing the competitor's architecture, the Hitter must explain his claim in technical terms the audience understands. He describes how the single-machine address solution works in comparison to his. He also introduces the differentiation between the two architectures, which is less traffic and faster performance. In essence, the first sentence is a general sentence that is operated on by the second and third sentences.

The Heavy Hitter continues to explain why his solution is better. *"In your four-node implementation, this would result in 75 percent less network traffic."* Up to this point, all of the arguments have been theoretical, and you can assume they have been received logically by the network engineers. From previous discussions, the Heavy Hitter knows they have a technical environment that consists of a network of four computer systems. He then makes a specific claim about the impact of his product in their environment. He ties both direct benefits of the generic term "performance" to the engineers' specific technical implementation. He wants them to understand the distinct advantage that his product would bring to their environment.

"For example, the ABC Company recently switched from a single-machine address architecture and improved their network performance by over 60 percent." To further validate his argument, the Heavy Hitter offers a specific customer example to illustrate his claims and, equally important, have his claim accepted as the truth. Customer anecdotes and references are a powerful way to add credibility to his product claims. Think for a moment about the last major personal purchase you made, such as a car, a boat, or even a vacation. Most likely, you wanted to talk to someone who already owned the product or had been to the destination you were considering.

Using Customer Examples

In our current example, the Heavy Hitter is making a presentation to a group of network engineers who work at a financial institution based in New York. The personal connection between the customer example (ABC Company) and its relevancy to the network engineers will determine to what extent the Hitter's claims are received and accepted. Therefore, the pertinence of the example chosen is very important. Presenting a company that closely mirrors the customer's business or technical environment will make the statements more powerful. Presenting a company that the network engineers don't recognize will have less impact. In reality, it may actually hinder the argument because the engineers might think the technology is not pervasive or mainstream enough.

At the lowest level of relevance, the example used could be a well-known organization, such as Coca-Cola or Shell Oil. Certainly, these are companies that would be known by the network engineers. The level of relevance improves when the example company is known for its past innovations in technology, such as Federal Express or Intel, or is well respected for its quality and brand, such as Mercedes-Benz or Nordstrom. By providing as examples customers that have a dominant position in an unrelated technology segment, such as Amazon, eBay, or Yahoo, you also receive implicit technical approval since it is highly likely the network engineers have successfully used the services or products of these companies personally. Therefore, they make the logical assumption that the Heavy Hitter's technology also works successfully.

The company example could also have a technical environment similar to the network engineers'. In this case, the company's name or business is de-emphasized while its technical environment is highlighted. Let's assume the network engineers are using Sun computers, a specific version of an operating system, and Cisco routers. By providing a customer example that identically matches their system, the Heavy Hitter is able to validate his technical claims that his product works in their exact technical environment.

The Heavy Hitter can also offer customer examples that have similar technical attributes. Suppose the network engineers' network traffic consists mainly of large FTP (File Transfer Protocol) files being sent around the world between 12 A.M. to 4 A.M. nightly. By referring to a company performing a similar function, the Heavy Hitter also validates his claims.

Geographic proximity is a very compelling attribute of a reference. If the customer's company is based in New York, a reference to a company that is based in Los Angeles is not nearly as strong as a reference to one that is based in New York.

The ideal reference is a customer's direct competitor. This example provides the highest level of relevance and the most persuasive argument to use the Heavy Hitter's product. The best customer reference of all is a company in the same business, with the same infrastructure, in close geographic proximity, and with the same business initiatives or technical tasks.

The Heavy Hitter is careful with name-dropping. He knows that once he offers a customer's name, he has obligated himself to give the network engineers contact information should they ask for it, and he has given the prospect the right to call the customer as a reference.

He knows that once he extends any customer's name he is offering that company as a reference. Anytime he inserts another person into the sales cycle on his behalf, it adds an element of risk.

One exception to this rule is when he gives a prospect the name of a company that is its direct competitor. For example, if the network engineers were given the name of their biggest competitor from across town, the rule of thumb is that they will not call the rival company, and the Heavy Hitter does not have to provide contact information. In fact, two direct competitors almost never share information about a critical project. That's what makes these customer examples so useful. The Hitter is able to validate the product claims without adding risk to the sales cycle.

The high-tech industry is consumed with communicating at the content layer with good reason. If I tell you to connect to my network using Internet protocol address 190.111.1234, you need to use this exact number. Use any slight deviation from it and you won't succeed. As a result, every industry has developed its own language to ensure exact meaning of the content of words. This unique language is called the "technical specification language." Whether you are selling airplanes, computer chips, or platform drilling equipment, you need to know the terms and nomenclature of your industry. These form one of the primary languages your customer speaks.

The technical specification language has four major characteristics. First, words within the technical specification language have very narrow meanings. This is distinctly different from the normal day-to-day language you use. It is a precise and exact language where "100 Mbps" means "100 megabits per second," not 99 or 101. Second, the meaning of general words can be completely changed by the addition of operators. For example, a general term like "computer" completely changes in meaning when the word "mainframe" or "personal" is added in front of it and keeps changing meaning when additional operators such as "Sun" or "IBM" are added. Third, the language is completely androgynous. No reference is made to feminine or masculine characteristics (outside of cable connectors, that is). Finally, the language is nonpersonal. After all, it's referring to machines, not humans.

Unfortunately for Hitters, the technical specification language has been adopted by customers as the default standard for all of their communication. This presents Heavy Hitters with a significant problem. They are trying to create a personal relationship with the buyer. However, the buyer is communicating in an androgynous, nonpersonal, technical language. More importantly, given the use of this unusual language, Heavy Hitters must somehow decipher the underlying meaning and intent of what the customer is saying.

In addition, the technical content of the language is the yardstick by which a customer's technical peer group (the team selecting a product) measures a person's relevant knowledge. Outside of formal titles, it's another way members of the peer group will establish a hierarchy. It's also how they will validate the sales team's value to them. Conversely, it is how the sales team members will present their product's features and the technical reasons for selecting their product.

So how do you determine if your technical arguments are actually being understood? Obviously, you can ask a content-level question, such as, "Do you understand?" However, most technical people are very reluctant to publicly admit they don't understand something. Doing so could affect their position within the group, particularly in a presentation environment that includes their peers and management.

More importantly, how can you determine if a customer really agrees with your arguments? In the story earlier about the grueling two-hour sales meeting, at the end of the presentation Bob said he would find some lab time to evaluate the product. However, he didn't mean it. The Heavy Hitter determined that the content layer of his words were incongruent with the phonetic layer of his communication. Bob was at odds with himself. Heavy Hitters are constantly trying to determine if any of the layers of the human communication model disagree with one another.

PURPOSE LAYER

So far we have discussed the phonetic and content layers of the human communication model. The third layer involves the purpose of communication. Words are assembled to communicate an idea or experience. Every sentence of every conversation between Heavy Hitters and customers is purpose driven. One way to think of this is that they have an ulterior motive for everything they say. Of course, you and I have been communicating with selfish interests all of our lives.

For example, before my children were old enough to talk, they would cry to let the world know of their unhappiness. As parents, we would then proceed down our mental checklist of what they might be crying about. Through the process of elimination, we determined whether they were hungry, wet or cold or just needed to be held.

As my children were learning how to talk, their language capability was limited to labeling. They would see a dog and say, "Doggie." My wife and I would excitedly confirm, "Yes, doggie!" Soon thereafter, they learned they could use words to get things they wanted. They were able to grasp that if they said, "Cookie?" with a certain enunciation, they would frequently receive a cookie. They were able to communicate with a self-centered purpose.

Heavy Hitters and customers are just as self-centered in their communications. Each is constantly trying to extract information from the other. Heavy Hitters will collect this information to create their account strategy, the long-term plan to win a deal. They are trying to uncover technical, political, and personal information in order to assess their current position and continually refine their strategy. To implement the strategy, they will determine a tactical plan and the daily tasks that are required.

Meanwhile, customers are trying to obtain information about the Heavy Hitter's company, products, and customers. Their main goal is information assessment. Whether formally or informally, they have developed and prioritized their needs. They need information in order to measure the fit of the Heavy Hitter's solution.

The Heavy Hitter and the customer have two different purposes for communicating. This results in interactions between customers and Hitters that can be thought of as circular "vignettes." These vignettes are small dramas, short interactions between the customer and the Heavy Hitter. Usually they are about one topic or one conversational theme. They are considered circular because every vignette will come to an end and close as the topic of conversation is exhausted.

These vignettes are not static models. Rather, they are very fluid and incredibly dynamic. The customer and the Heavy Hitter can be thought of almost like two boxers who are constantly punching and counterpunching based on their opponent's last movement. Each vignette is composed of a series of actions the Heavy Hitter or the customer may execute. Each party can *gather* additional information, make an *assessment* as to what a question means, put forth a *response* to information, *present* additional information, or use *persuasion* to influence the other party's thinking.

Gathering is how one party tries to find out information about the other. It is usually done with a question but can be done in a variety of ways, such as a drawing on a whiteboard, presenting a slide, or acquiring a drawing of the customer's environment (network schematic,

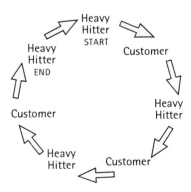

Figure 2.5 Customer Interaction Vignette

accounts payable process, or chip design drawing). Basically, gathering is the passing of any knowledge about a specific subject.

Assessments are done when both parties analyze a question (or any other information that has been gathered) prior to making a response. Assessment is the filtering process to find the "right" answer. An assessment can be as straightforward as trying to determine the right words to use to construct the best response to the question. Or it could be a calculated editing process to limit or camouflage a response. The assessment may or may not result in a truthful answer. How long it takes for a customer to complete the assessment is a good indication of the amount of editing needed to produce an answer (and how true it is). Customers may give untruthful information because they simply do not know the answer, aren't in a political position to answer, don't want to answer, or don't understand the question.

Meanwhile, Hitters do their own mental assessment of all the different potential answers to a customer's question, and they will present the response they feel will help strengthen their position the most. The Hitter's response is very calculated. Most amazingly, it requires a series of complex comparisons to be carried out in a fraction of a second, which makes it seem natural to the customer. Heavy Hitters are like chess players making a move. They are constantly thinking three steps ahead and beyond.

Four types of Heavy Hitter replies are possible. First, the response may be as simple and straightforward as "Yes" or "No." This is a content-level response that specifically answers the question asked. Second, the response can be a presentation of additional facts or information. Third, Hitters can use persuasion to influence another person's thinking. And finally, on rare occasions, the response may even be an objection to the question being asked.

From all of these possible replies, the Heavy Hitter will do a quick assessment to determine which response will present the most applicable or strongest answer. Does it make sense to answer yes or no and move on to the next vignette? Should he keep gathering additional information? Or should he use persuasion to make a point and try to bring the vignette to a close?

A sales call is a collection of these circular vignettes. A typical sales presentation will begin with individual vignettes about the company's history, milestones, and customer references before moving into vignettes explaining specific technical features of the product.

Vignettes typically change when the subject changes or when an implied agreement on the current topic of discussion is reached. The implied agreement may or may not mean that the issue or discussion point is resolved. Often, it is an agreement to move on for the sake of time.

Every sales call will have several critical vignettes that will determine whether the call is a success or failure. While every vignette will close, the issues associated with some vignettes will remain open. Heavy Hitters know that unresolved issues will come up again later in the sales cycle, usually when they least want an objection. Therefore, they always try to address these awkward points early. They want them out in the open. They want to know whether an issue will inhibit the purchase of the product, and they want to know as soon as possible.

Here's an example of a very simple vignette involving only the Heavy Hitter and one person from the customer's company. Most vignettes involve a team of people from both the vendor and the customer, such as technical engineers who work with the Hitter and a team of people who are responsible for evaluating the solution. As with previous examples, don't be concerned with the technical specification language being used. Instead, follow the flow of the vignette. Actions being taken are given in parentheses.

Vignette #1

HEAVY HITTER: *(Gathering)* What platforms are you running?

CUSTOMER: *(Assessment plus Response)* We are using Sun and NT servers.

HEAVY HITTER: *(Assessment plus Presentation)* Our product runs on Sun and NT servers, and we can manage both platforms through a single console.

CUSTOMER: *(Assessment plus Gathering)* We are planning to migrate the NT servers to Linux later this year. Do you support Linux?

HEAVY HITTER: *(Assessment plus Presentation)* Yes, we do. Since our management console runs under a Netscape or Microsoft browser, we can also manage the servers remotely.

CUSTOMER: *(Assessment plus Gathering)* How do you ensure the security of remote administration?

HEAVY HITTER: *(Assessment plus Presentation plus Persuasion)* We encrypt the traffic being sent using Blowfish. Also, the management console can manage roles and responsibilities. We have a customer, XYZ Company, that is managing its entire worldwide network of sixty servers with three administrators based here.

You will notice in the above vignette the customer is primarily on the offensive, asking for information. This vignette closes when the Heavy Hitter satisfies the questions being asked and changes the topic to further investigate why the customer is moving to Linux. He also wants to know who made the Linux decision in order to determine if this person will influence the selection process he is involved in. Now he moves from a defensive position to an offensive position.

Vignette #2

HEAVY HITTER: *(Assessment plus Gathering)* Where are the servers located and who will manage them?

CUSTOMER: *(Assessment plus Response)* We have four Sun servers here, two Sun servers in Chicago, two NT servers in New York, and I think four servers running in Europe. We manage the U.S.-based servers here, and we have an administrator in London.

HEAVY HITTER: *(Assessment plus Gathering)* What platform are the European servers on?

CUSTOMER: *(Assessment plus Response)* They are currently on NT but moving to Linux.

HEAVY HITTER: *(Assessment plus Gathering)* Why are they migrating the NT servers?

CUSTOMER: *(Assessment plus Response)* They did some testing with Linux servers and found they were quite a bit faster than their older NT servers.

HEAVY HITTER: *(Assessment plus Gathering)* Do you see yourself migrating any servers to Linux in the U.S.?

CUSTOMER: *(Assessment plus Response)* No. If anything, it looks like we'll be moving everything to Sun. Sun is our standard here.

HEAVY HITTER: *(Assessment plus Presentation plus Persuasion)* Sun is our primary development platform. We have developed our new products using Java and found we were able to port them to other platforms much faster than if we had built them on NT.

After each customer response in the vignette above, the Heavy Hitter assesses whether he should gather further information, present a solution or feature, or use persuasion. The persuasion he uses will be either visible or transparent to the customer. In the first vignette he explained that the XYZ Company is managing its entire worldwide network of servers with three administrators. This is an example of visible persuasion. The XYZ Company physically exists.

When Heavy Hitters use logic, reasoning, or examples that cannot be seen, they are using transparent persuasion. For example, in the second vignette, the Heavy Hitter provides commentary about how Java-based products are easier to develop than NT-based platforms. He is implicitly validating the customer's decision to use Sun computers as a standard. He is using transparent persuasion in order to let the customer know they share similar views, in the hope of positively influencing the customer's opinion.

Although the conversation seems natural and free flowing, the Heavy Hitter is guiding the interaction to the topics he feels will influence the customer's perception of his solution. Each vignette is very dynamic. A vignette could consist of only two interactions or two hundred. It could include participation from everyone at the meeting or only two people. Since the use of PowerPoint is so pervasive in sales presentations today, most vignettes last as long as one slide or a series of several slides.

The complexity of a vignette is also directly related to the number of participants. For example, the two types of assessments are external and internal. In meetings involving teams of people, the assessments are frequently external. During a sales call, the customer's team members may have a discussion in front of the vendor to determine what their response should be. In the second vignette, the customers could have discussed among themselves whether or not they will be migrating to NT or exactly how many servers they have in London. When this happens, Heavy Hitters listen intently. They recognize this is a valuable opportunity to learn about the dynamics of the decision process and get a better understanding of a person's knowledge, credibility, and importance in the decision process.

The Heavy Hitter's sales team may also perform external assessments. He and his technical engineer may have a conversation about a technical detail associated with a response from the customer. Together, they use the vignette to make their points. Most importantly, the Heavy Hitter will manage all the vignettes as part of his tactical plan to complete his strategy for the call.

In internal assessments, information is analyzed solely within one person's mind. In vignettes #1 and #2, the Heavy Hitter listened to the customer's response and determined the next course of action in his mind. Likewise, the customer listened to the Hitter's response and determined privately what to say next. The decision of what words are selected and how they are said is intimately linked to the next layer of the human communication model, the representational system.

REPRESENTATIONAL SYSTEM LAYER

You have developed a lifetime of experiences that are unique. These experiences, both good and bad, have shaped your perception of the world. Through your senses, you are constantly adding to your cumulative knowledge of how your world functions. As you accumulate new experiences, they are edited and influenced by your history. As a result, it is accurate to say every person functions in his or her own unique world. Your world is your own personal reality. You use your representational systems to catalogue your experiences and describe your world to others.

Reality	Sensors	Influences	My Reality
As it is	Sight, sound, touch, taste, smell	Family, money, work, friends, schooling, spirituality	Experiences catalogued

Figure 2.6 Cataloguing Reality

Through language we represent our thoughts and experiences. We use words to represent the sensory experiences of sight, sound, touch, smell, and taste. The map we use to describe and interpret an experience is based upon one of three representational systems—visual, auditory, and kinesthetic. Visual refers to sight. Auditory refers to sound. Kinesthetic refers to touch and internal feelings.

Most people use one representational system more frequently than the others. This representational system has become their default, or "primary," mode of communication. You can identify someone's primary representational system by listening to the adjectives, adverbs, and nouns they use in conversation.

People who have a visual primary representational system will describe their experiences in visual terms. They are likely to say, "I see what you mean," "Looks good to me," or "Show me what to do." People with an auditory primary representational system will say, "Sounds great," "Talk to you later," or "Tell me what to do." People with a kinesthetic primary representational system will say, "I've got it handled," "We'll touch base later," or "I don't grasp what you mean."

Great benefits in communication and persuasion are gained if you understand your customer's primary representational system and adjust your communication to fit their world. This is an extremely important concept for salespeople to recognize. From this point forward, this book will refer to a person with a visual primary representational system as a Visual (or in the plural as Visuals). Similarly, people with auditory or kinesthetic primary representational systems will be referred to as Auditory(ies) or Kinesthetic(s).

Chapter 5 is dedicated to understanding and communicating with a customer's representational system. The representational system is directly related and inseparably linked to the next layer of the human communication model, the internal dialogue.

INTERNAL DIALOGUE LAYER

Every waking hour, a stream of communication is going on inside your mind. You are always talking to yourself. This conversation is an unedited, honest discussion that represents your deepest feelings. This is the fifth layer of the human communication model—the internal dialogue layer or simply the "internal dialogue."

Let's pretend you are at a party and you accidentally meet a person whom you despise. Since you don't want to create a scene, you exchange pleasantries with this person. Your internal dialogue may be cursing at this person, but your spoken dialogue is polite and well mannered.

Usually these internal conversations remain internal. Occasionally, they'll slip out. We are all familiar with the term "Freudian slip." A Freudian slip happens when you say one thing but mean another. Freudian slips often occur because you are having two simultaneous dialogues—the words you are speaking externally to others and the internal dialogue within your mind. Sometimes you accidentally substitute a word from your internal dialogue into your external dialogue. In other cases, you get confused between the two. You may create a new word that is a combination of the first syllable of your content word and the last syllable of your internal dialogue word. In either case, these slips can be very embarrassing.

Usually, the words being spoken externally are a subset of the internal dialogue. In between is an editing process to filter the precise statement. The Heavy Hitter's editing process is very well developed and so refined through repetitive use that it is automatic.

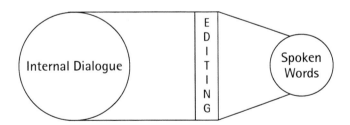

Figure 2.7 Spoken Works as a Subset of the Internal Dialogue after the Editing Process

PHYSICAL LAYER

Everyone is well aware of the final layer of the human communication model, the physical layer. You were introduced to this layer as a baby. When you were two days old, you were able to distinguish a happy face from a sad face. Soon thereafter, you naturally understood that a smile, hug, or kiss is to be interpreted as something very good.

The physical layer is also known as body language. Body language can be very subtle or more powerful than the actual words being spoken. Let's go back to the party in the previous example. Suppose the person you despise sees you first at the party. This person gives you a glare and starts pushing people out of the way to get to you. Those actions probably communicate one idea to you—run!

Body language is unique in that it is a three-dimensional language. One form of body language is sign language, which is a physical recreation of the content layer of communication. Sign language is the third most common language in the United States behind English and Spanish. Contrary to popular belief, sign language is not a universal language. Like spoken language, different countries have entirely different sign languages.

A sign is created by combining four different hand parameters— hand shape, palm orientation, hand location, and hand movement. The meaning of a sign changes based on the use of each of the parameters. Like the spoken word, sign language has grammatical structures, syntax, and rules. Essentially, anything you can communicate in the spoken word can be communicated in sign language.

Just as you can communicate any word in sign language, other forms of body language can communicate meaning. Heavy Hitters are masters at reading body language and using their own bodies to communicate. When considered in conjunction with the other layers of the human communication model, body language plays an important role.

With or without conscious effort, you most likely have mastered each of the six layers of the human communication model. However, the *interaction* between the layers is of particular interest to Heavy Hitters. Let's take another look at the communication model of computers.

Within the computer model, all seven layers of the stack must be in place before information can be sent between machines. Each layer talks directly only to the corresponding layer on the other machine. You can think of them as physically connecting with each of the respective layers.

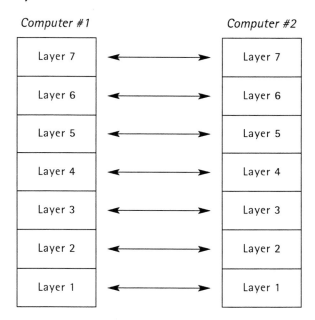

Figure 2.8 Computer Communication

The physical layer (layer 1) cannot communicate with the application layer (layer 7) and vice versa. It is a very structured model that requires the preceding layer for communication to occur.

However, when people speak, the layers are totally interactive, and any layer can communicate with any other layer. The layers can also be combined to form complex statements that can convey additional or different meanings than the content-level words would have by themselves.

It's truly a remarkable, flexible model. By combining or eliminating layers, greater efficiencies and a wide range of communication are possible.

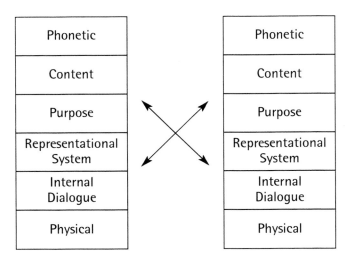

Figure 2.9 Human Communication

Here's an example of how the various layers can be combined, using the example of asking Mary for a report. Suppose Mary is coming to my desk to give me the report. As I see her coming, my internal dialogue assesses what my response will be. Here are some of the ways I could respond to her.

1. Physical. I could give her a big smile and a "high-five." She would obviously interpret this to mean I was pleased. My communication is congruent because my facial expression and hand slapping are communicating the same message.

2. Physical. I could do absolutely nothing. When she comes to my desk I could continue to do whatever I was doing. How would Mary interpret this? Would she think I was too busy with my tasks to notice her? Or wonder if the report was really not important after all? Maybe she would ask herself if I was ignoring her and communicating my displeasure about the report. Mary truly wouldn't know what I was communicating. However, if my established behavior had always been congenial, then this response would be incongruent with our prior interactions.

3. Content plus phonetic plus physical. I could say "Thanks" in my normal tone of voice but present a very forced, fake smile. Mary would have to do some internal assessment as to what I was trying to communicate. Why was my communication incongruent?

4. Physical plus content plus phonetic. I could plan and mentally rehearse how I would embarrass Mary when she finally gave me the report. Holding my arms over my head, I could say at the top of my voice, "I see I *finally* have my report!" This would definitely get the point across about my unhappiness and would surely elicit a response. This response requires planning after an internal assessment and some extra effort and energy commensurate with the level of frustration I experienced. My desire is to convey this frustration to Mary.

CONCLUSION

In this chapter, we introduced the six unique layers of the human communication model. These layers are the fundamental building blocks that we will continually refer to throughout the book. They help explain how Heavy Hitters structure their message and discern when they are being misled. As we'll examine later, they also determine the intensity of the Hitter's intuition.

We also reviewed the concept of the technical specification language. Heavy Hitters are selling to people who are technical by nature. Their formal education backgrounds are in the sciences, such as computer science, engineering, and mathematics. They are trained to speak at the content level and unfortunately have adopted the attributes of this language for all their communications. They are also judged by their peer group based upon their personal knowledge of their industry's unique technical specification language.

The content layer represents only a fraction of the total communication spectrum that is being presented during any conversation.

Additional layers can be added on top of each other to convey even greater meaning. They can be aligned to create holistic, congruent communication. Heavy Hitters interpret congruent messages as being honest and true. However, if the layers are at odds with each other, or incongruent, further investigation is required.

Finally, to further complicate the process, human communication is always occurring in several different forms and on several different levels. An immense amount of information is being conveyed, phonetically, verbally, physically, consciously, and subconsciously.

Heavy Hitters have developed the ability to listen and sense all of the information a customer is projecting, regardless of whether it is being delivered consciously or subconsciously. They evaluate each layer's message to determine its meaning. Another term for this ability is "sales intuition." Heavy Hitters will use their intuition to create the strategy that gives them the highest likelihood of winning a deal. Based upon their intuition, they will invest more time, develop individual relationships further, and select a plan of action. This is why Heavy Hitters are successful.

Ensuring you have received the correct message isn't as easy as it seems. Even the elite scientists at NASA make embarrassing mistakes. "Clearly something is wrong, and we have to understand it," NASA administrator Daniel Goldin pronounced after the loss of the $165 million Mars Polar Lander. "These failures in the Mars program have given us a wake-up call and we are going to respond to it,"[3] said Edward Weiler, deputy director of NASA's Office of Space Sciences. The Mars climate orbiter burned up in the Martian atmosphere because technicians at Lockheed-Martin and at Jet Propulsion Laboratory (JPL) used different units of measurement for navigation. Lockheed-Martin transmitted English units to JPL engineers, who thought they were getting metric units.

Sometimes it takes the loss of millions of dollars to understand that people aren't necessarily speaking the same language. In sales, failure is a lot less expensive. We simply lose the deal.

3

How People Are "Wired"

After initial introductions, the salesperson started her standard presentation. As usual, she planned to introduce the company, describe how it was formed, and give a brief overview of the success it had enjoyed. She planned on highlighting a few prominent installations to illustrate her product's benefits. She would close the presentation by outlining the key features of her product.

However, after the first slide, she was interrupted by the prospective customer, who said, "Could you tell me how your product manages large numbers of users?"

The salesperson responded, "I have a slide that shows our benchmark performance later in the presentation," and continued. A couple of slides later, she was interrupted again.

"Could you explain how your product maintains the status connections of users in an environment with ten thousand concurrent users?"

The salesperson jumped forward a few slides to show a high-level profile of one of her largest accounts. After showing the slide, she went back to her planned presentation.

The customer was growing frustrated. "I heard your product doesn't scale when there are large numbers of concurrent users. Is this true?"

Fifteen minutes into the sales presentation, the meeting was at a complete standstill.

In the last chapter, we introduced the concept that everyone lives in his or her own world. The world you experience is not the real world but rather your perception of the world. The way in which you perceive your world is intricately connected to the language you use. You use your senses to define everyday experiences for storage in your brain. Your representational systems are the storage-and-retrieval mechanisms used to access these experiences. They are also responsible for the words you select to communicate your world to others.

Because our past experiences are unique, our views of the same situation may be very different. For example, we may have grown up in the same town and even gone to the same schools. However, our recollection of our childhoods will be distinct since we both have a unique ability to interpret, classify, store, and retrieve information in our brains.

Every day, you receive an infinite amount of information. This information constantly influences the decisions you make. Think about the first few minutes after you awoke today. You got out of bed. You may have casually glanced outside to determine what would be appropriate to wear. Perhaps you went to the bathroom and proceeded to take a shower.

We experience the world through three main representational systems: kinesthetic (touch, taste, and smell), auditory (sound), and visual (sight). We continuously process information from our senses. The senses can't be turned off, and the large amount of information they gather can overwhelm our conscious mind's ability to process and catalogue it. Therefore, not all information is treated equally. Some information is ignored, some information is misinterpreted, and some information is generalized.

Let's take another look at your morning experience with this in mind. We process kinesthetic information from all parts of our bodies at all times. Our skin alone is a sixteen-square-foot sensory blanket. When you awoke, were your feet cold? Was the weight of the blankets heavy or light? What was the temperature under versus above the blankets? How did the floor feel as you walked to the shower? Was the shower handle cold? Was it easy or hard to move? What was the taste in your mouth?

We also process auditory information continuously. Was the clock radio alarm set to play music or to buzz? Were sounds coming from outside your window? Were sounds coming from other parts of your house? What sound did the water make as it came through the showerhead? Our ears have the ability to hear an infinite number of diverse sounds.

What visual information did you receive? Was the room light or dark? What was the time on the clock? What color were the numbers on the clock? Was sunlight beaming through the window? Did you notice anything on the floor in your path to the shower? Was it bright or dark in the shower? Did the steam vapors fog the bathroom? Our eyes can see stars millions of light-years away, as well as a speck of dust on a computer screen.

In the first few minutes of your day, you were exposed to thousands of pieces of information. It would be very inefficient if you had to process each piece of information and catalogue it. You therefore process the minimal amount of information you need to accomplish the task at hand. The other information is tuned out or ignored, deleted from your conscious mind. However, the subconscious mind still collects all the information, just in case it is needed later.

By retrieving information from past experiences, you can extrapolate what to do in an entirely new situation. For example, let's pretend I gave you car keys and placed you in a parking lot with a hundred different cars. You would know what to do with the keys based upon your knowledge of how cars work. You would be able to open the car door, start the car, and drive it away, even though you may have never driven or seen this type of car before. You have developed a model based upon your cumulative experience of driving and being in cars. Now suppose a hundred different kinds of tractors are in the same parking lot. Your model may or may not work, depending on how close a particular tractor's operation mirrors that of a car.

TRIANGULATION

Up to this point, we have learned that we all operate in our own world, which is our perception of reality. We also filter information all the time. While most salespeople operate in a world of incomplete or incorrect customer information, Heavy Hitters have a different strategy, called "triangulation."

Triangulation is the process of identifying your position by using three or more data points. If you are sailing across the ocean, you can calculate your latitude and longitude by forming an imaginary triangle with certain stars. In sales, we do the same, with the stars being the members of our project team assembled to win an account. In most cases, the team consists of a Hitter, a system engineer, an inside sales team, and a sales manager.

Sailors continuously take readings from different stars to ensure their position is accurate. In the same way, Heavy Hitters may even talk about a deal with someone who has never met the customer or isn't even in sales, such as a spouse or friend. Heavy Hitters constantly try to triangulate their position by answering these questions: Is there a deal? Am I winning? Who do I have to watch out for, and what can ruin this deal?

In sales, triangulation is the process of checking all information that has been gathered about a customer with other people. Through triangulation, Heavy Hitters try to identify the pieces of information that their representational system may have ignored, generalized, or misinterpreted. It's a calibration technique for finding "reality." Before we take an in-depth look at triangulation, we should identify the main participants involved in a Hitter's triangulation process.

Heavy Hitter or Salesperson

The Heavy Hitter is the customer's main point of contact for all customer communication. The Hitter coordinates all meetings and events, such as presentations and technical evaluations. She is in charge of all of the company resources that are assembled to win the account, regardless of their departmental origin. In essence, she is the project manager. The project is to win the account. To accomplish this, she can pull from any department in the company, including management, engineering, support, consulting, marketing, and product management. The project team may also include partners from outside the company.

The Heavy Hitter is responsible for creating a proposed solution and ensuring that the solution matches the customer's needs. As the team leader, she confirms the customer is qualified from a business and technical perspective to the rest of her project team, motivates the team, and takes responsibility for the overall relationship with the customer and ongoing account satisfaction.

Presales Engineer or System Engineer

The presales engineer is mainly responsible for understanding the customer's technical profile and presenting the company's technical solution. The system engineer conducts the process that determines the level of technical fit between the vendor's product and the customer's technical environment. The system engineer is also responsible for the solution design, product evaluation, and implementation of the project. Members from other departments, such as consulting or support, may also perform certain tasks at the system engineer's direction. Most importantly, the system engineer is responsible for the technical relationship with the customer and the ongoing technical satisfaction with the product. In this role of a customer advocate, the system engineer will represent the customer and facilitate meetings with the technical support department.

Inside Sales Team—Telesales or Telemarketing

The inside sales group will play a different role depending upon the complexity of the Hitter's product. With technically complex products that require longer implementations, the inside sales team members generate leads by making cold calls or sending e-mails and direct mail. They also provide the Heavy Hitter with a support system at the corporate office. The support functions may be administrative, such as sending marketing collateral, providing order follow-up, or tracking down specific information the Hitter may need. In any case, members of the inside sales group work at the direction of the Heavy Hitter, even though they may have an immediate supervisor.

If the products are less complicated to install and sell, the inside sales team will be able to perform a telesales function. In this case, the inside sales team is made up of salespeople with a quota who close new business and search their customer base for additional sales. Depending on the nature of the product, the team members may be closely integrated with the Hitter's territory, or they could work independently on smaller deals, freeing the Heavy Hitter to pursue major accounts. Most likely, the inside sales team will be involved in the triangulation process at the beginning of the sales cycle. Once their information has been passed on to the Heavy Hitter, their role is less active.

Sales Manager

The final person involved in triangulation is the Hitter's sales manager. Sales managers have been involved in more sales cycles and have experienced a more diverse set of sales scenarios than most salespeople. Therefore, they can draw upon these experiences and compare them to the existing sales cycle.

The various members of the customer's evaluation team are going to give contradictory information. Since we all have our own perception of reality, this isn't surprising. Disagreements will occur, and as the saying goes, "When two men in business always agree, one of them is unnecessary." The intent of the triangulation process is to identify these subtle or obvious differences. Areas of contention or contradiction require further analysis, so the issue is assigned to a member of the Hitter's team to investigate.

TRIANGULATION DIAMOND

The following discussion shows how Heavy Hitters carry out the triangulation process. It is based on the analogy of a baseball diamond. (After all, Heavy Hitters are trying to score a home run!)

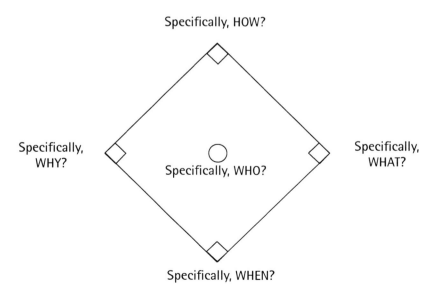

Figure 3.1 The Triangulation Diamond

First Base

On the triangulation diamond, first base is the "What" base. What are the content-level words being spoken by the prospects? What specifically do they mean? The Heavy Hitter is trying to determine as specifically as possible what the customers mean when they speak. The Heavy Hitter will do this by asking, *specifically* what they mean. Questions asked on first base include the following:

- Specifically, what are you trying to accomplish?
- Specifically, what business problem are you trying to solve?
- Specifically, what technical problem are you trying to solve?

As the customers answer these questions, the Heavy Hitter is trying to decipher their high-level requirements into very specific targeted needs. For example, let's say a Heavy Hitter sells a financial application and is meeting with prospects who are unhappy with their company's accounting system. She will help them define exactly what is making them unhappy. Is it functionality, performance, ease of use, support, or flexibility? Suppose it's functionality. Is it accounts payable, accounts receivable, human resources, or integration? Suppose it's accounts receivable. Is it customer creation, payment application, or delinquent accounts reporting?

The Heavy Hitter is trying to get to the very specific cause of pain. Members of the triangulation team will each have their own prioritized list of the customer's pain points. Once the Heavy Hitter has triangulated with the group about the pain points, she can determine whether her product can solve that pain, particularly in comparison with other solutions being evaluated.

Second Base

Second base is the "How" base. The Heavy Hitter uses second base to understand how the customers will take action. Again, she is trying to determine in as much detail as possible how the sales process will happen. She does this by asking specifically how the customers will accomplish a task. Questions on second base include the following:

- Specifically, how will you make a decision?
- Specifically, how will you implement the solution?
- Specifically, how will you determine if it is successful?

Suppose the prospects have decided to evaluate the Heavy Hitter's financial application. She will want to know the prospects' evaluation criteria, the steps of the evaluation, and how they will determine if the evaluation is successful. Members of her triangulation team will gather this information from their respective contacts. Together, they will assimilate the results. From this exercise, the Heavy Hitter will identify areas of product strength, weakness, and information she doesn't know.

Third Base

Now that the Heavy Hitter knows specifically what the customers are planning and how they intend to accomplish their goal, she needs to understand why third base is the "Why" base. Hitters want to understand "Why" from the company's perspective.

- Specifically, why is the company evaluating a new financial system?
- Specifically, why is our product a better fit than our competitor's?
- Specifically, why would the company select our product?

The second element of "Why" is the personal agendas of the individuals involved with the initiative. Items on these agendas are called "benefactions," personal benefits that come from taking a particular action. The dictionary definition of "benefaction" is "The act of doing good or helping others, especially by giving money."[4] Clearly, the Heavy Hitter wants customers to feel good about giving her money when they buy her product. Nonetheless, the Heavy Hitter's definition is more intricate: "To derive an advantage that contributes to one's well-being, such as happiness, esteem, power, or wealth, that results in influencing the way the person behaves during the sales cycle." We will explore benefactions in more detail later in the chapter. At the personal level, the Heavy Hitter will ask the following questions about each participant in the customer's selection process:

- Specifically, why is this particular person on the evaluation team?

- Specifically, why would this person endorse our product?

- Specifically, why would this person oppose our product?

Home Plate

After rounding third base, you are headed for home plate. Home is the "When" base. Even if you reach third base every time you hit the ball, you don't score until you reach home. All the work the Heavy Hitter has done on the account is moot if the customer doesn't have a time frame to evaluate, decide, and purchase. On home plate, the questions include the following:

- Specifically, when will the evaluation start and finish?

- Specifically, when will a decision be made?

- Specifically, when will the customer buy?

The Pitcher

In baseball, the pitcher can throw the ball to any base at any time. The pitcher's position represents "Who." "Who" can be applied to each base. The Heavy Hitter will determine who decided on the criteria, who will perform the evaluation, who will make the decision, and who will buy. At each base, triangulation is used to compare the various responses from each of the sales team members. Hitters triangulate incessantly and with everybody.

THE HITTER'S BENEFACTION

Heavy Hitters' goal is to win the deal at hand. In order to win the deal, they form an account strategy based upon information they have accumulated about the account and their knowledge of the products they are selling. Whether formally or informally, they will plan a series of tactics that they believe will give them the best opportunity to win at the least possible expense in terms of precious resources. The most precious resource is their time and the time of their project team. As they continually gather more information about an account, they will adjust their strategy and the associated tactics.

Heavy Hitters have their own personal benefactions associated with winning a deal. Maybe they dream about using the commission to buy a new car. Perhaps they envision themselves driving to the office in a Ferrari or Porsche. Maybe they are eager for the accolades they will garner by winning a large and prestigious customer. Possibly, they can hear the applause as they are handed an award at the next sales meeting. A benefaction is something strongly desired, defined in a personal way, that is important to you.

Professional athletes understand benefactions. Sprinters will visualize an entire race and see themselves on the winner's stand (their benefaction) receiving the gold medal. College basketball coaches will ask their team to mentally rehearse cutting down the net after they win the national championship (their benefaction).

Athletes describe their field of vision narrowing while they are focused on their benefaction. A professional baseball player will see the stitches on a ninety-mile-per-hour fastball. Golfers that are surrounded by members of the gallery won't hear or see them while they focus on the next putt.

Understanding your benefaction affects your conscious activities, as well as your subconscious mind. Your conscious mind is obsessed with achieving benefactions. Meanwhile, your subconscious mind is constantly sensing and filtering data that is necessary to achieving important benefactions.

In computer terms, the conscious mind is like a point-to-point model. For example, a salesperson wants to check her e-mail while traveling on the road. Using her laptop, she makes a dial-up connection to the host computer. Her only concern is to get her e-mail, and once she checks it, she disconnects the phone line. This point-to-point connection is similar to the conscious mind focused on a specific benefaction.

The subconscious mind is more like a broadband connection that is always on, such as a cable modem. The modem has a wider band of data and processes at a higher speed than a dial-up connection. The modem is always on, always receiving information. In the e-mail example, the salesperson always receives e-mail in real time. She doesn't have to dial up a connection.

The subconscious mind retains information that the conscious mind doesn't. It simply isn't efficient to store everything in your conscious mind. Remember the last time you misplaced an important item (your keys, wallet, glasses)? At first, you employed a conscious strategy to find it. You may have thought about where you had recently been and gone back to those locations. If you didn't find the item, hours, days, or weeks may have gone by. Then suddenly, without specifically thinking about it, you knew exactly where it was. Your subconscious mind found it. In the same way, when your prospective customers say, "Let me sleep on it," they are actually saying, "Let me see if my subconscious mind has any objections since it has some additional information that I don't have right now."

PERSONAL BENEFACTIONS

Let's assume a Heavy Hitter has a scheduled meeting with a prospective customer. The goal of the meeting is to present her company's product to the customer team. In the process of presenting the product, she expects to collect additional data and further define her account strategy. Obviously, she wants the presentation to go well. Ideally, she wants to have the team members get so excited that they progress to the next step in the sale process, such as a product evaluation or, better yet, a close. Meanwhile, the customers' goal is to limit their investment to a finite number of relationships. They are trying to use the meeting as part of the courting process to determine the quality of the suitor.

To measure the success of the meeting, the Heavy Hitter creates a personal benefaction. It may be to have the key decision maker tell her at the end of the presentation, "It looks great. Send me your final quote!" In this example, the Heavy Hitter may have a picture of the person in her mind. She hears those words being said and perhaps feels the excitement of closing the deal. This is her benefaction for the meeting. She can measure the success of the call based upon what actually happens and how closely that matches her benefaction. In other words, she will know she has achieved her benefaction when the sensory information she has collected confirms it.

Each meeting participant from the customer team also has a benefaction. The manager of the department may view the cost savings of implementing the product as the main goal. His benefaction may be being rewarded with a bonus for reducing the department's expense structure (which he will use to take his family to Hawaii). The person in charge of implementing the solution may view manageability as the goal. Since she will have to devote less time to managing the new product than the current one, her benefaction may be to have more time to spend on the projects she enjoys (or less time at work and more time at home with her family). Notice all these people's benefactions are personal, regardless of whether they are the buyer or the seller.

The Heavy Hitter uses her representational systems to determine the benefactions of each individual. And she also uses her representational systems to determine if her benefaction for the meeting has been achieved.

THE PYRAMID OF MEETING SUCCESS

At the heart of every successful sales call are mutual trust between both parties, the competence of the participants, and the identification of personal benefactions. The pyramid of meeting success illustrates this concept.

All sales calls start with a handshake. The tradition of the handshake started as a way of physically validating that a person wasn't carrying any weapons. Since both sides shook hands freely, it was a mutual event, a ritual that occurred very quickly at the beginning of a meeting. Unfortunately for Heavy Hitters, mutual trust is not achieved as quickly. It is earned over time and not freely granted. Depending on the product you are selling, it may take many meetings or several demonstrations over many months to gain a customer's

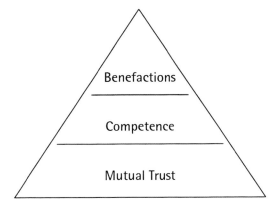

Figure 3.2 The Pyramid of Meeting Success

trust. Once achieved, it can be lost or weakened if commitments given by either party are not honored or if information given is proven false.

The next level of the pyramid is competence. The first aspect of competence is the personal fit between people. Since the sales team members are a direct reflection of their company's competence and culture, the customer wonders if this team will capably manage their long-term relationship. Are they technically competent? Do they understand my problem? Are they pleasant to be around? The sales team, on the other hand, determines if the customer's selection team has the wherewithal to make the decision, purchase the product, and implement it.

The other aspect of competence is the fit between the product and the customer. How well does the product solve the customer's technical problem? Will it operate as promised? What features of the product is the customer unsure of? How good is the product's technical support? What is the product's future release schedule? The questions regarding personal and product fit must be answered satisfactorily at the competence level.

At the top of the pyramid are benefactions. Entering into a meeting, each party knows what the overriding goal of the sales team is. It's to sell the product. What's the customer's goal? More specifically, what are the benefactions each participant has for achieving this goal? Decisions are influenced by politics. Politics are based upon self-interests. Hitters will attempt to find out and understand these self-interests. They will incorporate all participants' desires into their strategy to help them achieve their individual benefactions.

A sale will most likely occur when three criteria are met. First, an adequate level of mutual trust must be established. Second, both parties must be assured of the competence of each other. And third, the Hitter's solution must be aligned with the benefactions of the individuals involved in the decision process. The formula is shown below.

| Mutual Trust | + | Product and Personal Competence | + | Understanding Benefactions | = | POSSIBLE SALE |

Figure 3.3 Criteria for Making a Sale

However, one more key part of the formula is needed in order for the equation to actually work. Rapport must be underneath the entire process to actually close the deal.

| Mutual Trust | + | Product and Personal Competence | + | Understanding Benefactions | = | SALE |

R A P P O R T

Figure 3.4 The Importance of Rapport

In the early '90s, I had the opportunity to work for one of the fastest growing software companies of that time. For five straight years, the company was a darling on Wall Street. For two of those years, it was one of the top five appreciating technology stocks on NASDAQ. In every office in the company, a plaque with a quote from the president was posted: "Always take the customer's point of view." The plaque covered only half the point. It should have read, "Always work to help the customers achieve their benefactions!"

Let's take another look at the pyramid of meeting success. With the addition of rapport, it actually is a pyramid, not just a triangle.

REPRESENTATIONAL SYSTEMS AND RAPPORT

How do you establish rapport? By speaking individuals' different languages, understanding their distinct representational systems (their "wiring") and relating to them in their world.

Most likely, you are being introduced to the details of their representational systems for the first time. The information may surprise or even startle you.

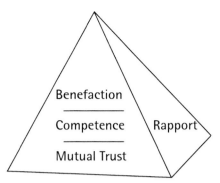

Figure 3.5 The Complete Pyramid of Meeting Success

Why is it important for you to learn and use this information? Understanding a person's representational system can aid you in achieving your benefaction by helping you create rapport. By being conscious of people's representational systems and communicating with them in the same meaningful terms they use, you will facilitate mutual trust and help demonstrate your competence. Customers will understand you better and, in fact, like you more because you are speaking the same language.

This chapter includes exercises to help you create rapport with your customers. Remember that learning something new always takes time. By honestly completing the exercises, you will be taking the first step in learning something very powerful.

Some people are left-handed and some are right-handed. The dominant hand you use was not your conscious choice. Your brain was "wired" to use that hand. In addition, over time you have grown comfortable and proficient in using it more than the other.

Some people also have a more dominant ear (perhaps the one you use when you talk on the telephone), a more dominant eye, and even a more dominant leg. Similarly, people have a dominant or primary representational system. They also have a weaker secondary system and finally, a recessive system. People process information with their representational systems using pictures, feelings, or words according to the strength of each system.

However, people do not use one representational system exclusively. Instead, they use all three representational systems. Because spoken language is the system we use to communicate our experiences, people will describe their experiences and convey their thoughts in terms that match their representational system wiring.

You can tell what people's representational system wiring is by noting the adjectives and verbs they use in their conversations. An adjective is a word used to modify a noun, and a verb is an action word. However, some words can be used as either a noun, verb, or adjective, and this usage will significantly change the interpretation of the representational system. The sentences in the left-hand column represent a visual, auditory, or kinesthetic usage, while those in the right-hand column do not imply any particular representational system.

Please *outline* your strategy.	He's finished with the *outline*.
Bob will *call* a meeting for tomorrow.	Did you get the phone *call*?
Let's *copy* what they're doing!	Please make me a *copy*.
Please *watch* your mouth.	His *watch* is broken.

The italicized words in the sentences in the left-hand column are verbs or adjectives that imply a particular representational system. Although the same words are used in the right-hand column, they are used as nouns. As you know, a noun is a word that describes a person, place, or thing. In general, nouns do not imply any particular representational system.

For example, people with a visual primary system will use visual keywords more frequently to describe their experiences than they will use auditory or kinesthetic words. Here are some examples of visual keywords:

Beaming	Demonstrate	Frame	Imagine	See
Bleak	Diagram	Gaze	Light	Shine
Bleary	Diffuse	Glance	Look	Show
Blight	Disappear	Glare	Magnify	Sight
Blind	Discern	Glimpse	Map	Snapshot
Bright	Display	Graph	Murky	Spectacle
Brilliant	Distinguish	Hallucinate	Observe	Spot
Chart	Dreary	Hazy	Outlook	Stare
Clarify	Emit	Highlight	Perspective	Survey
Clear	Expose	Illuminate	Preview	View
Cloudy	Fade	Illustrate	Reflect	Viewpoint
Dazzle	Focus	Image	Scan	Watch

People with an auditory primary system will use auditory keywords like these in their conversations:

Accent	Bark	Denounce	Note	Say
Amplify	Berate	Dictate	Paraphrase	Shout
Articulate	Bicker	Digress	Persuade	Slur
Ask	Blare	Discuss	Plead	Snap
Assert	Boast	Drone	Profess	Sound
Attune	Cajole	Edit	Promise	Speak
Audacious	Call	Giggle	Quiet	Spell
Audible	Chime	Hum	Rave	Talk
Backfire	Chord	Implore	Recap	Tell
Back-talk	Crunch	Loud	Retract	Vague
Banter	Cry	Noise	Ring	Yell

People with a kinesthetic primary system will use kinesthetic keywords like the following:

Ache	Catch	Hard	Pique	Smile
Bash	Chafe	Heart	Plug	Smooth
Bask	Chew	Heavy	Post	Spit
Bat	Choke	Hit	Press	Squash
Bend	Chop	Hold	Pull	Sticky
Bind	Clinch	Impact	Push	Stink
Bit	Cough	Impress	Queasy	Strike
Blink	Crawl	Irritate	Rough	Taste
Boot	Draw	Kick	Rub	Thaw
Bounce	Feel	Leap	Scratch	Throw
Bow	Friction	Mark	Sense	Touch
Breathe	Gnaw	Move	Sharp	Walk
Caress	Grab	Nip	Smell	Weigh

EXERCISE 1: HOW ARE YOU WIRED?

What is your primary representational system? Here's an exercise that will help you understand how you are wired. Print out the last ten business e-mails you sent to colleagues within your company and the last ten personal e-mails you sent to friends or family. Write the letters *V, A,* and *K* at the top of a piece of paper. In the left column write "Work," "Personal," and "Total." The chart should look like this.

	V	A	K
Work			
Personal			
Total			

Figure 3.6 VAK Keyword Count Chart

You are now ready to perform a "VAK keyword count." Examine the e-mails and circle each occurrence of a visual, auditory, or kinesthetic word. Remember to circle the usage of the word only when it is used in the context of an action or description ("you *light* up my life," not "please turn the *light* on"). As you circle the words, add a tally in the appropriate column. The chart may look something like this when you are done.

	V	A	K
Work	III	ℍℍ I	III
Personal	ℍℍ	ℍℍ ℍℍ	ℍℍ IIII
Total	ℍℍ III	ℍℍ ℍℍ ℍℍ I	ℍℍ ℍℍ II

Figure 3.7 Sample Results of a VAK Keyword Count

Was there a difference between the tallies from the work and personal e-mails? In the example above, the person is primary auditory, secondary kinesthetic, and recessive visual. Most likely, the language in your work e-mails is more androgynous and technical; therefore, the counts will be lower. Were the counts evenly dispersed or clustered under one system? You can do a similar exercise with the e-mails you receive to determine a sender's representational system wiring.

DETERMINING SOMEONE'S REPRESENTATIONAL SYSTEM

Although nouns do not usually imply any particular representational system, there are exceptions to this rule. When a person's communication is dominated by nouns that can be associated with one of the representational systems, it is a good indication of a person's wiring. For example, if an e-mail had a pervasive or repetitive use of nouns such as "photograph," "picture," or "maps," this would provide additional clues that the person is a Visual.

Other nuances about VAK keywords are helpful. Here are three separate e-mails I received from the same individual. All the VAK keywords are italicized.

E-MAIL #1

I *saw* Jeff's note on the good news about version eight and our token support. However, I would like to *see* us run a test to verify that the cluster is running *smoothly*. Can we do that?

E-MAIL #2

We have this gal *handled*. I *called* her and updated her with all the appropriate info right away. I have been working with a few folks including her around Q2 & Q3. *Looks* like we will be getting a deal from them. Will verify if it is a new opportunity or the one I have had in the pipeline for a while now.

E-MAIL #3

MAN. . . . I think we are *hearing* it all these days!!
I do not even want to know what we will *hear* next!!

If you do a VAK keyword count on these e-mails you will notice that the categories are almost equal (three visual, three auditory, and two kinesthetic). Since the VAK count is evenly distributed, how can you tell what this person's primary system is? The more stressful or tense a situation is, the more likely people will communicate in their primary representational system. The third e-mail was sent under very distressing circumstances. The sender had just been told he lost a deal in which he had invested a lot of time and effort. This person is wired as primary auditory, secondary visual, and recessive kinesthetic. I have validated this through my many conversations and interactions with him.

Bring a notebook to your next meeting, and perform a VAK count to determine the primary, secondary, and recessive representational systems of each of the participants. While people are being introduced, write their names down. In the left-hand margin of the paper, conduct a VAK count for each person. Another trick is to place their business cards inside your binder and write the VAK counts directly on them (in tiny print). Later, you can review the cards and refresh your memory about the people's wiring. The results of your VAK counts will be fascinating. You will begin to be able to identify a person's representational systems in a very short time. You will also spot patterns and similarities between people who share the same representational systems.

Everyone uses all three representational systems, just in different increments and priority. You have a primary representational system, which is your "default" method for accessing your catalogue of experiences. It is the system used most often. Visuals think in terms of pictures, Auditories in sounds, and Kinesthetics in terms of feelings. Your secondary representational system is your next strongest method for accessing your catalogue. Finally, your recessive system is your least used and least developed access method.

Many people make prejudiced generalizations about representational systems based upon their experiences with a small sample of people. For example, people may associate being kinesthetic with being more emotional. This may or may not be the case. Just because people's primary representational system is kinesthetic does not mean they are more emotional or temperamental than anyone else. It simply means they catalogue experiences and express themselves in terms of their feelings.

Whether people are introverted, extroverted, or emotionally mature is a function of their personality. While your customers' personalities are influenced by their representational systems, a person's personality is a complex matrix of different traits. In other words, you will meet introverted Visuals, and you will meet extroverted Visuals. You will interact with selfish and unselfish Kinesthetics. In chapter 9, we will review personality traits in further detail.

VAK KEYWORD COUNT PATTERNS

As you begin to perform VAK keyword counts, you will notice some patterns developing. At a sales meeting, I asked my entire sales force to perform VAK counts for three speakers making forty-five-minute presentations to the group. Interestingly, their VAK counts were representative of the three major types of VAK count patterns: balanced, strong secondary, and dominating primary.

Title	Visual	Auditory	Kinesthetic
President/CEO	20	17	14
Vice President of Engineering	16	20	2
Product Manager	5	34	4

Figure 3.8 Sample VAK Keyword Counts

We found that the president has a visual primary system along with strong auditory and kinesthetic systems. This is a very balanced pattern. This wiring suits him well in his position. As president, he is responsible for the vision of the company, and it makes sense to have a Visual in that role. Other responsibilities of the president are company communication and consensus building. His well-developed auditory and kinesthetic systems help him to naturally accomplish these two tasks with people who are not visually wired.

The vice president of engineering has an auditory primary system and a strong secondary visual system. His kinesthetic recessive system is almost nonexistent. The nature of the vice president of engineering's position is both analytical and visionary. He has to be able to give specific direction to the programming teams in order to build products. Since the communication framework by which this is done is a functional specification (a detailed description of the product in the form of words), having an auditory primary system helps.

Meanwhile, he has to chart the product road map; therefore, having a strong visual secondary is desirable. Since the vice president of engineering is consumed in the technical specification language (described earlier as precise, androgynous, nonpersonal language that uses technical operators to modify general words), a strong kinesthetic system is not necessarily needed in this position and, in fact, could even be a detriment.

The product manager has an overwhelmingly primary system that is so dominating that the secondary and recessive systems are very rarely used. This pattern is called a "dominating primary." In this example, the person has a dominating auditory primary system. A dominating system could be visual or kinesthetic just as well.

This person's role is primarily technical. One of his main job functions is to create detailed technical collateral, such as white papers, data sheets, and technical content for the company's Web site. Having a strong auditory primary system is helpful in accomplishing these tasks.

In addition to the VAK keywords, catch phrases, descriptions, and clichés also reveal a speaker's representational systems. Some individuals use an unusually high number of clichés, for example. These people tend to be strong Auditories, and they actually repeat a cliché to themselves first before repeating it externally. In fact, Auditories actually spend more time listening to themselves speak than Visuals and Kinesthetics because the volume of their internal dialogues is higher.

Sayings, descriptions, and clichés may be used by people from all three systems. However, usually a phrase is more often used by people with one particular system. For example, "sizzling hot" is most likely to be said by Auditories. They hear the sizzling sound. Upon hearing this phrase, Visuals might picture a grill with something sizzling on it, and Kinesthetics might think of a finger actually touching the grill (particularly if they have burnt themselves in the past).

EXERCISE 2: SAYINGS AND CLICHÉS

Let's do another exercise. Below is a list of sayings and clichés. After each phrase, mark a *V* for visual, *A* for auditory, and *K* for kinesthetic. If you think the phrase has multiple interpretations, write the order of what you believe is the priority usage. Here are some examples:

"music to my ears," A   "from their perspective," V
"windows are opening," V, K   "that's alarming news," A

The answers follow, but don't look at them until you finish the entire list.

"tough nut to crack" *A, k*   "juggling so many balls" *V*
"balls in the air" *V|C*   "iron out the problem" *K*
"we'll keep pinging him" *A(k4)*   "play it back for me" *A*
"push the deal" *K*   "look them in the eye" *V*
"we'll hammer it out" *KA*   "banging the phones" *A,*
"coin rattling down the pipe" *A*   "see how the smoke clears" *V*
"die a slow death" *K, N*   "they want to vent" *A*
"level playing field" *K*   "domino effect" *k V*
"I'm listening to this feedback" *A*   "ear to the ground" *A*
"he's sharp" *k*   "that's a new twist" *k V*
"bottom line, in a nutshell" *V K*   "echos what I say" *A*
"dream state" *K V*   "close-knit" *K*
"breathe some life" *V*   "after my own heart" *k*
"talk it through" *A*   "crunch time" *K, A*
"touch it every day" *k*   "harping on this" *A*
"flying off the shelves" *V*   "newly charted territory" *K, V*
"recipe in the cookbook" *A V*   "talk a little bit about" *A*
"take that to heart" *V A*   "carry the flag" *k, V*
"talk the talk" *V, A*   "in the crosshairs"
"from their perspective" *V*   "that resonates with me"
"kick them when they're down" *k*   "bubble to the top"

Based on my experience, here is the most likely usage of these phrases matched to the representational system:

"tough nut to crack," A, K   "juggling so many balls," K, V
"balls in the air," V, K   "iron out the problem," K

"we'll keep pinging him," A

"push the deal," K

"we'll hammer it out," K, A

"coin rattling down the pipe," A

"die a slow death," K, V

"level playing field," V, K

"I'm listening to this feedback," A

"he's sharp," K

"bottom line, in a nutshell," K

"dream state," V

"breathe some life," K,V

"talk it through," A

"touch it everyday," K

"flying off the shelves," V

"recipe in the cookbook," A, V

"take that to heart," K

"talk the talk," A

"from their perspective," V

"kick them when they're down," K

"play it back for me," A

"look them in the eye," V, K

"banging the phones," A

"see how the smoke clears," V

"they want to vent," A

"domino effect," K, V

"ear to the ground," A

"that's a new twist," K

"echos what I say," A

"close-knit," K

"after my own heart," K

"crunch time," A, K

"harping on this," A

"newly charted territory," V

"talk a little bit about," A

"carry the flag," K

"in the crosshairs," V

"that resonates with me," A

"bubble to the top," V, A

There is another very interesting way to learn about a person's representational wiring. To understand this, it is helpful to revisit how computers work. Computer systems store data in two areas, either in short-term random access memory (RAM chips) or in long-term storage (hard drives). Since RAM has no mechanical parts, it is much quicker to access RAM. However, RAM is more expensive than long-term storage. Therefore, it is impractical to keep all your data in RAM. When you turn off your computer system, you lose the contents of your RAM. However, the information in long-term storage is still stored on the hard drive, regardless of whether the computer is on or off.

If I ask you what you had for dinner last night, you will easily be able to give me an answer. In a way, you can think of this information as being stored in your brain's short-term RAM because of its recent occurrence. However, if I ask you what the most memorable dinner you have ever had was, you will have to access your long-term storage to process and compare different memorable dinners. You would access and remember the dinner using your primary representational system, whether you think of the appearance of the restaurant, the taste of the food, or the conversation during the meal (pictures, feelings, and sounds). Like a computer, you use your input and output systems (senses) to gather information and form an answer.

You can think of your primary representational system as the default method of cataloging your experiences. It is your personal search engine for your brain. With an Internet search engine (such as Yahoo), you start your search based on a topic and receive a list of results. From this list, you can access more detailed information (such as Web sites). Similarly, your primary representational system is the key by which you can retrieve a complete experience (or memory). For example, if you are a Visual, your initial search would be through mental images. Once the correct mental image is found, you could access the auditory and kinesthetic portions of the experience.

Suppose you are asked, "What was the best day of your life?" If your primary system is visual, you may search your memory, looking at many stored pictures before finally deciding on the day your first child was born. To make this decision, you retrieved a picture of the hospital room, which then may have triggered the feeling of holding your baby for the first time and being both joyous and nervous. The experience may have been further embellished by hearing the sound of the baby crying in your mind.

Take a minute and think about the best deal you ever closed. Pay close attention and try to follow the path of your representational

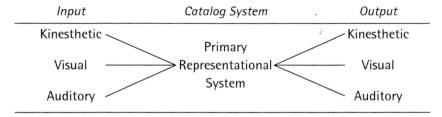

Figure 3.9 Cataloging Experiences

systems. What did you experience? Depending on how you are wired (as an Auditory, Visual, or Kinesthetic), here are examples of what might have happened:

- Auditory—You thought of being told by the customer you won the deal or telling your manager or your spouse you won the deal.

- Visual—You saw a picture of the company's building or the people who bought your products.

- Kinesthetic—You thought of holding the signed contract or your commission check or shaking hands with the customer or your colleagues.

Your brain has a very efficient technique of searching for information using your primary system. When compared to your primary system, your secondary and recessive systems are less developed. Since your recessive system is the least used, you may find you have the most difficulty accessing it. However, if you start to incorporate the use of language associated with your secondary and recessive systems daily, it becomes easier (as they become more developed), and you will find your use of all three systems more balanced. Exercising these other parts of the brain makes them grow, much like exercising any muscle.

Representational systems are physically powerful. If you became particularly ill while eating a certain food, the smell or sight of that food may trigger queasiness. To this day, I can barely stand the sight and smell of salmon, bacon bits, or gin because they trigger very bad past experiences. Conversely, the smell of freshly cut grass always reminds me of football and being part of a team.

Even people can be triggers. Think for a moment about someone who has seriously mistreated you or whom you are deeply in love with. Every time you see this person, the corresponding emotion is triggered.

EXERCISE 3: ANCHORS

Let's do another exercise. Think of the best day of your business career. Have a very specific day in your mind. Remember how great you felt on this day. Perhaps it was a day you received an award or were promoted. Whatever it is, try to relive the feelings, hear the sounds, and recreate a picture of it in your mind. Take a minute to do this. While holding these thoughts, take your right hand and pinch the back of your left hand. You have now created an "anchor." An anchor is the process of associating a certain feeling to an object. Unlike triggers, anchors are conscious, premeditated associations.

USING ANCHORS

Here's a personal story about how I use anchors. I had been asked by my sales office in Boston to speak to a group of one hundred people at a seminar. I was very apprehensive about this presentation for three reasons. First, the audience was a gathering of very senior technical people. This alone took me out of my comfort zone. Second, I was to give an entirely new presentation based on a subject in which I do not consider myself an expert. And finally, a well-known and widely respected author of several books on this subject would be speaking immediately following my presentation.

The pressure was definitely on. I prepared and rehearsed my presentation many, many times. Although I felt confident I knew the content, I was still nervous. I was very tense when I walked into the meeting room and saw the crowd. Immediately prior to my presentation, I spent a few minutes replaying the tapes in my mind from previous successful presentations. I chose one event in particular and anchored it to my left hand (by pinching the back of it). As the announcer introduced me, I pinched my anchor. I became calm, confident, and relaxed. The presentation was a huge success.

Anchors are valuable tools, and I use them all the time. For example, when someone on my staff did something great, I gently put my hand on his shoulder and let him know how much I appreciated his hard work. Later, perhaps when he was feeling down, I put my hand on his shoulder in the same manner and his spirits changed noticeably. Hitters naturally anchor with their customers in a similar manner. When Heavy Hitters take their clients to play golf or out to dinner, they are actually attempting to anchor themselves to a positive experience in the customer's mind.

You've probably already noticed my name is Steve Martin. When I introduce myself, people almost always smile. I am very lucky to have a name that triggers a positive recollection of such a humorous person.

Over the years, I have noticed an interesting pattern after I am introduced. An Auditory will most likely say "Excuuuse me!" while a Visual will be more likely to ask where my arrow is. For me, my name is also my personal anchor. I feel good when I say my name, as I hope you do when you say your own.

Conversely, I once had a business meeting with a fellow named Jesse James. Sharing the name of a famous outlaw is obviously a lot less desirable way to start a meeting.

In sales, we are frequently placed in uncomfortable situations where rapport is nonexistent. Under these circumstances, the Hitter's job is to create a receptive environment. Using humor is a great way to start the process. When people laugh, at some level they agree with you or they have shared the same experience.

In particular, self-effacing humor, where Heavy Hitters poke fun at themselves, is particularly effective. For example, if my name were Jesse James I would try to make light of the situation and might say, "Be careful, I'm meaner than a sidewinder in molting season." Being able to turning a negative into positive is a fundamental part of selling.

EXERCISE 4: IDENTIFY YOUR CUSTOMER'S WIRING

We are going to finish this chapter with another exercise. It is critical that you be able to identify your customer's wiring. Like the earlier exercise, after each phrase write a *V* for visual, *A* for auditory, and *K* for kinesthetic in the order of priority usage:

"what we are shooting for"   "in a later discussion"
"glimpse of the future"   "one thing to mention"
"across the company"   "look at the numbers"
"put our finger on it"   "the question is"
"we're cooking now"   "take a step back"
"want to point out"   "through the tunnel"
"they're hooked,"   "what's the angle"
"flowing through"   "train left the station"
"humming along"   "hindsight is always 20/20"
"tell you what"   "walk through"
"concrete example"   "cry on your shoulder"
"apples and oranges"   "weigh the possibilities"

Following are the answers to exercise 4:

"what we are shooting for," V, A, K   "in a later discussion," A
"glimpse of the future," V   "one thing to mention," A

"across the company," V

"put our finger on it," K

"we're cooking now," K, A

"want to point out," V

"they're hooked," K, A

"flowing through," K, A

"humming along," A

"tell you what," A

"concrete example," K, V

"apples and oranges," V

"look at the numbers," V

"the question is," A

"take a step back," K

"through the tunnel," V, K

"what's the angle," V

"train left the station," K, V, A

"hindsight is always 20/20," V

"walk through," K, V

"cry on your shoulder," K

"weigh the possibilities," K

CONCLUSION

Let's review some of the key concepts introduced in this chapter. We experience the world by receiving constant streams of information from our visual, auditory, and kinesthetic senses. However, this information can overwhelm our conscious mind's ability to process it. Therefore, information is ignored, misinterpreted, or generalized. In order to have accurate and complete information about a deal, Heavy Hitters triangulate with the other members of the sales team. Through this process, they further define the account strategy.

A key factor in formulating the strategy is identifying the individual benefactions of the customers. A benefaction is the self-centered interest of each person involved in the selection process. When Heavy Hitters meet with a customer, they know they must establish mutual trust and demonstrate competence in order to align themselves with their customer's benefaction. Most importantly, rapport must be present. By understanding how people use their representational systems, you can help create rapport.

People's representational systems are responsible for how they process information (in words, sounds, or pictures) and relate to the world. They will always have a primary, secondary, and recessive representational system. To identify their systems, you can perform a

VAK count of the most frequent descriptive or action words they use. Their sayings, descriptions, and clichés will also reveal their wiring.

People catalogue experiences using their primary representational system. Once catalogued, the primary system triggers the retrieval of the other aspects of the experiences. Also, you can use your representational systems to purposely anchor a past experience. By doing so, you will be able to recreate the total experience on demand.

By storing past experiences, people create personal histories that are used in the decision-making process. Or as Bill Walsh, one of the most successful coaches in the history of professional football, described it, "History is our collective memory. It is our accumulated experiences. It is invoked constantly and unconsciously by every person, every day, to help them make decisions based, to some extent, on what has gone on before in their lives."[5]

Finally, we learned that language is a direct reflection of how the brain operates and is organized. In addition to examining a person's language usage, there's another, even more interesting, way to determine how someone is wired. Amazingly, you can actually watch the brain access information. We'll cover this technique in the next chapter.

4

How People Think

In the last week alone, Darren had made more than two dozen cold calls to the chief technology officer (CTO) of a prominent bank. Finally, on a Tuesday around 7 P.M. he caught him at his desk.

"This is George," said the CTO as he answered his telephone.

"Hello, George, this is Darren from ABC Computer Company and I have been trying to reach you for some time."

"Oh, you're the one who's been *calling* me night and day. Do you realize how many *calls* I get? It's simply impossible to *talk* to everyone who *calls* me," lectured George.

"And I wouldn't bother you unless I had something important to *say*," Darren said sincerely. "Eight of the top ten largest banks use our software. They *tell* us that we have helped reduce their systems' downtime by an average of 25 percent. I have been *calling* you to schedule a meeting to *discuss* how we might possibly help you."

"Well, I'm very busy."

"I understand and I *promise* it will be worth your time."

"Hmmm . . . as long as it is brief. *Call* my assistant tomorrow to schedule an appointment."

Every day, you speak and listen to thousands of words. Through the words you speak, you are able to explain your ideas, recount your past experiences, and share your personality with others. Since it comes so naturally, it is easy to take the communication process for granted. However, its complexity is quickly remembered when you travel abroad and have to communicate with someone who doesn't know your language.

You are an expert at conveying information. Since you do it all the time, you have learned the most efficient way to transmit and receive a message or several messages at once. You have also mastered how to conduct simultaneous conversations while performing different physical activities. For example, you are able to drive your car, listen to the radio, and talk on your cellular telephone at the same time. Undoubtedly, you have typed an e-mail and conducted a meeting concurrently.

Most of the time, you probably don't think about the specific meaning of the words you are using. Since they are so integrated with your being, they just seem to happen. However, your words represent your attitude, outlook, and perspective about life. For example, sitting in my backyard on a moonless night, I can describe the light emanating from a galaxy as a "pinpoint." Looking at the same stars, an astronomer might talk about the apparent magnitude of the Horsehead Nebula in the Orion constellation. A physicist might explain the complex principles of nuclear fusion. Meanwhile, an astrologer might view the same stars as an apparition of the future. While we are all viewing the same stars, the language we use to describe our viewpoint will reflect our individual orientation.

In the last chapter, we learned how we organize the world according to the information received by our senses (sight, sound, touch, taste, and smell) and that we use language as the method to describe what we have experienced. The language we use is dependent upon an individual's representational system, and each person has a primary, secondary, and recessive system that determines how his or her brain processes and stores information. In this chapter, we are going to take the next step in understanding the connection between the brain and the communication process. You will learn how you can actually "watch" the mechanical movements of the brain as they access a particular representational system and how this enables you to identify a person's wiring. Once identified, you can then adjust your communication style to build rapport using the customer's own language. After you have mastered this technique, you will be able to tell when a person's communication is congruent (truthful) or incongruent (misleading). Here's a hint at how it's done. It all starts with looking your customer in the eye!

Ralph Waldo Emerson once said, "Tell me what you know."[6] In my case, I feel I know three subjects very well: people, sales, and computers. Therefore, I tend to use examples from these areas to explain concepts of "how things work." By way of illustration, let's review how a computer works as a logical model to understand how the brain operates.

My first computer (back in the '70s) wasn't very powerful by today's standards. However, it had the same architecture that you find in state-of-the-art computers today. Here's a list of the major components of a computer:

- CPU (central processing unit)—The chips that process information, perform calculations, and control the other computer components.

- I/O (input/output)—The hardware components by which information enters and exits the computer (keyboard, mouse, monitor, network port, and printer).

- OS (operating system)—Software that tells hardware what to do.

- Short-Term Storage (random-access memory, or RAM)—Data storage that is kept on chips electronically.

- Long-Term Storage (hard disk drive)—Data storage that is kept on devices magnetically.

Here's a simplistic overview of how computers work. The CPU can process a finite number of instructions or requests each second.

Each of the components—input/output, storage, and operating system—is continually requesting processing time from the CPU for its own needs. Although the CPU is processing at a very high speed, it is capable of serving only one component at a time. However, since it handles these requests at such a fast pace, from the outside it looks like everything is happening simultaneously.

The slowest parts of a computer have moving or mechanical parts. Storing and retrieving data electronically from RAM (short-term memory) is much faster than storing and retrieving data magnetically on a hard drive (long-term memory). Since the hard drive has to position a mechanical arm to a precise spot on a spinning disk and physically manipulate the surface of the disk, it takes more time to read and write information.

Although it weighs only three pounds, our brain is infinitely more complex than any computer. It's an intricate architecture of one hundred million neurons (nerve cells) and one hundred thousand connectors or pathways that control all of our body's components. These components include the nervous system, muscular system, respiratory system, digestive system, and circulatory system. These systems are also responsible for gathering data via our senses.

The brain has three major parts: the cerebrum, cerebellum, and brainstem. From a sales perspective, we are most interested in what is happening within the cerebrum. The cerebrum controls our voluntary actions, such as body sensations, learning, emotions, and pain. Two hemispheres make up the cerebrum. The right side controls the left side of the body. The left side controls the right side of the body. This cross-management occurs because the nerves connecting the brain to the body cross the spinal cord. The cerebellum coordinates our movement and keeps us in balance. The brainstem controls our automatic functions, such as breathing, heartbeat, and circulation.

If you are right-handed, you have a dominant left side of the brain. You are more likely to have a higher proficiency in solving problems, doing math, and using language. If you are left-handed, you have a dominant right side of the brain. You are more likely to have a higher proficiency in the arts, such as music, writing, and drawing. Your brain is wired a certain way. You were born with this wiring and you cannot change or camouflage it.

The brain has an incredible capacity to sort, prioritize, and process information. As you read this book, your lungs are breathing, your food is digesting, and your heart is pumping blood to all parts of your body, without your having to think about it. Meanwhile, you are consciously moving your eyes to the next word to be read and saying that word to yourself. When you reach the bottom of the page, your hand and arm will execute a complex series of muscle movements in response to commands from the brain to turn the page.

While it is interesting to know the parts of the brain and understand their physiological function, it is helpful to think of the brain's architecture as being much like the structure of a computer. However, as shown in the following diagram, the brain's design actually has two CPUs. A computer with two or more CPUs is called a Symmetric Multi-Processor machine, or SMP machine. In an SMP machine, each CPU has access to all the components, and each CPU can process information independently of or in conjunction with the other.

The following diagram represents the "computerized" architecture of the brain. You will notice one CPU processor is solely dedicated to the internal dialogue, while the other CPU is busy servicing all the systems of the body (nervous, muscular, respiratory, digestive, and circulatory). In addition, each of the CPUs has a conscious or "controllable" side and a subconscious or "uncontrollable" side.

It's helpful for a salesperson to think in terms of this diagram. The first CPU, or your internal dialogue, is very dominating. It's always on, always engaged, and always talking to you. It drives the language being used and the actions of the Heavy Hitter during the sales call. Likewise, the customer's internal dialogue is equally active.

The second CPU, which is in charge of managing all the body's components, is working independently most of the time. However,

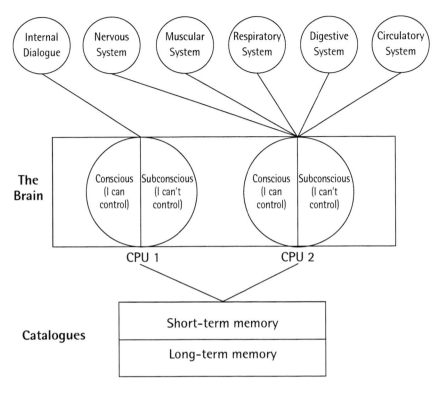

Figure 4.1 The Brain Compared to a Computer

during a sales call, the words spoken and actions of the participants can have an immense affect on this CPU, which results in changes to the body. Heavy Hitters monitor all of the sales call participants for these bodily changes. Are they tense or relaxed? Are they breathing faster or slower? Finally and most importantly, understanding how each CPU accesses short-term and long-term memory enables Heavy Hitters to validate their customers' representational system wiring. Once they understand, Heavy Hitters can be assured they are communicating effectively to build rapport and even determine when they are being told the truth.

As you read each sentence of this book, your internal dialogue repeats the content, assesses the content, and makes a decision about whether it is meaningful, believable, and applicable. After the assessment, your internal dialogue prepares a response to the words it just heard based upon what it thinks. The same process is true for conversation during a sales call. The internal dialogue requires the full-time processing and the attention of a dedicated CPU.

You can't turn off your internal dialogue. It's always there, always working consciously. It's also being affected by subconscious memories of past experiences. When you make a sales call, you are not talking to people. You are talking to their internal dialogue. Understanding this is crucial to becoming a Heavy Hitter.

During the sales call, the Hitter's internal dialogue is at its loudest. It is constantly communicating, telling the Hitter what to say next and how to respond to questions. It also monitors the rapport being established with participants.

OBSERVING INTERNAL DIALOGUES

The airport is a fascinating place to study internal dialogues. If you are in sales, you undoubtedly spend a great deal of time there. The travelers are most likely thinking about where they are going, and their internal dialogue is consumed with the success of their personal benefaction (whether it is going home to family or off to an important meeting). Airports are also stressful places because we are in a situation where we have little control. Our subconscious is always preparing us for bad news (primarily based upon previous experiences). Hence, the internal dialogue of travelers can be very nasty. It also quickly surfaces to reveal itself in their spoken words.

Groups of travelers have a completely different demeanor from that of someone traveling alone. Having someone to share your internal dialogue with reduces the stress (one reason to bring someone along on your next sales call). If you take a moment to stand by the flight arrival and departure monitors, you will notice people traveling alone will be talking to themselves, repeating aloud their flight and gate numbers. Watch them as they walk through the airport. You can almost hear their internal dialogues calculating the time and distance to the gate.

THE BRAIN'S OTHER CPU

While one CPU is controlling the internal dialogue, a second CPU is managing the systems that control body functions. Normally, this CPU doesn't require any direct conscious involvement. For example, it is controlling your next breath and moving blood throughout your body on its own. However, each of the systems can be impacted or overridden by the first CPU (the internal dialogue). Here's another way to explain this: the words you say and the words other people say to you affect your entire body. As a result, the body is continuously transmitting valuable information about a person's mental state.

When people are discussing issues they are passionate about, their hearts pump more blood and their skin flushes. The volume of their voices may rise and their speech quicken. Conversely, people who are bored or apathetic will fidget or become lethargic. People who are worried may feel sick to their stomachs, and their bodies will broadcast this. Consequently, Heavy Hitters are astutely aware of the physical communication of the body. The next chapter is devoted to understanding how Heavy Hitters interpret and manage this important channel of communication.

EYE MOVEMENTS

Here is the most interesting and relevant part of the diagram to understand. Both CPUs can access short-term and long-term memory to recreate an experience. For example, when you sleep, your mind can create vivid dreams. You can be transported back to your childhood to relive an experience that is stored in your long-term memory, or you can replay yesterday's sales call that resides in your short-term memory. Although they are just dreams, they seem equally real.

Similarly, when you are awake, you are constantly accessing your short-term and long-term memory. However, it is much easier to access your short-term memory. Accessing your long-term memory is harder and slower. Much like the computer's disk drive, it requires some "mechanical" movements. Short-term storage is accessed "electronically" and is therefore unobservable. However, access to long-term memory can be seen. Amazingly, by observing people's eye movements, you can follow the mechanical movements of the brain that happen when they access their long-term memory. By watching their eyes move, you can determine if they are making pictures in their mind, listening to themselves speak, or experiencing feelings. From this information, you can determine their representational system wiring.

When people remember pictures, their eyes will move up. When people remember sounds, they will move their eyes down to the left, straight to the right, or straight to the left. When people remember feelings, their eyes will move down to the right. Take a minute and do the following eye movements. After each movement, make a mental note if it was more comfortable than the others.

- Up and to the right
- Straight to the right
- Down and to the right
- Down and to the left
- Straight to the left
- Up and to the left

What happened? Did some movements feel strained while others were easy? Suppose that in the analysis of your e-mails you performed earlier, your VAK count indicated that you have a visual primary, kinesthetic secondary, and auditory recessive wiring. Most likely, the auditory eye movements were noticeably more uncomfortable to make than the others. If your VAK count indicated you are wired with an auditory primary, kinesthetic secondary, and visual recessive, then the visual movements were most likely harder to do. Eye movements reflect how the brain is processing information.

When remembering pictures, people will move their eyes up to the right, keep their eyes straight while defocusing their pupils, or move them up to the left.

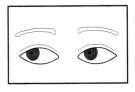 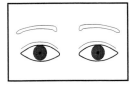 

Figure 4.2 Visual Representational System Eye Movements

When remembering sounds, people will move their eyes straight to the right, down to the left, or straight to the left.

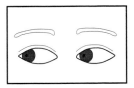 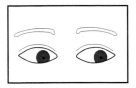 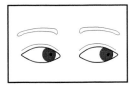

Figure 4.3 Auditory Representational System Eye Movements

People will move their eyes down to the right when remembering feelings.

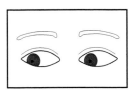

Figure 4.4 Kinesthetic Representational System Eye Movements

Recall the earlier example of someone being asked, "What was the best day of your life?" Visuals may start searching their memory by looking for stored pictures before finally deciding on a specific day, such as the day their first child was born. To search their memory bank of pictures, their eyes would move up to the right, move up to the left, or look straight ahead with the pupils defocused. Once retrieved, the picture could then trigger the feeling they had of holding the baby for the first time. Their eyes would move down to the right to get the feeling. Finally, to recreate the entire experience, their eyes may move down to the left or straight to the right or left to actually recall the sound of the baby crying.

Have you ever tried to have conversations with people who would not look at you? Perhaps they tilted their heads down and stared at the ground during the entire discussion. Maybe they turned their heads slightly to the right or left so that it seemed they were looking at something behind you. Or they could have cocked their heads back, as if they were looking at the sky. Each of these scenarios is an example of someone who has an exceptionally strong or dominant primary system. These people have a single system that is so controlling that their heads become an extension of their eye movements. If their eyes move down and to the right, that indicates they are dominant Kinesthetics, while people who always tilt their heads up are dominant Visuals. When people stare down and to the left or laterally away from you for the majority of your conversation, you can assume they are dominant Auditories. The person you may have thought of as being "shifty eyed," or untrustworthy, may actually just be an Auditory.

SHORT-TERM AND LONG-TERM MEMORY

Two categories of information are kept in your long-term memory, date-dependent experiences and minutiae. Just like a computer's RAM memory, your short-term memory has a limited amount of space. In comparison to RAM, the computer's disk drive (long-term storage) has much more space available. Similarly, your long-term memory is almost infinite. Therefore, your brain is continually optimizing what is kept in short-term memory and "writing," or transferring, it to your long-term memory. As time goes by following an event, its relevance diminishes, causing it to be reclassified into long-term memory. In addition, your brain will place small details that are considered trivial directly into long-term storage. In this case, the date of the experience has nothing to do with where the experience is stored. It is being stored based solely upon its importance.

Every morning, I read the business section of the local newspaper. While I ignore most of the information, news I consider important is placed into my short-term memory. This morning, for example, I made a mental note that the next Federal Reserve meeting is on the twenty-seventh. If it lowers rates again, I may want to pursue refinancing my home loan. Therefore, I placed this important date in my short-term memory. Once the date passes, this information will become trivial and be moved into long-term storage. However, all the other minutiae from today's business section was immediately placed into my long-term memory. If later in the day someone asked me what I had read that morning, it would require the identical eye movements to access the information as if I read it a year ago. Remember, some information is placed into long-term memory regardless of the date it is experienced.

EXERCISE 5: YOUR EYE MOVEMENTS

At this point, you may still be skeptical about whether eye movements can really explain what is happening in the brain. Try this experiment. However, before you start you will need to find a mirror. This exercise is much more meaningful when you can watch yourself, so don't proceed until you are in front of a mirror.

Below, you will find a list of questions. All of these questions are intended to make you access your long-term memory. However, it is possible that an answer is actually stored in your short-term memory. Finding answers in short-term memory doesn't require any specific eye movements. For example, if I ask, "When did you wake up this morning?" the answer is available instantaneously without much work. However, if I ask you what time you woke up last Saturday, that answer may require some additional thought.

As you read each question, try to follow your eye movements. Specifically, concentrate on where your eyes move first to "search" for the answer and make a notation of it. Use *UL* to reflect upper left and *UR* for upper right. Write *SL* for straight left, *S* for straight center, *SD* for straight defocused, and *SR* for straight right. Write *DL* for down left, *DR* for down right, and *DC* for down center. Also try to pay specific attention to the exact position of your eyes when you actually "find" the answer.

1. What did you have for dinner last Friday?

2. What was the name of your third-grade teacher?

3. What was your favorite vacation?

4. What was the best job you ever had?

5. What was the best sports event you ever attended?

6. Who is your favorite music group?

7. Where were you when you received your first real kiss?

8. What was the worst day of your life?

9. What was your SAT verbal score?

10. What was the color and license plate number of your first car?

What happened? Did you have to look away from your reflection to answer a question? Where did your eyes move first? What was the last position of your eyes when you found an answer?

Let's examine the questions further. They are all date dependent and designed to access your long-term memory. However, it's possible that some of the answers were in your short-term memory. It depends on you. If you're reading this book on Saturday, it's easy to remember what you had for dinner yesterday. However, if you're reading it on Thursday, the answer may be in long-term memory. If you had Friday's dinner at your favorite restaurant or ate with a classmate you hadn't seen in ten years, then it would be more likely that the experience would be in short-term memory. If there wasn't anything particularly eventful about the meal, it was probably placed in long-term memory.

I could not tell you who my third-grade teacher was. However, I do know a person who can name each of her teachers, even though she attended school over forty years ago. Not surprisingly, she is now a counselor and has dedicated herself to helping others. Obviously, her teachers had a lasting impact on her and this information has been stored to reflect its importance.

If it has been a long time since you took a vacation, you probably had to do a complex mental search to determine your favorite one. If you were on vacation last week, you may have recently performed this comparison, and the results are still in your short-term memory. If all of your vacations have been indistinguishable or you had a problem selecting the correct answer, you may have continued in a "search loop."

It's easy to spot people using their search loop. Their eyes are moving around in a circle, going from system to system. They'll start in the primary system, move to the secondary system, then the recessive system, and then repeat the process. Someone with a particularly strong dominant primary will get stuck with his eyes in the primary representational position. When this happens in the sales call, the

Heavy Hitter knows that the customer is trying to "find" the answer. Since the answer wasn't immediately retrievable, most likely it represents the customer's best guess and the answer needs to be validated.

This experiment was intended to make you aware of your own eye movements. This exercise should have helped you understand and validate your own representational wiring. Don't be concerned if you were unable to complete every question, as it is hard to track eye movements when you can't look yourself in the eye.

EXERCISE 6: SHORT-TERM MEMORY

Now, let's do another experiment. Look in the mirror and ask yourself these questions:

1. What did you have for breakfast today?

2. What color is your car?

3. What is your birthday?

4. What is your zip code?

5. What is your social security number?

Did you notice completely different eye movements or no movement at all? While the first set of questions required you to access your long-term memory, the second set of questions probably didn't. Most likely, the answers were already in your short-term memory because the experience happened recently or you use this information all the time. In computer terms, the answers for the first set of questions required you to access the hard drive, while the second set of answers was already cached (held temporarily) in your RAM.

Now, take the first list of ten questions to some friends you know very well. Without telling them why, ask them the same questions. However, instruct them not to tell you the answers. Rather, at the instant they know the answer have them say, "Got it!" After each question make two notations—where their eyes went first and where their eyes were when they said, "Got it." You should get a very consistent pattern. Once again, the direction their eyes consistently move indicates a person's primary representation system. Most likely, it will also be the same place they find the answer.

CALIBRATING EYE MOVEMENTS

Twenty years ago, it was more common for companies with expensive merchandise to require potential employees to take a polygraph (lie detector) test, and when I joined a large computer firm, I had this requirement imposed on me. The polygraph measures the body's response (breathing, heart rate, and temperature) as you answer questions. At the beginning of the polygraph test, the administrator asks a certain number of questions he knows to be true, such as your name and where you live. These questions calibrate your response of a known answer to the machine's measurements.

Similarly, you can calibrate eye movements of individuals by watching their response to known answers. By doing this, you are establishing a baseline measurement of their truthfulness. For example, you just finished a great meeting with the decision maker who is responsible for buying your product. Based on the presentation, you know he is auditory primary, kinesthetic secondary, and visual recessive.

HITTER: How long have you been evaluating solutions?
DECISION MAKER: (eyes left, momentary pause) "Well, we started last . . . November."

Analysis: Since the evaluation started over ten months ago, this question was a date-dependent event stored in long-term memory.

HITTER: When do you plan to roll out the first systems?
DECISION MAKER: (eyes straight, not defocused, instantaneous answer) "Our plan is to be up and running by the end of Q2."

Analysis: This is another date-dependent question. However, the answer was in short-term memory. This is probably an important project date, and it is always on his mind.

> HITTER: Where will the first system be implemented?
> DECISION MAKER: (in a search loop, eyes move left, down left, upper right) "Probably . . . Los Angeles."

Analysis: This question may have caused him to search for an answer. He was actually making his best guess as the decision is not final.

> HITTER: What other companies are you talking to?
> DECISION MAKER: (eyes straight, not defocused) "We are looking at Acme, Beta Company, and ABC Company."

Analysis: The answer resided in short-term memory. He's probably talking to all the vendors on a regular basis.

> HITTER: Does one of the solutions sound better than the rest?
> DECISION MAKER: (eyes up to the right) "No, they all sound the same."

Analysis: Incongruence! Or as the robot from the classic television series *Lost in Space* would say, "Danger! Danger!"

In the preceding example, the first four questions established the baseline measurement. The decision maker's eyes moved to the left when he accessed his long-term memory. They were straight center (not defocused) when he accessed his short-term memory. Any eye movements outside these two ranges must be evaluated in context with the answer.

We can assume that the answers to the first three questions were truthful. The third answer was his best guess. Based on the nonpolitical content of the question, this would be an appropriate assumption. The answer to the fourth question, about which companies he is evaluating, should be in short-term memory. If the answers "Acme,

Beta Company, and ABC Company" were given extemporaneously at a quick tempo, then you would assume the answer is truthful. If he went into a thirty-second search loop to produce the other vendors, he's editing his response, which is another form of incongruence, and this requires further investigation. If you observe very complex eye movements for seemingly simple questions or no eye movement to questions for which you would expect movement, then you need to investigate further to ensure the person is being truthful.

The fifth question is the interesting one. The collection of these five questions represents one vignette as previously described in chapter 2. The questions from this vignette may seem free flowing, but they were purposely constructed and orchestrated by the Heavy Hitter. He wanted to know if the playing field was level or if there was a favored vendor. His goal was to find the truth. The first four questions established the baseline to set up the fifth question. This is reminiscent of the boxer who throws a series of right jabs in order to land a big left hook. While the first four questions provide valuable content-level information about the sales process, they also give the Heavy Hitter a chance to calibrate the answers to the customer's representational system. The answer he gave to the fifth question is most likely a lie.

While answering the fifth question, his eyes went up to the right to his visual recessive system. This is the first incongruence. Based on the previous questions, we would have expected that his eyes would either go to short-term memory (straight, not defocused) or long-term memory (straight left). Since his eyes went to the visual position instead, it can be assumed he was "imagining" or creating an answer.

The second incongruence is that the visual eye movements do not match the content language he is using. "No, they all sound the same" is an auditory statement. However, when he said this, his eyes were in a visual position. The two incongruencies would suggest that this person is not telling the entire truth. This type of incongruence happens all the time during sales meetings. Most Hitters rely on their intuition to tell them they are being misled. With this methodology, anyone can develop the same skill by tracking eye movements and matching these movements to spoken words.

If you are a salesperson armed with this information, you have two courses of action. First, you could introduce a new round of questioning to further determine the extent of the bias. For example, you could ask, "Has the company used other products from one of the vendors?" "Has anyone on the selection team used products from one of the vendors?" Or you can take a greater risk approach by confronting the customer with your suspicions that one vendor is favored.

Second, you could take this information and incorporate it into your account strategy. You could implement account tactics that would require the customers to make extraordinary commitments, above what is normally required in terms of their time and resources, before you committed any more of your resources. For example, if your product requires a customer questionnaire or preimplementation plan, you could demand the completion of the document before you provided them an evaluation product. Your goal may be to consume as much of their time as possible. Either they will push back and by doing so reveal their bias, or you will have an opportunity to build the relationship.

Before you select any strategy, you need to determine if you can find a coach (friend) within the customer company to help you win the deal. If you can't develop a coach, it does not make sense to invest your time in any account. Also, you should always be gaining momentum with the account and need to have tangible evidence that the deal is moving in your direction. Evidence of this includes vendors being eliminated, meetings with upper management or people involved in procurement, and other buying signs. We'll cover more sales cycle strategies in chapter 6 and discuss how to develop a coach in chapter 9. Remember, customers want a finite number of relationships. In the evaluation process, they will spend the majority of the time with the person they believe will provide them with the "best" relationship.

EXERCISE 7: EYE MOVEMENTS AND VAK COUNTS

You have probably been exposed to something new in this chapter. The interpretation of eye movements and understanding their relationship to representational systems is a new set of tools to add to your sales survival kit. However, before you use them in the real world with customers and colleagues, you need some additional practice. Your first assignment is to watch four hours of television interview programs. They could include any interview show, such as *The Tonight Show, Oprah,* or *Larry King Live.* However, watch these shows from a new perspective. Specifically, study the guests' eye movements when they are answering questions. While you are doing this, perform a VAK count and try to correlate keywords with the eye movements.

One night, I happened to watch Colin Powell on a television interview program. Prior to his becoming secretary of state, he had spent his entire career in the military. Most certainly, this molded the way he speaks and his calm, cool, collected demeanor. Most government employees operate in an impersonal, bureaucratic world and their use of language reflects this. They speak with carefully selected words to form their own type of "government specification language." However, even though they may be able to edit their words, they cannot edit the eye movements of their representational systems. If I were negotiating a treaty with Colin Powell, knowing he has strong visual and auditory systems would help me "tell my story" (auditory) in the "best possible light" (visual).

Several months following the TV interview, *Time* magazine published an interview with Colin Powell that confirmed my previous assessment about his wiring. Here are some of the more revealing quotations from the interview.

I would like to see our alliances strengthened. I would like to see NATO expanded. I would like to see us develop a very, very strong relationship with China. I would like to find a solution to the problems of the Middle East and the Persian Gulf . . .

In every administration, there are many voices, but the only voice I really listen to is the voice of President George W. Bush.

Let's just say, if there were another situation that approached the Rwandan level, I think in light of what has happened in the past, we'd have to take a very, very hard look at doing something.[7]

CONCLUSION

Another famous American statesman, Thomas Jefferson, said, "Knowledge is happiness . . . Knowledge is power."[8] Learning how to use representational systems to create rapport and determine the truthfulness of someone's communication is advantageous. Most often, power is associated with the use of physical force and the one-sided domination of someone or something else. However, Heavy Hitters achieve their power by creating a harmonious relationship with a customer and having the confidence in their product and themselves to be honest at all times. After all, it was Jefferson who also declared, "Honesty is the first chapter in the book of wisdom."[9]

5

Finding the Truth

We were in search of a new vice president of marketing. Since the candidate had worked in the same market segment for the past five years, her background matched our requirements. The interviews had gone well enough with the other members of the management team, but we wanted to be very sure that we were hiring the right person. The previous vice president of marketing had lacked the aptitude to build our brand. More importantly, she had difficulty relating with other members of the company and was not integrated with the management team.

The first portion of the interview went fine. Then the candidate was asked, "What part of marketing do you enjoy?" She answered, "Hmmm . . . I like to work with the press and analysts . . . I enjoy creating new market awareness programs and collateral . . . and I really enjoy working with the sales force." As she was answering the question she nodded her head up and down until she said, "I really like working with the sales force," when she began to shake it back and forth as if saying no. Something wasn't right. "What specifically do you like about working with the sales force?" I asked. She immediately gave me a "deer in the headlights" look. She fumbled for an answer because she honestly didn't have one. That question led to a lengthy round of questioning about how she worked with others within the company. The discussion left us feeling unsatisfied, and we ultimately passed on the candidate.

Everyone is familiar with the basics of body language, the physical layer of the human communication model. Body language is defined as communicating through gestures or poses. People communicate using many different parts of their bodies. Someone who is smiling at you is assumed to be friendly. Conversely, someone who is approaching you with a very serious look and fists clenched is considered a threat. Children who strike out in baseball may hunch their shoulders with shame and depression. When a home run is hit, there are "high-fives" throughout the dugout. These are just a few of the many ways we communicate nonverbal messages. However, the body language salespeople need to be able to recognize and interpret is much more subtle than these explicit examples.

In chapter 2, we identified the six different layers of the human communication model. To review, the phonetic layer is the manner in which words are pronounced. The actual words spoken are the content layer. Words are assembled to communicate a particular message or purpose. The representational system catalogues your life's experiences and influences your communication choices. And all of these processes are the result of a never-ending internal dialogue, or conversation, inside your conscious mind. This leads us to the final layer of the human communication model, the physical layer. In this chapter, we will study the physical layer of communication, more commonly referred to as body language.

Earlier, we learned that each of these layers may communicate knowingly or unknowingly with other layers. For example, a conversation at the content level is a purpose-driven communication that your conscious mind knowingly creates. Phonetics are then consciously applied to spoken words to create greater impact or to clarify the meaning. Telling a customer, "Yeah, we have the feature too" is different from exclaiming to a customer, "Yes! We have that feature!" The last statement exudes confidence and excitement and was said with a different purpose.

In addition to phonetics, another form of underlying communication occurs in every conversation. It is typically not recognized as part of the communication event except when it becomes so obvious that it changes or contradicts the meaning of the words spoken. For example, the candidate for vice president of marketing was nodding her head up and down as she spoke about what she enjoyed. When she began to speak about working with the sales force, her head began to move back and forth, communicating no. In this chapter, we will review the different types of nonverbal communication and learn how to interpret them.

Your conscious mind is obsessed with benefactions. The most vital benefactions are driven by your physical well-being. If you are hungry at the moment, you may have difficulty concentrating on reading these words. If you haven't eaten for the past twenty-four hours, you would definitely be more interested in food than any concepts on these pages. The conscious mind is fixated with the avoidance of pain, the preservation of self, and self-gratification.

The conscious mind is on a mission to satisfy the most urgent benefactions first. As a result, it will instruct the senses to collect the relevant data needed to accomplish this urgent sortie. In this regard, typical salespeople and Heavy Hitters share the same desire and sense of urgency to close the deal. However, one of the primary differences between most salespeople and Hitters is the amount and range of data that is collected by the senses. Heavy Hitters gather data from all levels of the human communication model. Armed with this information, they are better able to determine their course of action based upon the data they have collected and past comparable experiences. By doing this, they can determine the sales strategy that offers the highest probability of winning. This process is most commonly referred to as "sales intuition."

Most likely, the Heavy Hitter's process of assimilating all these data points is not formalized. Rather, it is both a conscious and subconscious process. Although the subconscious mind is not actively assertive, it is always vigilant and capable of influencing actions. The ability to effectively send and receive information from each layer of the human communication model is a critical component for developing sales intuition. While it is easy to recognize the communication being sent consciously, the subconscious information being sent is just as expressive, but it's much harder to recognize and interpret. It is important to realize that the subconscious and conscious are communicating at all times, internally within the self and externally to others.

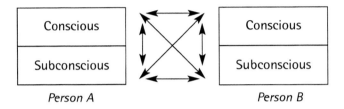

Person A   Person B

Figure 5.1 Conscious and Subconscious Communication

Each of the communication layers can also communicate both consciously and subconsciously between themselves. For example, when people lie, the subconscious mind will affect the phonetic and physical layers of communication. The pitch, tone, and volume of their voice may change along with their posture, demeanor, and skin tone. The subconscious mind is very influential. It is your subconscious mind that keeps you from falling out of your bed at night.

Most people equate physical communication with the term "body language." Unfortunately, this term has been sensationalized over the years in books on everything from dating to cosmetic surgery. However, since it is the more widely recognized term, I use it interchangeably.

Hitters want to communicate with a customer's physical layer in order to develop rapport. They are aware of a customer's body language and analyze it to ensure they are communicating effectively. They also try to understand any communication from the customer's subconscious that may be revealed physically. These unintentional messages will help them determine their chance of closing the deal.

Heavy Hitters are always trying to understand the physical layer for three reasons:

1. Heavy Hitters know the key to developing long-term successful relationships is rapport. Just as they develop rapport at the content layer by using the customer's language, they also desire to develop rapport at the physical layer. In other words, we want rapport with the customer's body as well as her mind.

2. Heavy Hitters are continuously searching for feedback on the prospect's receptivity to their solution. Body language provides another visible checkpoint that can be used to ensure everyone participating in the meeting understands and agrees with the topic of discussion.

3. Heavy Hitters want to "perceptively persuade." They want to win to satisfy not only their own benefaction but the benefaction of the customer as well. They honestly feel their solution serves the best interest of the customer. Therefore, they want to use all of the tools at their disposal to ensure the "right" solution is selected. Perceptive persuasion involves leading another person (the customer) to do something on your behalf (buy your product).

A CAVEAT

Up to this point, you have been introduced to the fundamentals of how people communicate and how they are wired. In the remainder of the book, you will be introduced to strategies and techniques that will enable you to directly influence another person's behavior. These techniques should be used only when the customer's benefaction is best served by your solution. Heavy Hitters use perceptive persuasion to defeat their competitors because they deem them inferior.

Understanding how to influence another person is powerful knowledge. If you use this to selfishly accomplish your benefaction and not the customer's, there will be consequences. Manipulation results in remorse and vilification. It is the exact opposite of rapport. Remember the old adage that a customer who buys a product and likes it will tell five people, while the customer who dislikes it will tell twenty-five.

Heavy Hitters also know their biggest competitor is time. They want to learn as soon as possible if rapport is not present. They want to know immediately if the information being discussed was not understood or agreed to by the customer. At the end of a sales call, many salespeople do not truly understand where they stand in terms of the competition. Often, customers say all the right things but do not follow up with any meaningful action. Heavy Hitters assimilate physical communication as a key part of their decision whether to continue on with the sales process.

PHYSICAL CHANGES

Many physical changes occur while we communicate. Our skin becomes flushed when we are embarrassed or mad. Our breathing becomes slower when we are relaxed and faster when we are excited. Our facial muscles become tight when we are stressed or in disagreement. The response on the outside of our bodies represents what's going on inside our minds. Our body posture indicates our comfort level in any particular situation.

Understanding the nuances of these changes is a tricky proposition. First, you cannot assume that each body movement means the same thing for everybody. For example, I worked with an individual who moves his right foot constantly during every meeting. This is his "rapport posture," or the position he assumes when he is in a receptive state to receive information. This is very different from someone who would be showing impatience by moving in the identical way.

Second, the way to understand the meaning of a physical movement is by observing the movement over time. The time period could be as long as days or as short as a few minutes. The vice president of marketing candidate was vigorously nodding her head up and down and talking enthusiastically about certain aspects of the jobs she liked. She was able to give specific examples instantaneously. She was telling the truth. When she was asked about working with the sales force, her physical behavior shifted completely.

Just like a polygraph examiner, you must establish a "control group" of movements your customer makes. You want to link a specific movement to a known meaning. By doing this, you create the default meaning of the movement. More importantly, you are trying to specifically understand if the default meaning of the movement is in congruence with the words spoken at the content layer. For example, the candidate's head nodding changed in conjunction with her statements about working with the sales force. When a person's physical communication is incongruent with (not matching) their content-level communication, then that person is not telling the truth!

IS IT THE TRUTH?

Over the years, I have had the opportunity to participate in thousands of sales calls with both typical salespeople and Hitters. A key difference between Heavy Hitters and most salespeople is their ability to determine if they are being told the truth. Truth is an interesting concept. Truth is defined as "genuine and authentic in accordance with a person's reality."

For a moment, let's put ourselves in the position of the customer. As the customer, you are going to meet with multiple vendors, watch their presentations, and read their marketing collateral. Each vendor, most likely, has equally talented, friendly, and professional salespeople who come to your office. However, you will select only one product.

Given that, how will you behave with each vendor? Will you tell each one the truth? Probably not.

It is basic human nature to want to avoid confrontation. This is particularly true when you are meeting in person, face-to-face. In addition, our society has implicit guidelines of behavior. We are taught at an early age that if we have nothing nice to say, then we shouldn't say anything at all. If you (the prospect) are not interested in the product after the meeting, it is much more comfortable to tell the nonwinning vendors about your decision over the phone or just do nothing. The problem is that all of the vendors may have to continue to spend an equal amount of time and effort to win the business when a decision for one vendor was most likely made early on in the sales cycle.

Our definition of truth also includes the phrase "in accordance with a person's reality." The problem here is that multiple realities are at work. The company reality may be that product sales are disappointing and the economy has slowed. Given this reality, the previously approved information technology budget may have just been slashed, even though the lower-level personnel of the information technology group may not know of the cuts or believe they can work around the budget issues, so they continue with their product evaluation.

Most likely, the decision to buy your product rests with a team of individuals. Since everyone has a unique map of reality, what reality—and whose—will be pervasive within the evaluation group?

TYPES OF BODY LANGUAGE

The ability to recognize and interpret a person's body language can help you validate the quality and truthfulness of the information you are receiving. Let's examine the seven major types of body language we use and observe daily as salespeople.

- Handshakes
- Hand movements
- Breathing
- Facial expressions
- Skin color
- Body posture
- Speech

It could be argued that a person's handwriting is also a valid form of body language. Since the brain determines the content and form of what is written, handwriting also reflects certain personality tendencies, such as orientation to detail. However, in the world of sales today, handwriting has been almost eliminated by laptops and personal digital assistants. Therefore, it is not a major point of our discussion.

Handshakes

How many times have you participated in a flawed handshake at the beginning of the meeting? Perhaps the other person was more aggressive and you were too limp-wristed? Perhaps one person grabbed the other person's fingers instead of the palm? If you were at fault, this event probably ruined your ability to concentrate for a few moments. Undoubtedly, you planned that when the meeting ended, you were going to correct the earlier mistake with a solid handshake.

You can learn a lot from someone's handshake. Here are some observations. Kinesthetic people tend to shake hands a little longer than Visuals and Auditories. Dominant Kinesthetics will put their other hand on top of the handshake or pat the person on the shoulder or arm. Visuals tend to shake hands with a faster up and down movement. Recessive Kinesthetics tend to not make eye contact when they shake, almost as if they want to end the unpleasant process as soon as possible.

One of the more obvious signs of a person being nervous is the temperature of the skin. Colder hands may indicate nervousness (unless the person has just been outside). We are all familiar with the term "sweaty palms," which indicates a person is in a stressful situation. It is difficult to know what to do after you've shaken someone's wringing-wet hand. Such people know they are nervous, and if they see you wipe your hand off, they will feel even worse. It's human nature to want to make people feel comfortable, not to embarrass them.

Culture plays a role in handshakes. In Japan, the handshake is replaced by a card presentation. A handshake in New York City is different from a handshake in Atlanta. Some people overaccentuate the handshake. They'll lock your hand into their vicelike grip or hold your hand too long, as if you were shackled together. They're either insecure or trying to establish an overpowering position. Neither of these actions helps build rapport.

Save an imprint of the handshake from the beginning of the meeting and compare it with the handshake at the end of the meeting. Was it more sensual or colder? Longer or shorter? Was there a change in the amount of direct eye contact? Was there more than one handshake? Did the person actually pat you on the back or touch you in some other way during the handshake? Handshakes provide instant feedback about how a meeting went. Like a kiss with your lover before boarding a plane, the longer and more emotional, the better. From now on, be conscious of handshakes.

Hand Movements

Hand movements will vary based on a person's representational system. Visuals and Kinesthetics will use hand movements while speaking much more frequently than Auditories. The position of the Visuals' hands will be high in context to their bodies, usually at the chest or above. They will use their hands to point to things. They want to make sure you see whatever it is that is important to them. The fingers of their hands are usually straight or pointed out. They have no problem extending their arms and hands as far as they can because they want you to see the "big picture." They will use their hands as an imaginary marker to help draw a picture of the content they are trying to communicate. Visuals' hand movements will be quicker because they are exploding with thoughts that must be communicated quickly.

Kinesthetics will make "deep" hand gestures while they communicate their feelings. That is, their gestures will be lower on their bodies in accordance with their feelings on a subject. The fingers of their hands will be in a closed or interlocked position. They will be touching and holding their bodies while they speak. They may use their hands to cradle their heads or use their arms to hug their bodies. Their hand movements tend to be slower and more deliberate than Visuals' or Auditories' because formulating feelings takes more time than creating pictures or assembling words.

Auditory people are listening to themselves speak. This alone is a full-time job. Therefore, they will use fewer hand movements. When they do use them, they tend to keep their hands closer to their bodies. Another term for this is "dinosaur hands," since they are being held like the arms of a *Tyrannosaurus rex*. Their hand gestures will tend to be at the middle of the body, lower than Visuals' hand gestures but higher than Kinesthetics'. Their hand movements also tend to keep time with or be at the pace of their voice tempo.

Breathing

You may not have noticed this, but people actually breathe quite differently. Obviously, people breathe at a different pace depending on whether or not they are performing a physical activity. The aspect of breathing that we are interested in, however, is the changes in breathing patterns while customers are in their normal state (when most business meetings take place), and these changes can be quite subtle.

If a customer is wearing a suit or jacket or if glancing at the customer's chest would be considered inappropriate, breathing patterns can be observed by watching people's shoulders rise as they inhale and exhale.

Different breathing paces can be observed by watching different areas of the abdomen. Some people breathe fast and some slow. Some people have a repetitive rhythm to their breathing: deep breath, pause, deep breath, pause. Some people's breaths are quick and shallow. Visuals tend to breathe shallower and higher in the chest, while Kinesthetics breathe deeper and lower in the belly. Auditories' breathing is somewhere in between.

How someone breathes is really not that important. What is important is trying to spot a change in a breathing pattern. A change is a signal that a person's internal communication state has changed and the level of rapport has fluctuated. Meeting new people is stressful and people's breathing will speed up under stress. As they relax, breathing slows. At this point, Heavy Hitters calibrate the pace of the customer's breathing and use it as the baseline to monitor if the respiration is speeding up, slowing down, becoming deeper or shallower, or staying the same. This is valuable information to help identify a customer's state of rapport. People experiencing rapport are relaxed and their breathing reflects this.

Facial Expressions

Regardless of what country you may travel to and what language is spoken, you are still able to communicate with the locals via your universal communication mechanism, otherwise known as your face. Your face is the only part of the body where muscle is directly attached to skin, thereby making possible a wide range of diverse expressions. Since you have been using facial expressions successfully for all of your life, you are already a trained expert.

Our faces represent the emotions we are experiencing. When I am happy, I smile. When I am serious, I may lower my eyebrows. When I am startled, I open my eyes wider. When I am in pain, my entire face tightens. When I am very sad, I cry. We are all familiar with reading these types of highly visible facial expressions. However, in the business world, people rarely express their true emotions outwardly. Facial muscles are used more to inhibit the public display of emotion rather than to show it. Therefore, a salesperson only has small variations of a customer's facial expressions to study.

EXERCISE 8: FACIAL EXPRESSIONS

Let's do a short facial expression exercise. I am going to ask you to think of different emotions and to make the corresponding facial expression. (Don't worry if you are in a public area. Those around you will think you are reading a very interesting book!) While you are making the expressions, pay particular attention to the following: Is your forehead getting smaller or larger? Are the corners of your eyes becoming tight or relaxed? Are your eyebrows rising or lowering? Is your nose moving up or down? Are your nostrils flaring? Are your cheeks rising or lowering? Becoming flat or round? Are your lips, chin, and jaw becoming relaxed or tight? Are your ears and hair moving up and down? Ideally, you want to do this exercise in front of a mirror. Try to hold each expression for five seconds.

Happy	Sad
Frustrated	Hurt
Scared	Laughing
Ecstatic	Peaceful

If you earnestly did this experiment, you may have learned something new. First, you may have become aware of some subtle feature of your face that you hadn't noticed before. We see our faces a lot but usually with only one or two expressions, such as ones we use while shaving, putting on makeup, or smiling for a photo.

Second, as you made each new facial expression, you may have felt a subtle impact on your emotional state since our feelings are "connected" to our faces. With some practice, you will be able to recognize small facial expressions and be able to link the facial expressions back to an individual's communication layers. This is how gamblers tell their opponent is holding four aces.

Fortunately, you have already had a lot of practice recognizing facial expressions. If you are married, you can probably tell the exact emotional state of your spouse with a quick glance. Some people call this intuition. Actually, after numerous interactions, you have categorized every possible combination of facial expressions and have developed a behavioral model. You can also do this with your customers. It's an instantaneous feedback loop to help you understand their reaction to what you are presenting.

Skin Color

To a lesser extent than facial expressions, skin color can also give subtle clues to a person's emotional state. In a tense meeting, for example, you may witness the skin tone of someone who is scared or unnerved turn ashen gray. When successful sales calls conclude, the participants' skin tone may seem warmer. However, this observation may be influenced by your perception of the meeting's results.

Body Posture

A person's body posture is one of the primary communication features of the physical communication layer. Regardless of the activity (sitting, standing, walking, or sleeping), a person's body posture sends a message to the outside world. People are normally in a continuous pose, and the manner in which they hold and shape their figures reflects their mental state.

The airport makes a great laboratory to study and interpret body posture. At the check-in lines, study the different ways people stand. Some will stand with a defiant or impatient posture, with arms akimbo (hands on hips and elbows turned outward). Some will slouch in quiet resignation, and others will stand comfortably. Watch people walk. Some people saunter gracefully while others trudge as if they were carrying the weight of the world. Some wander and some are on a march, as if they have to reach the summit of K2 by nightfall.

Airplanes are also good places to reflect on the importance of understanding body language. Once, I boarded a Monday morning flight at 6:45 A.M. from Los Angeles to San Jose. I had planned to work on the plane to prepare for my meetings that day. I boarded early, sat down in my window seat, and started working. The seat next to me was empty at the time. A few minutes later, a business-man approached my row. On this day, I didn't have time for small talk, and I used my body position to communicate I wasn't interested in talking. I did this by "closing" my body posture. I had my arms on the tray table, head down, and my body faced straight ahead. I was intensely focused on my work.

However, it would have been incredibly rude not to acknowledge the person who would be sitting beside me for the next hour. As he sat down, I gave him a very quick smile of acknowledgment. It wasn't a warm and friendly "How are you doing today?" smile. Rather, it was an acknowledgment of his presence, an "I come in peace" kind of smile.

He recognized my presence briefly with a very similar greeting. He said nothing and I was relieved. Based on that small physical inter-action, he communicated the following message: "I am a seasoned traveler who also has a lot of work to do and I don't plan on bother-ing you." He unpacked his briefcase and immediately started to work.

Even though we did not exchange a single word during the flight, there was very good rapport between us. We both shared the same benefaction and helped the other accomplish it. It would have been uncomfortable for either of us to explain, "I'm too busy to talk." Even this small exchange would have taken time and energy away from accomplishing our more important tasks. I know he felt the same way that I did. You can have meaningful communication between people solely using body language.

Recently, I had another interesting "conversation" on an airplane. After a long day of meetings, I sat down in my seat on a flight that was barely one-third full. Unlike my closed posture in the previous example, I was sitting normally, as one usually does on an airplane. I had the window seat and a young woman sat down next to me in the middle seat. I greeted her with the customary, "Hello." However, it was an awkward situation since there were so many open seats, and we were going to be crammed together for the next couple of hours.

For the next few minutes, she continually looked at all the open seats. I could almost hear her internal dialogue telling herself that it would be "okay to move." As the departure time approached, her scanning of the open seats became more frequent and urgent.

Finally, she stood up and blurted to me, "You don't stink or anything, but I'm going to move over there." While I did not laugh aloud, she clearly was embarrassed over what she had said. She gave me a facial expression that said, "I don't know where that came from!" and quickly collected her belongings and moved.

What happened? Well, she had just finished an intense internal discussion about whether it would be rude to move. After all, she had rationalized, there were plenty of open seats. However, she didn't want me to interpret her moving as an insult. Most likely, what she said to me were her exact words from her internal dialogue. The pressure mounted for her to make a decision because the plane's door would soon be closed for take off. Once that happened, she probably felt she would be "stuck" in this seat for the entire flight. She acted impulsively, making a quick final decision to move. However, I don't believe she intended to offend me. She simply repeated her internal dialogue word for word. Most likely, she was a Kinesthetic. The fact she used a kinesthetic word, "stink," also suggests this.

What can you learn from this story? First, by observing the physical communication layer, you can anticipate someone's future actions. When the young woman was sitting in the plane, she was not relaxed like the rest of the passengers. She was agitated, scanning the open seats. This was incongruent with the natural sitting position on an airplane. Something wasn't right, and I needed to be on guard.

Also, observing the physical communication layer helps to explain verbal communication. Let's assume I had not paid any attention to her movements. She would have blindsided me with her comment. How would I have interpreted it?

BODY LANGUAGE AND GROUP MEETINGS

In sales, we are interested in three main aspects of body language. First, we want to interpret people's state of receptiveness to our ideas. Second, we want to observe body language to help validate our assumptions about people's primary, secondary, and recessive representational systems. And third, we want to match their body language with the content of their spoken words in order to identify congruencies or potential incongruencies.

The sales world normally uses one of three prevalent meeting positions: when all the participants at a meeting are sitting, when one person is making a classroom-style presentation to a group of people who are sitting, and when two or more people are standing in a conversation. These settings cover the majority of sales situations and are worth studying in more detail.

Group dynamics are very complex. Earlier, we introduced the concept of technical specification language and discussed how technical people's position in their group is determined by the technical content of the words they use. In group meetings, the pecking order is also reflected in where a person sits. Whether at a round table or in a classroom setting, the person with the most influence will choose a dominant place to sit. For example, at a long, boardroom-style table, these people will be found at the center of the table, and a spot will be left for them there even if they are late. If the table is shorter, dominant people will sit at one of the ends, while their subordinates will cluster around them.

At a round table, the dominant position may be the seat facing the door or the one with the best view outside. In a large classroom-style setting, dominant people will sit in the front of the room or in the most visible position. This is the position that provides the best location to see the presentation and to be seen by the audience. Occasionally, dominant people will sit in the very last row so they can be in the position of leaving whenever they please. Regardless of the table type, where a person sits is of primary importance.

Now that you know where influential people will sit, let's examine their posture. Most meetings start with people in a "closed" posture versus an "open" posture. A closed posture is when the body is folded up on itself. Probably the most familiar one is when the arms are crossed on the chest. More subtle closed positions are legs crossed, ankles crossed, hands interlocked on the table, or both hands touching the face. A person in a closed position may also face away from the focus point of the meeting or presenter.

A closed posture does not necessarily indicate a negative attitude. Rather, it is a natural position of skepticism that shifts to an open position as rapport is created. The open position represents the best environment to communicate your message. When people change to an open position, it may be as obvious as their uncrossing their arms and lowering them to the table. More likely, the change will be a lot more subtle. They may relax the tightness of the parts of the body that are folded: arms, hands, legs, ankles, feet, and even lips. They could also move their folded arms from their chest to their waist. Or they could switch position, such as going from legs crossed with the right leg on top to legs crossed with the left leg on top. Watch for these subtle changes and make a mental notation of when they happen. Who was speaking? What was the topic? Was there a variation in facial expression that accompanied the move?

People are opening and closing their positions all the time throughout a meeting. It's important to identify a person's closed and open state and watch for patterns of reoccurrence during the meeting. Heavy Hitters know they need to investigate why they lost a person's open state and will pause to ask the person if she has any questions or try to solicit an opinion on the topic.

Heavy Hitters are constantly surveying all of the meeting participants to see if they are receptive to the presentation. The goal is to uncover any confusion and uncover objections as early as possible. They do not want objections to remain hidden until it is too late to address them successfully. Even if someone else is making the presentation, Hitters do not relax but carefully and continuously examine everyone's physical state. Therefore, Heavy Hitters always take a position in a meeting that affords them the best viewpoint to observe all of the meeting participants.

Think about the last time you were in an elevator with a group of strangers. You assumed the natural elevator position where everyone is facing forward toward the door, watching the floor numbers. No one speaks. Everyone is on hold, almost as if in a trance. This is the acceptable body position in an elevator.

Standing conversation also has a natural position. An acceptable distance is kept between the talkers. A comfortable way of presenting the body is found. Usually, it's by mimicking the other person's posture. However, frequently an ongoing negotiation is taking place between the body positions of the people engaged in a conversation. Explaining this negotiation process requires the introduction of three concepts known as pacing, mirroring, and leading.

PACING, MIRRORING, AND LEADING

I drive to the local mountains to go boating during the summer and ski in winter. The trip takes several hours each way. While I am driving, my speed or pace will be determined by several factors besides the speed limit. Usually, I will drive at the pace of the car in front of me, keeping a distance between that car and mine that I feel comfortable with. I will automatically maintain this distance until the pace of the car in front of me becomes too fast or too slow. In either case, this will cause our driving rapport to break.

Sometimes, I will keep pace to the music on the radio and find myself speeding up to the tempo of the song. Suddenly, I'll be jolted into action upon realizing that I am driving faster than the legal limit.

Pacing can be thought of as the natural process of adjusting your tempo to your environment. In both examples, my behavior was being influenced by something else (the car in front of me and the music), and even though I am mindful of how I am driving, I'm not solely concentrating on it. It's as if I have passed the responsibility to my subconscious mind.

On remote roads, cars tend to cluster together instead of being evenly dispersed. It seems that the cars act together as a group and will accelerate or slow down together. I like to drive in these groups because I believe it reduces my odds of getting a traffic ticket. Therefore, when I drive on long stretches of highway, I will adjust my speed to fit into one of these groups of cars. This is mirroring, which can be thought of as the conscious act of modifying your behavior to fit your surroundings. As opposed to pacing, where your subconscious mind is in control, mirroring requires a physical effort at the direction of the conscious mind.

The car in front of me is also "leading" my behavior. Let's assume I have been mirroring the car in front of me for the last ten minutes. Suddenly, the driver swerves to the right. I will follow her lead and prepare to swerve to the right, even though I have not actually seen the danger. Leading is the process of influencing another person's action by yours. In this example, if the other driver had been driving erratically as if under the influence of alcohol, I would not have swerved. However, for the past ten minutes she had demonstrated she was a capable driver. She created a "driver's rapport" so that when she swerved, I followed. Leading requires rapport.

Let's pretend we are driving on a desert highway and see a group of cars in front of us. First, we mirror the speed of the group to stay with them. Once we are part of the pack, we naturally keep the pace to maintain our position. After many miles of driving within the pack, we decide to lead the group by gradually speeding up and taking the pole position. Now all the cars behind us have to mirror our speed.

In terms of the sales call, Heavy Hitters will mirror and pace a customer's speed and tempo to help establish rapport, for example, by mirroring the customer's posture and maintaining the same tempo or pace of breathing. Once rapport is established in conjunction with the dialogue of the meeting, they lead the customer into an even deeper rapport. The customer relaxes, lowers her defensive guard against the salesperson, and an even more meaningful dialogue takes place. The ability to consciously develop a formalized process of pacing, mirroring, and leading and integrating these actions naturally into sales meetings is an extremely powerful sales tool.

Most likely, the Heavy Hitter doesn't have a formalized process to accomplish this. It comes naturally. Salespeople with strong kinesthetic systems do this instinctively. However, this process can be learned by anyone with any representational system.

Heavy Hitters use pacing, mirroring, and leading to gain rapport with their customer. They are constantly monitoring the customer's physical communication—handshakes, hand movements, breathing, facial expressions, and body posture. Hitters know that by changing their style to match the customer's, they will create more effective communication because the customer does not have to expend additional effort to translate the Hitters' message.

Mirroring breathing styles is the first step to helping you create rapport because it makes you recreate the customer's world with your body. If someone breathes slowly, you have no choice but to slow down the pace of your speech and movements along with your breathing. If a person breathes faster than you, your actions will naturally speed up.

Mirroring body posture is accomplished by making a subtle reflection of the customer. The most obvious mirroring is a direct reflection, like the opposite image in a mirror. For example, when someone sits with legs crossed, you sit in the identical position with your legs crossed oppositely. Or you cross your arms tightly to your chest, in the exact opposite position of your counterpart during a conversation while standing.

However, this type of mirroring is too obvious and can potentially be perceived as patronizing. Rather, the mirroring we want to use is much more discreet. Instead of crossing your legs to directly mirror someone, cross your legs at the ankles or even cross your arms. Instead of standing with your arms tightly folded, cross your arms in a looser fold at the waist or stand with your legs crossed.

Let's think about handshakes in the context of mirroring. You start a handshake using a medium grip and instantaneously react to the other person's. If her grip is firmer, you grip harder, and vice versa. The length of the handshake and degree of hand motion you use are also equally matched to the other person's. You have instinctively been doing this mirroring for your entire career.

Assuming you have been successfully mirroring your customer, now it's time to test whether you have rapport by leading. Leading can be thought of as the process of using your actions to guide another person's behavior. Let's assume that you are fifteen minutes into a meeting. You have been successfully mirroring the customer's breathing and body positions. You feel you have gained rapport and now want to test if this is true. Slowly, you start varying your breathing, and the other person follows your lead. Slowly, you change your body position, and the other person changes as well. It's just like the example of taking the pole position, leading the cars through the desert.

Through the process of leading, you can determine the level of rapport that exists between you and your customers. If they don't follow you, it doesn't necessarily mean there's a problem. It's normal for people to fall in and out of rapport during meetings. Simply start mirroring again.

Most importantly, through the process of leading, you can influence a person's state to be more open or receptive to your message. Earlier, we discussed how people are opening and closing their body postures throughout meetings. A Hitter's intuition is constantly scanning for closed positions. When it senses someone is closed, it becomes curious and wants to know why. It initiates the investigative process by asking questions or soliciting the opinion of the person in the closed position. The goal of this questioning is to understand what the person's internal dialogue is saying.

Remember, people are always communicating at the physical layer (whether consciously or subconsciously). The physical layer will enable you to validate a person's open or closed state. It also works in conjunction with your content-level dialogue to move someone from a closed state to an open state.

MIRRORING AND LEADING CASE STUDY

The best way to understand the concepts of physical communication is to see how these techniques can be applied in a real-world scenario. Let's return to the story of an actual sales meeting recounted at the beginning of chapter 2 and describe how pacing, mirroring, and leading influenced the meeting results.

The meeting was held in a small rectangular room on the lower floor of an old brick building. The layout of the room was not conducive to a presentation for a group of people. It was narrow and cluttered with obsolete computers. At first, we were unsure which wall would serve as our projector screen.

The sales team consisted of Karl, a local field sales representative, his presales engineer, and me. The customer consisted of the technical team leaders, Mark and Beth, and their manager, Bart. While Karl had had several telephone conversations with Mark about the company's technical environment, this was our first face-to-face meeting. Mark and Beth entered the room first and took their seats. There was small talk before the meeting began among Karl, Mark, and Beth. Mark and Beth seemed at ease.

Bart entered a couple of minutes later. Immediately, Mark and Beth assumed a more formal body posture. Clearly, Bart was in charge. Bart's demeanor also communicated that he was a busy person. He threw himself into the open chair next to Mark and Beth. His posture plainly indicated that his time was valuable and suggested he had better things to do. I assumed from this hurried behavior that this meeting was probably more of an interruption than a scheduled event. While he was physically at the meeting, mentally he was somewhere else. It was obvious that we would have very little time to impress him and get our message across.

The narrowness of the room made conversation with others difficult. From my seat, I couldn't see Bart, nor could he see me. At this point, I announced that I wouldn't be able to view the presentation from my seat and moved to the open chair next to Bart. Karl (the salesperson) was anxious to begin the meeting, but we needed to get some information about Bart in order to try to develop some receptivity to our message.

Just before Karl commenced the meeting, I had a chance to ask, "Bart, how long have you been with the company?" On the surface, this question seems innocent enough, and Bart answered, "Over twenty years. I started out of New Jersey." His answer was very informative from several different aspects. With twenty years of tenure, I surmised, he probably has both political and business savvy. He must know the political structure of the company and must have worked on many different projects. Therefore, he should know how to evaluate vendors, their products, and the process to procure them. This was great content-level information.

When Bart answered the question, his eyes went up and to the right for an instant. As you know from chapter 4, this is the eye movement of a Visual. Although you cannot make a conclusion about a person's primary system from one question, this gave me more information than I previously had. I suspected he was a visual primary.

When he volunteered his origins, it gave me the opportunity to ask another natural question. "Where did you grow up?" I asked. Once again, on the content level, this seems like a very natural follow-up question. However, it is actually a very complex question because it can be interpreted on several different levels.

His content-level answer was two words, "New Jersey." Again, his eyes momentarily went up and to the right, which provided further evidence that his primary representational system was visual. However, the question had another important aspect.

When I asked Bart where he grew up, for a split second he physically had to access his catalogue to remember the experience by either recreating a mental picture, a feeling, or a sound about where he grew up. To recreate the experience, he actually had to regress back to when he was growing up (at least for a moment, anyway). Now, I didn't know whether Bart had a pleasant or unpleasant childhood. However, when I asked the question, I knew two responses would happen.

First, through this regression, his current frame of mind would be altered, albeit slightly. If he had a happy childhood, most likely it would affect his current state positively and make him slightly more receptive to our presentation. On the other hand, recalling an unhappy childhood would certainly not help us. Second, by having him regress back to when he was growing up, he would offer additional insights about his representational system.

His reaction to the question was revealing. He only gave a two-word response; however, he communicated a lot. As he regressed to get his childhood experience, his eyes went up and to the right, where he saw a picture of something (perhaps his family, house, or school). Then, his eyes went down and to the right (the kinesthetic position), where he momentarily experienced a positive feeling. I interpreted it as positive because his facial tone relaxed slightly, and his next two breaths were a little deeper and slower than his previous ones.

Unlike people searching for something specific, like the best day of their life, he also had to interpret what the phrase "grow up" meant. Did it mean where he was born, where he spent his boyhood, or where he spent his years as a teenager? Perhaps he lived in several different places and had to select the best answer. Since his eye movements were very rapid, I had to pay very close attention or I would have missed them.

These two questions were purposely asked to gain rapport. I was trying to get him to slow down and change the way he was thinking prior to our presentation. Also, these two questions had another benefit. Most people enjoy talking about themselves, and I wanted him to know that we were interested in him. We still had a long way to go to gain rapport with him, but at least we were ready to start the meeting.

What if he had responded differently? If he was raised in an unhappy home or suffered some trauma when he was a youth, most likely he would have tensed up even more. At that point, my response would have been to "mirror" his experience. I could have said something like, "I grew up in Los Angeles and hated it." But since his response was positive, I said, "I was in Princeton last Halloween. It was beautiful."

The meeting began with Karl's confirming what he had learned about the customer's environment from his previous phone calls with Mark. Mark answered most of Karl's questions and Bart participated very little. He sat with his arms crossed at his chest, his right leg crossed over the left. He frequently looked up at the ceiling. This would make any salesperson more nervous, and Karl became slightly flustered. I started mirroring Bart's breathing rate and the shallowness of his breaths. I mirrored his closed position, with my hands folded on top of my notebook, my pencil in my right hand, and my legs crossed at the ankles. I also started a VAK count of the meeting's participants. It would later validate my assessment of Bart's systems as visual, kinesthetic, and auditory.

After pacing his breathing for a few minutes, I was ready to check to see if we had developed any rapport. To do this, I started leading him by slowing down my breathing. His breathing followed. "Ah, we're making some progress," I said to myself.

The meeting format consisted of Karl presenting the company overview followed by a technical presentation from his presales engineer. I knew the company overview would be challenging, as Karl was an Auditory and he was also relatively new to the company. Because his presales engineer was a Visual, I knew this portion of the presentation would fare better with Bart.

Given this scenario, my internal dialogue told me also to undertake three tasks. First, I would continue to do everything in my power to improve Bart's receptiveness to our presentation. Second, throughout the meeting, I would observe the openings and closings of the posture of each of the meeting participants and further investigate them to find out why they were occurring. And finally, I would serve as Bart's personal interpreter to translate Karl's auditory presentation into Bart's visual world. I would be illustrating Karl's pitch. When Karl made an important comment, I would put it into Bart's language. If Karl said, "Our customers tell us all the time we have great support," I would reiterate his point by saying, "I see reports on all of our support cases, and the average time to fix the problem is two hours."

As the presentation started, Bart's right leg was still crossed over his left leg, and his foot moved every two to three seconds. While mirroring his breathing, I began to tap my pencil in time with his foot movements. After a few minutes of tapping my pencil in rhythm with his foot, once again I took the lead. I slowed down the time between taps. He slowed too. I stopped, and he stopped.

At this point, I felt sufficient physical rapport had been established. However, Bart still wasn't actively participating in the meeting. It was now time to test the depth of our rapport. I yawned, and he soon followed. I frequently will use a yawn during presentations or meetings as a checkpoint for rapport. If someone yawns when you do, you can assume they are relatively comfortable. A few more minutes of mirroring passed. Then I took my left hand from the table and slowly held it to my left cheek. A couple of moments later, Bart uncrossed his left hand and held it to his ear. We were making great progress. I knew he was listening!

A minute or so later, I uncrossed my legs, leaned forward, and put my arms on the table. A few moments later, Bart uncrossed his legs, leaned forward, and put his arms on the table. From that point on, his participation in the meeting increased. He began asking questions and sharing his opinions. He stayed the entire length of the meeting, which was over an hour and a half.

During this meeting with Bart, my internal dialogue was constantly active. I was listening to the presenter and the other participants and inserting myself in the flow of the conversation. I was identifying the closed and open states of the participants and investigating why. I was planning what I would say next and managing the process of building rapport with Bart. Obviously, I was multitasking many different physical and mental activities. Most importantly, I wasn't solely focused on or exclusively listening to the content of the words being spoken (a frequent mistake of an inexperienced salesperson). I was cognizant of the entire spectrum of communication taking place. A Hitter's internal dialogue is so fully developed that it can do multiple tasks instinctively, intuitively, and naturally. It takes practice, but it can be learned.

You can perform exercises to help build this skill set. At your next meeting, choose one person and spend the entire meeting mirroring and leading the breathing of that person. Similarly, in other meetings, pick a body position, such as a position of a person's hands or feet, and mirror it along with breathing through the entire meeting. Continually add new layers of sophistication to your mirroring and leading. You can even mirror how a person speaks!

Speech

One of the most interesting and revealing aspects of body language is a person's speech. People speak in different tones of voice, speeds, and volumes. People's primary system and the strength of their secondary system will greatly affect their manner of speech.

SPEAKING CHARACTERISTICS OF AUDITORIES

Auditories are actually talking to themselves and tend to speak in repetitious patterns. The pattern could be melodic or more like Morse code. The Morse code–type pattern tends to be monotone. Certain words are enunciated in the pattern. In the following examples, all the "dot's" are enunciated in a similar way, and all the "dash's" are accented in a different way:

- We are committed to your satisfaction.

  (Dot...dot...dash...dot...dot...dash)
- We guarantee high performance and availability.

  (Dot...dash...dot...dash...dot...dash)

- Some Auditories speak in a monotone voice.

  (Dot...dot...dot...dot...dot...dot...dot)

Other Auditories have speech patterns that are more melodic. Their sentences are more wavelike. Word sizes represent the "crest" of the wave and vary in pitch, tone, or even pronunciation.

- We guarantee high *performance* and availability.
- We are *committed* to your *satisfaction*.

Auditories tend to be very proficient masters of the technical specification language, the nonpersonal, androgynous, technical talk used in the customer's industry. In chapter 3, we introduced the concept of VAK keywords. These keywords are nouns, adjectives, and verbs that reflect a person's representational wiring. Auditories tend to not "leak" or show their representational systems through the use of VAK keywords as much as Kinesthetics or Visuals. However, when their secondary system is kinesthetic, more "leakage" or VAK keywords will be embedded in their conversations.

Auditories also tend to quote what they have been told by others. They will also quote themselves in their conversations.

Here are more examples of auditory sentence structures:

- "Our meeting went great. Bob told us, 'We did a great job and everyone is excited to work with us.'"
- "The meeting was going really well and then 'Boom, boom, boom,' we were asked some really tough questions."
- "And I started to ask myself, 'Are they still a partner of ours?'"

SPEAKING CHARACTERISTICS OF VISUALS

The speech pattern of a Visual is quite different from that of an Auditory. Strong Visuals are being bombarded with pictures inside their brains. As a result, it is very difficult for them to keep the pace of the words being said synchronized with the pictures being created in their minds. This condition is somewhat analogous to a computer's CPU having to wait for the mechanical movements of the disk drive to be complete before it can further process any information. As a result, strong Visuals are constantly trying to speed up the mechanical process of speaking. Therefore, they usually talk faster than Auditories or Kinesthetics. Here are examples of sentence structures of strong Visuals:

- "WE ARE COMMITTED TO YOUR SATISFACTION."

- "VISUALSHAVEALOTTOSAYANDASHORTTIME-TOSAYIT."

To Visuals, words are an interruption of the pictures or ideas in their minds. They have to get them out of their internal dialogue as fast as possible because thoughts are constantly getting stacked up. Therefore, they speak with energy and a sense of urgency.

In presentation situations they tend to speak even faster. Their stream of speech may be interrupted only by the necessity to breathe. Have you ever heard someone insert "um's" in every other sentence? Visuals have a tendency to do this more than Auditories or Kinesthetics. These filler words are basically used as a checkpoint to synchronize the images in their minds with their spoken dialogue. The um's are also said at the same speed and tone as the other words. Conversely, a Kinesthetics says "um" much slower and in a deeper tone than the other words. Their um's are actually synchronized with their feelings, and this takes more time. You also may notice them looking down when they say "um."

Visuals tend to not only talk faster but also louder. Visuals are painting a picture for their audience. When they are telling their story, they are trying to make the language represent all the detail and complexity of a picture. You've heard the saying "A picture is worth a thousand words." For Visuals, it's true, and they have to communicate all of the thousand words to convey the picture they are seeing. Therefore, Visuals are the most talkative too!

Having to "always" communicate a thousand words at a time creates a lot of energy. When Visuals are making presentations they will move back and forth across the stage, Auditories will stand in one place or a small space, and Kinesthetics will shift their weight back and forth. Visuals' arm gestures are more exaggerated since they are illustrating a picture with their bodies. They'll outstretch their arms as far as they can horizontally (so that they resemble a cross) to make their point. Kinesthetics are more likely to make the same point by holding their hands vertically (with one hand over the head and one hand at the waist). Auditories hold their hands closer to their bodies and will use arm gestures sparingly.

While making a PowerPoint presentation, Visuals will point at the screen frequently and may use an index finger like a flashlight. Kinesthetics will extend an arm, using the entire hand or palm. Auditories will most likely point an arm (in the locked position of a push-up) straight in front of the body or from the shoulder horizontally. You will notice that Visuals' arms are held higher on the body or over the head. Kinesthetics will cradle or hold themselves with their arms and hold them lower, at the waist.

SPEAKING CHARACTERISTICS OF KINESTHETICS

Most people wrongly assume that people with a kinesthetic primary system are overly emotional, introverted, or extroverted. This may or may not be the case. Being kinesthetic simply means that they catalogue their experiences in terms of feelings. However, people who are strongly kinesthetic will reflect this in their speech patterns, and in turn their personality will be affected.

Kinesthetics tend to speak slower than Auditories and Visuals. Their speech is slower because they are frequently checking their feelings while they speak. Their speech pattern may also be frequently accentuated by their breathing, which is deeper than that of Visuals and Auditories. When speaking to a group, they tend to talk directly to a single person in the audience, while Visuals will constantly scan the audience. When talking about issues, Kinesthetics are more likely to associate a person with the issue or task at hand.

Strong Kinesthetics tend to be more dramatic in their speech patterns and inflections. They commonly insert pauses and voice inflections. Unlike Auditories with their Morse code patterns, Kinesthetics are "feeling" the words they are speaking. As a result, their tone of voice tends to be lower. This is because they are constantly validating and comparing their feelings with what they are hearing and saying.

Here are examples of sentence structures of strong Kinesthetics:

- *We* are committed to *your* satisfaction!"
- *I enjoyed* meeting with *you.*"

Every communication with Kinesthetics is personal. The emphasis is on the words "we," "your," "I," "enjoyed," and "you" as they directly correlate with the Kinesthetics' feelings. For example, their interpretation of "we" is actually "myself and my company," and their interpretation of "you" is "you and your company." These words represent very personal feelings, so their enunciation is likely to be slower or in a lower tone than the other words in the sentence. Kinesthetics' speech has other patterns. For example, Kinesthetics' voices will tend to rise at the end of sentences or fall and trail off.

CONGRUENCE

How a person speaks is also a good indicator of congruence. When people aren't telling the truth, their tempo speeds up or slows down, their volume gets louder or softer, and their tone is higher or lower than normal. For example, Visuals may slow down their speaking,

Kinesthetics may speak faster, and Auditories may change their tone. In addition, people's choice of words will change when they are not telling the truth. People telling the truth will talk in a straightforward manner using ordinary terms. When creating misrepresentations, their word selection is more careful, and they tend to use more sophisticated words. They also speak with precision and are mindful not to repeat the same word twice, unlike natural conversation.

CONCLUSION

Obviously, using all of the different aspects of physical communication (handshakes, hand movements, breathing, facial expressions, skin color, body posture, and speech) is critical to establishing rapport. At this point, it makes sense to summarize what we have learned in order to emphasize the three most important points about developing rapport.

First, you cannot mirror or lead someone effectively until you understand your own wiring. By knowing your representational systems, you will be able to compensate for your weaknesses and take advantage of your natural strengths. You must identify your primary, secondary, and recessive systems. You need to determine if you have balanced systems, a strong secondary system, or a dominant primary system.

Second, you must be able to identify the systems of the person to whom you are speaking. As we discussed in chapter 4, you can ask questions that require people to access their long-term memories. Based upon their eye movements, you can determine their representational systems. You can also perform VAK counts to determine their representational system prioritization. While this is easy to do in meetings with few participants, you need a different model for larger groups. In chapters 10 and 11, we will introduce the concepts of successfully speaking to large groups.

Finally, you are trying to establish rapport through the physical communication layer, and this requires mirroring body postures, breathing, and speech. If you are a Visual talking to a Kinesthetic, slow down and speak in terms of feelings; this will naturally lower your voice tone and decrease your volume. If you are a Kinesthetic talking to a Visual, speed up and speak in terms of pictures; this will naturally raise your voice tone and increase your volume.

If you are talking with people who are wired exactly as you are, you are already mirroring them. Most likely, these are people you naturally communicate with, who are the easiest for you to sell to. However, it takes skill and effort to communicate with someone who has a primary system that is the same as your recessive system. Ultimately, you want to become a communication chameleon. You want to speak in the customer's language (VAK keywords) and adopt all of the customer's physical communication attributes (body, speech, and breathing).

Certain representational system combinations communicate better with each other than others. For example, strong Visuals and strong Kinesthetics naturally communicate together better than strong Visuals and strong Auditories. Auditories naturally communicate better with Kinesthetics than with Visuals. Kinesthetics have an intrinsic communication advantage since they are always in touch with their own feelings and are sensitive about the feelings of others. This consideration is incorporated into their communication process.

Auditory salespeople face more of a challenge in presenting thoughts to customers than Visuals or Kinesthetics. If you are an Auditory, you must make a conscious effort to watch the people you are talking to in order to make sure they are grasping what you are saying. To put it another way, your internal dialogue is so developed that it overwhelms your ability to sense how your message is being received. What sounds good to you may not look good to a Visual or feel right to a Kinesthetic. Sometimes, it can be entertaining to watch two strong Auditories hold a conversation. They are so selfishly consumed with their own words that two separate conversations can occur simultaneously. Good advice to Auditories is to stop listening to yourself talk and make sure you are hearing what the customer is saying.

Conversely, Visuals and Kinesthetics should adopt auditory speech characteristics when they are speaking. Just as the chameleon changes colors to match its surroundings, your goal is to change your speaking mannerisms to match the person to whom you are speaking. By mirroring people, we are trying to continue the process of establishing rapport. If people are closed at the beginning of a meeting, we are trying to open them up to our ideas.

When all the observable and distinguishable layers of the human communication model are in agreement, meaning they are all sending the same message, people are unified in their communication and most likely telling the truth. For example, when their words match their physical demeanor and their language usage matches their representational systems, they are being truthful. If one of the layers is incongruent (does not match), you need to investigate further. The incongruence could be as obvious as that of the vice president of marketing candidate who drastically changed the ways she moved her head. Or it could be subtle, such as when she used words that did not match her representational wiring, perhaps using an auditory word when a visual one was expected.

Finally, this chapter has reviewed the physical layer of communication. Most likely, you were introduced to new concepts and ideas regarding the expression and the interpretation of the visible attributes of the body. Some aspects of this layer people consciously control and some they cannot. The key point is that the body is another means of communication, even without language.

For example, I have a special companion who is the preeminent expert on my own physical communication. This female has spent countless hours observing me. She can interpret each of my movements and perfectly anticipates my behavior based upon my slightest action. Who can this be? My dog, Blossom. Even though she can't speak a word of English, we enjoy great rapport!

6

Choosing Your Battles

Since the customer was already using his archrival's product, the
Heavy Hitter knew it would take a great deal of effort and a little luck to persuade the company to switch to his solution. In
order to win, he dedicated almost all of his sales team's time during the quarter to this one account. If it didn't close, the quarter
would be a failure. As the end of the quarter approached, the ten-
sion rose. Throughout the last day of the quarter, his manager
constantly wanted an update on the account. Everyone's nerves
were frayed. Finally, at 5:15 P.M. the fax machine started printing
the long-awaited purchase order.

People communicate differently. These differences are directly
related to biological factors such as intelligence, personality, and
representational system wiring. Environmental factors including
childhood, education, and where they live also play an important role
in shaping the ability to communicate. People's surroundings will also
greatly impact the demeanor of their speech. If you are in a library,
for example, you will soften your voice to a whisper. However, your
word selection and volume will be quite different if you are rooting
for your favorite team at a football game.

Even though there are over six billion people in the world, no
one is quite like you. You have had a completely unique set of experiences in your life. And you have kept a record of your past existence
by cataloging pictures, sounds, and feelings. As you make your way

through your daily life, you are interacting with the outside world by repeatedly sending and receiving messages. For Heavy Hitters, it's the ability to send meaningful messages and correctly interpret the messages being received that determines their success.

People communicate with a purpose, to achieve a specific benefaction. Benefactions are very personal prioritized needs. For Heavy Hitters the goal is to win the deal at hand. By doing so, they may achieve their benefaction of being the most respected salesperson or buying the new house they desperately want. In order to win the deal, they form an account strategy. The strategy is based upon information they have accumulated about the account, past sales experiences, and knowledge of the product they are selling. They plan a series of tactics that they believe will give them the highest opportunity to win in the shortest time frame and with the least amount of risk. By strategically performing these tasks, Heavy Hitters guide the prospect through the sales cycle.

THE SALES CYCLE

Sales cycle management has two aspects. First is the formalized process that the Heavy Hitters' company has established to win business. Most likely, your company has a defined methodology consisting of a series of steps to gather information about the customer and present information about your solution to the customer.

The second aspect of sales cycle management is the Hitters' personal contribution to the company's formal process—their ability to communicate and create rapport, their perceptiveness, and their past experience working sales cycles. Through repetitive motion, Heavy Hitters have developed a reservoir of experiences that they can draw upon to help manage the current deal. They recognize patterns of company and personal behavior and have developed a knowledge base of actions founded on previous similar encounters. Finally, Heavy Hitters know communication and rapport are critical components of every sales cycle. These two elements are prerequisites for a successful sale.

The sales cycle is a formalized information-and-activity exchange. Customers are trying to gather as much information about vendors in order to determine if they are appropriate long-term partners. Meanwhile, Heavy Hitters are trying to gather as much information about the customer in order to determine if they can win the deal. Information is communicated back and forth, and each message that is sent must also be received and interpreted correctly.

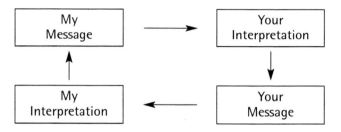

Figure 6.1 Communicating Information

However, an obstacle is inherent in this process. Since each message is subject to a person's interpretation, how do you know when your message has been interpreted correctly? Also, how do you know you have interpreted a customer's message correctly?

FOUR PREMISES OF THE SALES CYCLE

The solution is to apply the four fundamental premises of sales cycle management. First, all information we give and receive is subject to different interpretation. Second, through continual triangulation, we can ascertain the accuracy of information and determine our position in the account. Third, we need someone inside the customer's organization to help us win by providing reliable information we normally wouldn't have access to. Fourth, we must be flexible. If what we're doing isn't working, we'll change this strategy.

Sales Cycle Premise #1

All information communicated between customers and Heavy Hitters (and the sales team) is subject to interpretation and filtering. Here's an example of an e-mail that was sent from Jeff to two managers (Bob and Patti) to update them on the progress of a new salesperson (Mark). The e-mail describes the progress Mark is making with his territory, and it illustrates how the same message can create two entirely different interpretations. Jeff has worked with Bob and Patti for some time and has established rapport with each of them. Patti is an Auditory, Visual, and Kinesthetic. Bob is a Visual, Kinesthetic, and Auditory. As in many of the preceding examples, we are not as interested in the content of Bob and Patti's messages as we are in the message structure.

TO: Bob, Patti

FROM: Jeff

I met with Mark this afternoon for his territory review. We had a very long, somewhat pained discussion. He came on board six months ago and has sold very little. When I look at his strategy and examine his activities, they seem to be the same as everyone else's. On the sales calls I have attended, he establishes great relationships with the customers. Overall, I think he has done an admirable job under difficult circumstances. Obviously, I reiterated our company's commitment to him. Let me know your thoughts.

Here's Bob's response to the e-mail. Remember, Bob is a Visual, Kinesthetic, and Auditory.

TO: Jeff

FROM: Bob

Thanks for sharing with us the feedback and your thoughts on Mark. It isn't an easy situation. Do you think that it will get better as he establishes his territory?

Here's Patti's response to the same e-mail. Pat is an Auditory, Visual, and Kinesthetic.

> TO: Jeff
>
> FROM: Patti
>
> 1) What do you think that he will do in sales revenues this quarter?
> 2) Given the circumstances of his territory, what revenue should Mark do for the following two quarters?
> 3) Is his territory really that much worse than other territories?

The same e-mail solicited very different responses. Bob's response showed strong Kinesthetic traits. "Thanks for sharing with us the feedback," "isn't an easy situation," and "get better" all indicate that Bob read and understood this e-mail from the other person's point of view. He projected his concern to the sender of the e-mail (Jeff) as well as the subject of the e-mail (Mark). From his response, you could assume that Bob implicitly agreed with the statements made that Mark is doing an admirable job.

Meanwhile, Patti approached the e-mail differently. We knew ahead of time that Patti was an Auditory. In examining the e-mail, you will notice there are not any auditory keywords in her response. Instead, Patti is asking a series of questions. The questions are in fact the auditory keywords. She basically repeated her internal dialogue as the questions streamed into her consciousness. Most likely, this was the exact order in which she asked the questions of herself.

You will also notice that the point of view of Patti's e-mail is different. It could be inferred that Patti is not necessarily in agreement with Jeff's assessment that Mark "has done an admirable job under difficult circumstances." Her questions, particularly the last one asking if Mark's territory is worse than the others, indicate this, and her response requires further investigation.

People "filter" the information they give and receive all the time. In Patti's case, the process of filtering created a lot more questions.

Patti wanted more detailed information as she had several questions she needed answered. In Bob's case, he was more interested in the big picture and the welfare of others. The same e-mail message was interpreted in two distinct ways with two distinct sets of responses. Any information that is presented to the customer is similarly subject to different interpretations. This is the first premise of sales cycle management.

Sales Cycle Premise #2

Information must be triangulated to ensure the correct meaning is found. Now that we are aware the information we present and receive isn't 100 percent accurate, how do we validate that the customer received the message we intended? We accomplish this through "triangulation."

In chapter 3, the concept of the "triangulation diamond" was introduced. The Heavy Hitter is always swinging for a home run, to close the deal. Like a baseball diamond, the triangulation diamond has four bases. On first base, we ask, "Specifically what?" in order to understand the content level of the words being spoken. On second base we ask, "Specifically how?" to help us understand how the customer will take action. On third base, we ask, "Specifically why?" to determine history, perspective, and motivations. We reach home by asking, "Specifically when?" to determine time frames. Finally, the pitcher can throw to any base from the pitcher's mound. We ask, "Specifically who?" of any of the four bases in order to determine who sets the priorities, who makes the decision, or who will carry out the actions.

Triangulation is a repetitive process done over the life of a sales cycle. The Heavy Hitter's most frequent triangulation is with members of the immediate sales team including the system engineer and manager. Mostly, it occurs directly after a sales call while memories are still fresh. The Heavy Hitter's team members compare notes on their performance and evaluate the probability of winning the deal.

They'll also discuss their "read" of the customer participants from the meeting. Who is for them? Who is against them? And who can be swayed? This is analogous to lawyers during the jury selection process, who try to determine which potential jurors would react most favorably to their client's case. Of equal importance, lawyers want to eliminate those jurors who may be biased against their client. The information gathered from triangulation is continually factored into the strategy.

Whether formally or informally, customers are also doing their own triangulation about the vendor. They'll compare notes with their evaluation team, talk to customer references, and solicit opinions from consultants or industry analysts. They'll create a set of criteria a product must satisfy and guidelines to determine if a vendor will be a good business partner. They will grant a vendor further access based on how it compares against these standards and ranks against other vendors. The better the fit, the longer the time they will naturally be spending on a vendor.

The goal of Hitters' triangulation is to find out the truth about winning an account as early as possible. The sales cycle is a process that occurs over time, and Heavy Hitters are constantly reconfirming information they received earlier to ensure it is still correct. At the beginning of the sales cycle, they'll spend much effort evaluating the product's fit with the customer's need and qualifying the business opportunity. As the sales cycle progresses, Heavy Hitters will keep triangulating to ensure their information is still accurate by validating information they receive from one person with other people. They will also triangulate to determine the personal biases of each individual involved in the selection process. Finding the truth is a time-consuming process, and triangulation is a discipline that requires effort and time.

Sales Cycle Premise #3

You need a coach to win the deal. Heavy Hitters know they need a constant, accurate source of information revealing the internal machinations of the customer's selection process. The term "coach" is the popular name of a person who is the source of this inside information. The ability to locate, develop, and gain a coach is a skill the Heavy Hitter has acquired. Quite often, ordinary salespeople mistake someone for a coach when in fact the person isn't a loyal compatriot.

Several specific conditions must exist in order for a friendly evaluator to be considered a coach. First, coaches must have a personal reason for wanting the Heavy Hitter or his company to win. Second, coaches need to specifically say they want the Heavy Hitter to win and be willing to fight for the Hitter's cause. Finally, the information a coach provides must be accurate.

The ideal coach is the person with the highest authority or influence involved in the selection process. When this person becomes the coach, the Heavy Hitter will enjoy a unique advantage. However, the coach could be anybody inside the customer's company or even outside the company, such as a consultant working on the project.

A coach is the key to successful deal triangulation. Heavy Hitters know that without a coach, they will never truly be able to determine whether they are being told the truth. In chapter 9, we will review strategies and tactics for finding and developing a coach.

Sales Cycle Premise #4

Be flexible. If what you are doing isn't working, do something else! Heavy Hitters are constantly adding customer interactions to their knowledge base of experience. Depending upon the information and circumstances surrounding the account they are trying to close, they select the best course of action from this database by comparing the current deal with past wins and losses.

Throughout the sales cycle, Heavy Hitters are constantly responding and adapting to changing circumstances. If a situation changes, they'll change their strategy, tactics, and behavior. While they are solely responsible for winning the business, they are willing to assimilate advice from others into their strategy. When something isn't working, they'll try something else.

QUALIFYING AN ACCOUNT

Just as seasoned gamblers know which cards to discard and which to keep, Heavy Hitters know when to pursue and when to drop deals. They know their biggest competitor is time. Time is the enemy because time is finite. There are ninety days in a quarter. Hitters know that they can work only a finite number of deals during this time so they must invest time wisely in qualified accounts. Unfortunately, a qualified account can be disqualified at any time during the sales cycle. It takes a lot of flexibility to walk away from an account where there has been a heavy investment of time, energy, and emotions.

Heavy Hitters use a formal and intuitive qualification process for deciding which deals to work intensely and which ones to develop in the background. While the formal qualification process has most likely been supplied to them by their company, they have perfected their own instinctive method of qualification over time.

The formal qualification process involves determining the technical fit of the product to the customer's requirements and the business fit of the product to the customer's needs. This process may range from a checklist of technical questions to an in-depth evaluation of the customer's environment. Depending on the nature of the product, the Hitter may also have to determine whether the product fits the customer's current or planned business processes, for example, whether the order-entry module of his enterprise resource planning system matches the flow of the customer's order-entry process.

Of all the aspects of deal qualification, ascertaining the technical fit is probably the easiest. The criteria to determine if the account is technically qualified is developed either by product management, by product marketing, or within the sales organization. Through the completion of preimplementation checklists, technical questionnaires, and informal questioning, the sales team determines if the product meets the customer's technical requirements. From the technical perspective, Heavy Hitters position their product differently for each customer based upon each customer's criteria. They decide which features to emphasize and which to de-emphasize and how to position their company's story with the customer's technical needs in mind.

Another formal part of qualifying the account is asking basic business qualification questions. The answers to these questions will reflect the company's evaluation and procurement process. Below are typical business qualification questions. These types of questions are second nature to all salespeople.

- How much have you budgeted for your purchase?
- What is the decision process to select a vendor?
- When will a decision be made?
- What are the most important criteria in selecting a vendor?
- What other vendors are you evaluating?
- When will you be implementing the solution?

Heavy Hitters seek to understand what a customer is trying to accomplish from a business and technical perspective. Ideally, they want to actually change the customer's technical requirements to suit their product or, at a minimum, prove to the customer that the product meets a checklist of requirements. The process of qualifying a deal from a technical and business perspective is what most people outside the sales field associate with the term "qualification." When someone from engineering, accounting, or marketing asks if a deal is "qualified," they are referring to these formal processes.

The intuitive process of deal qualification is far more complex. Frequently, nonsalespeople within an organization have a hard time understanding that an entirely intuitive process surrounds the sales cycle. It's understandable since they operate in a more controllable, predictable world, such as accounting or engineering. Accountants know that both sides of a balance sheet must be equal. Software programmers code a series of statements in a logical, procedural manner. They don't necessarily understand why their company's salesperson still may not win the deal if the product technically fits the customer's environment and is priced competitively.

The Hitter's intuitive qualification process is far more important than the formal qualification process. The goal of the intuitive process is the successful search for the truth, and this is not a sequential process like marking items off a checklist. In fact, two competing salespeople could ask the same question and receive identical content-level answers. However, the salesperson with the ability to identify and interpret incongruencies, whether in language usage or physical contradictions of the body, is in a much better position to find the truth and win the deal. The preceding chapter was devoted to finding the truth by spotting these inconsistencies.

The sales cycle has a natural evolution. The first step for customers is to gather information from each vendor. As they gather more information, one vendor begins to look better than the others, its product sounds like it will work better, and they feel this vendor will be a better partner. Naturally, that vendor will enjoy an advantage throughout the remainder of the sales cycle.

However, customers have a dilemma. They still want to collect information from the other vendors to be 100 percent certain they are selecting the right vendor. Or they may want to complete the evaluation process to show others within or outside their organization (management, colleagues, consultants, or government agencies) that their evaluation was thorough and fair. As a result, they offer the other vendors the "customer placebo."

The customer placebo is present in literally every sales cycle. One vendor is in a unique position of receiving information from the customer that the others don't receive. As this favored vendor and the customer spend more time together, a higher level of rapport is developed. While this is happening, the customer is presenting misleading information to the other vendors about their position in the deal. Customers give salespeople false buying signs that they are more interested in the product then they actually are. Conversely, they may not share critical information or access to other people in the company as they do with the leading vendor. Unfortunately, the other vendors continue to spend additional resources and time on the account when a decision for one vendor has, for all intents and purposes, been made already.

Heavy Hitters' intuitive process is always triangulating the technical and business qualification questions. When they ask a person a content-level question like "What is your time frame to purchase?" they know they will receive a content-level answer. However, they use their intuition to determine the congruence (or truthfulness) of the person's answer. They will also ask other members of the evaluation team to gather information from their contacts and triangulate each response to form their own opinion. Finally, Heavy Hitters may even triangulate all data points about the account with other people whose judgment they trust, even if they have never met the customer or are completely outside the sales field. They are trying to gather as many opinions as possible to assess their position on the deal, determine their vulnerabilities, and set their course of action.

FIT

Up to this point, we have discussed the qualification of a customer from a business and technical perspective. A third element of fit is called "personal fit." Heavy Hitters are always trying to determine whether they have a personal fit with a customer. From an individual standpoint, they are trying to develop rapport with each member of the selection team evaluating the solution. They know without rapport, they will not win the deal.

They are also trying to develop rapport between the companies, or "company fit." The level of rapport developed between companies will depend upon how the cultures of the two companies match. The higher the level of rapport, the better the odds of winning the deal. However, the personal rapport developed by the Heavy Hitter (and his team) with each member of the evaluation team is more highly valued by both the customer and the Hitter than the rapport between companies.

After Heavy Hitters have determined the level of personal, technical, and business fit with a customer, they make the decision to pursue the deal. Whether formally on paper or mentally, they'll map out their ability to win based upon how they perceive their position in the deal.

SALES CYCLE QUADRANTS

In any account, Heavy Hitters will find themselves in four distinct situations, depending upon the amount of information they have acquired and the level of rapport they have developed. The sales cycle quadrants diagram helps illustrate how Heavy Hitters determine their bearings.

The vertical axis measures the amount of rapport Heavy Hitters enjoy with a customer. For example, a brand-new account would have low or no rapport. A high-rapport account would be one where the Hitter has personal friendships with members of the customer's team. The horizontal axis measures the amount of truthful information being shared by the customer. This is the Hitters' assessment of the quantity and quality of the information they are uncovering. It also includes any unique information from the coach.

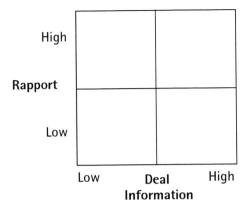

Figure 6.2 Sales Cycle Quadrants Diagram

The sales cycle quadrants correlate to the Hitters' competitiveness in the account. They are in the position of either being blind, competitive, or collaborative.

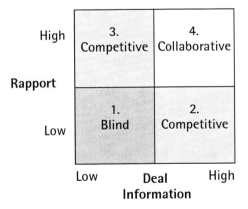

Figure 6.3 Sales Cycle Quadrants—Competitiveness

The blind quadrant is where Heavy Hitters have little information about the deal and little rapport has been established. In this unenviable position, they are "blind" about the deal. At the beginning of every new sales cycle, they find themselves in this position.

Their immediate goals are to collect information and start the process of developing rapport. As the sales cycle progresses, they know if they are unable to collect pertinent information or develop significant rapport, they should stop working the deal.

The amount of information Heavy Hitters receive from customers will vary. For example, the evaluation criteria could be extremely well documented. A request for proposal (RFP) may be three hundred pages long with descriptive narrations about the customers' environment and very detailed questions about the vendor. However, this is only the external aspect of the product selection. The internal political part of the product selection isn't publicly revealed. By establishing rapport, the Heavy Hitter will learn of the inner workings of the customer.

In the second quadrant, one of the two competitive ones, Hitters have a lot of information but little rapport. They know they must move quickly to establish rapport early in the sales cycle. Without rapport, the likelihood of winning the deal decreases as the sales cycle progresses.

In the third quadrant, Heavy Hitters have established rapport but have a low level of information about the customers' requirements or a high level of uncertainty whether the deal will happen. For example, the Heavy Hitter may have painstakingly developed relationships within the application group of the IT department of a Fortune 100 company. However, because of the IT department's immensity and bureaucracy, the application group members are unsure of the direction and approval of their project. Therefore, even though rapport is high and the application group has identified technical needs, the knowledge of whether there is actually a deal to be closed is low.

Ultimately, Heavy Hitters want to be in the fourth, or collaborative, quadrant. In this quadrant, they have established rapport and are receiving proprietary information that the other vendors aren't. In addition, an interesting paradigm shift occurs in the vendor-customer relationship. The customer begins working with the vendor as a long-term partner while still in the sales cycle. For example, when issues arise about the functionality of the product, the customer works with the vendor to find an acceptable solution. This shift, from being treated like one of the vendors to becoming part of the customer team, is very noticeable. At this point, Heavy Hitters know they have won the deal and update their forecast accordingly.

Hitters move from quadrant to quadrant as the sales cycle progresses. Moving from the blind quadrant to the competitive quadrants marks forward progress in the deal. During the sales cycle, they could also experience setbacks that move them back into being blind. For example, if the coach suddenly leaves the company or is reassigned, the Hitter is blind again.

ENEMIES

While Heavy Hitters know their true enemy is time, they are in daily fights with other enemies who are trying to vanquish them. Heavy Hitters always assume that someone is in the enviable position of being in the collaborative quadrant. Only one vendor can occupy this position. Everyone else is in one of the other quadrants.

Every high-technology company and every deal has an archenemy. Most often, it is the same company you compete against in deal after deal. You are probably very familiar with your archenemy and have no trouble identifying it. Most likely, it is the company you hate and fear the most. Your archenemy is also the one competitor who is most often present in the collaborative quadrant.

SALES CYCLE STRATEGIES

An implicit strategy is associated with each quadrant. In each quadrant, the Heavy Hitter executes a strategy that counteracts a competitor or corrects a weakness in the Hitter's current position. The

Heavy Hitter will execute one of the following strategies: attack/ retreat, seek, sustain, or protect.

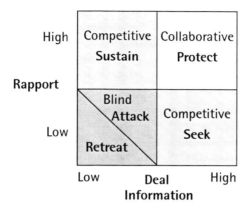

Figure 6.4 Sales Cycle Quadrants—Strategies

Attack/Retreat

If the Heavy Hitter is in the blind quadrant, he will either attack or retreat. The basic premise of the attack strategy is to hurt the competition. The methods are based on the creation of fear, uncertainty, and doubt (FUD). When Hitters are on the attack, they may furnish negative information about their competitors. This information may include bad references, negative press reports and reviews, critical industry analyst comments, and benchmarks showing poor performance.

To motivate a customer to spend additional time with them or to slow the sales process down, Heavy Hitters may attack the competition by drastically cutting the price and offering free services. Or Heavy Hitters can bypass the established evaluation process and present their case directly to the customer's key executives. The attack strategy may even include the conscious decision to do nothing. For example, customers may ask for information, but Heavy Hitters will not provide it until they get the information or commitments they want in return. Doing nothing sometimes frustrates the members of the selection team who are working against the Hitter as it forces them to spend additional time dealing with this disruptive person. Other times, it is exactly what they would like to have happen. They want the Hitter's solution to disappear quietly.

Customers may respond to the attack favorably. They may ask the "attacked" competitor to refute negative claims with direct proof. Thus the level of rapport that the attacked competitor previously enjoyed is reduced. At the very least, the sales cycle will be slowed down. This gives the Heavy Hitter additional time to find and develop a coach.

However, any attack strategy is very risky and will most likely fail. If the results are unsuccessful, the Hitter's own credibility is damaged, and the deal is lost. The Heavy Hitter actually welcomes this result as it makes no sense to work on deals where your involvement is not wanted or appreciated. It is the salesperson with the poor pipeline who continually tries to pry the customer's front door open with his broken foot.

Side by side with the attack strategy is the retreat strategy. After collecting enough information to know they cannot possibly win, Heavy Hitters want out of the deal as soon as possible to continue looking for other accounts.

Seek

Heavy Hitters will employ a seek strategy in the second sales quadrant, where they have a high amount of information but little customer rapport. The seek strategy is very simple: find a coach. Hitters will introduce themselves and their message to all the relevant people within the account. They will also ask the other members of the team (the system engineer, consultants, and manager) to assist in the search by infiltrating the account.

Sustain

In the third quadrant, the Hitter's strategy is to sustain rapport with the customer while continuing to gather more information. The "sustain" strategy involves using the coach not only as the on-site eyes and ears of the account (akin to a personal surveillance camera) but also as a go-between to disseminate information. The goal is for the coach to relay propaganda about the Hitter's product and to slander the competitor's. This strategy has a parallel in the presidential election process. Candidates for president will typically use their vice presidential running mates as "attack dogs" against their opponents. By doing this, the presidential candidates maintain their integrity and positive personas. Hitters and presidential candidates want negative information given out, but they can't do it themselves without looking bad.

Protect

Only one vendor at a time can be in the fourth, or collaborative, quadrant. Members of this vendor's team are trying to protect their position from the attack strategies of other vendors. They are trying to fortify their personal relationships to deflect the other seekers. Through the natural strength of this position, they are able to take the high ground over the other vendors by engaging in only positive tactics that emanate integrity or by directly influencing the selection process to favor their solution. They are in harmony with the customer and the customer will actually defend them against others. Once Heavy Hitters are in this quadrant, they obviously want to stay there for the remaining stages of the sales cycle.

Sales Cycle Stages

Heavy Hitters understand that every deal requires an investment of time and resources. The resources are tangible things like people, equipment, and money. Intangible items, including mental energy, credibility, and political capital, are also being expended. All of these items are finite. Through the managed use of these resources, Heavy Hitters gain momentum in a deal. However, as they gain momentum they have to expend more effort and resources. The following graph illustrates the expenditure of these resources.

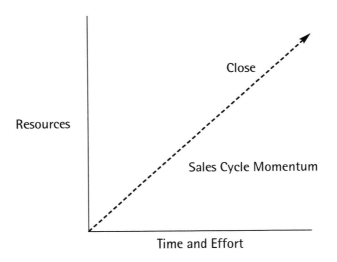

Figure 6.5 Sales Cycle Investments

In reality, the only two positions to be in at the end of the deal are first place, as the winner, or last place, as the first loser. Heavy Hitters would rather finish in last place than end in second place. Salespeople who are proud of a second-place finish are a detriment to their company. The next graph illustrates this point.

You may have noticed that the "momentum" line from the previous graph has been replaced with a "customer placebo" line. The only vendor who experiences momentum is the winner. All other vendors are interpreting the information they are receiving as the truth, when in actuality it is false evidence appearing real (FEAR). Remember the acronym because you will have a lot to FEAR when you are working on a deal using bad information.

Also notice that vendors disappear from the sales cycle at various stages of investment of time and effort. Clearly, last place is better than every place except winning. However, in most sales cycles the investment does not stop suddenly. Rather, a customer is more likely to become unresponsive or make a vendor perform some tasks that it cannot possibly complete. By continuing to jump through a customer's hoops or wasting valuable mental energy and emotions thinking about the deal, the salesperson continues to pour good resources on top of bad. In this situation, the vendor has no hope of protecting its investment to date. It is a sunk cost, and the expenditure of additional time and effort compounds the mistake. The mistake can be magnified even more depending on the sales cycle phase. Learning you are the loser in the eleventh hour of a deal is a frustrating, humbling, and embarrassing event.

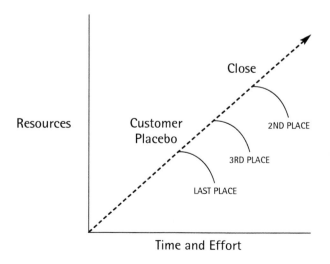

Figure 6.6 Investments by Winners and Losers

SALES CYCLE PHASES

Other distinct phases of the sales cycle are represented by the diagram below. The time frame of this entire process is dependent upon the complexity (and associated expense) of the product being sold. For a complex product, the period of time could be as long as a year. For a simple product, it could be as short as one hour.

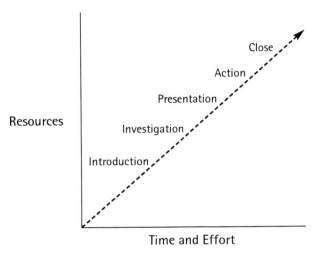

Figure 6.7 Sales Cycle Phases

Every sales cycle starts with an introduction—the action that was responsible for the Heavy Hitter finding the deal. The introduction may be an outbound activity such as a cold call, direct mail, a seminar, or an e-mail. An inbound introduction is when the customer searches out the vendor based upon an industry article, public relations, or word of mouth. Finally, an introduction could be made through a personal relationship such as a customer referral, through a partner referral, or from a consultant. These introductions take advantage of the attachment theory of relationships whereby the Hitter is attached to an existing relationship and bestowed with its same qualities, such as standing, character, and reputation. In other words, assuming the introductory relationship is positive, the Hitter is automatically thought of in the same manner. However, this theory also applies to negative introductory relationships. To Hitters, the source of an introduction is important. They know that relationship-based introductions provide them with the most credibility.

Following the introduction, Heavy Hitters try to gain as much information as possible about the customer's business and technical criteria. They will investigate the customer to determine if their product is a good fit. For a simple product, the investigation could merely be asking a few questions about the customer's environment, such as what hardware and operating systems they use. For a complex enterprise software application, the investigation could be a series of on-site meetings to determine the flow of the customer's business operations.

Assuming some level of cursory fit, Heavy Hitters will present their solution in the context of the customer's environment. Depending upon the reception to the solution, Heavy Hitters will introduce a call to action. This may include anything from providing additional documentation to arranging customer site visits for the evaluation of the product. Following the successful completion of the call to action, they are ready to negotiate and close the deal. Once again, the negotiation may include a complex legal process or simply asking for a purchase order.

Product, Fantasy, and Politics

Three underlying themes are present at each phase of the sales cycle: product, fantasy, and politics. These themes influence the vendor's ultimate selection, and they occur in different amounts and at different stages during the sales cycle.

In the early stages of the sales cycle, the customer focus is on the product. The customer wants to understand the underlying technology, feature set, and functionality. As the sales cycle progresses, the fantasy and political themes become more prevalent and important.

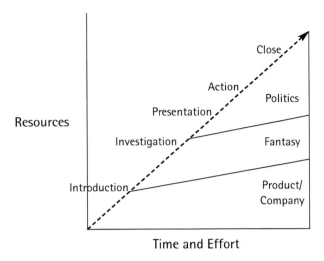

Figure 6.8 Sales Cycle Phases and Underlying Themes

All sales involve selling a fantasy. The fantasy is that somehow the product you are selling is going to make the customer's life easier, save the customer money, or enable the customer to make more money. The technology and feature set of your product validate the fantasy elements of your "story." They promote the customer's fantasy. During the sales cycle, you communicate how you can turn your customers' fantasies into a reality, but only when your product is selected.

Evaluation team members also have a "personal" fantasy. Maybe they want to master new technology to enrich their resumes. Maybe they want to earn bonuses for cutting costs or increasing revenue. Maybe they want to be perceived as heroes within the company or to spend more time at home and less at work. Everyone has a personal fantasy that is associated with the procurement of a product. Whatever the fantasy, it is tied to a very personal benefaction. Heavy Hitters understand and align their strategy with personal fantasies.

Heavy Hitters also understand the political nature of the sales cycle. They know that people will take sides for and against the product. They understand that people within the customer's organization are preoccupied with power or the status quo. As the sales cycle progresses, they know that the decision process will become more political. Ultimately, politics will play a large role in the final decision and only the vendor in the collaborative quadrant will win the political decision.

CONCLUSION

This chapter has been about how Heavy Hitters work the sales cycle to achieve their personal benefactions associated with closing deals. If you are interested in learning what these benefactions are, take a look at Heavy Hitters' work areas. They may have pictures of sailboats on the wall and dream about being free to sail the world. Pictures of family members may indicate a desire to provide security and a better way of life for them. Sales awards may be prominently displayed as a testament to their sales prowess or indicate their desire for power and prestige. By understanding benefactions you can anticipate the personal and political behavior of both the customer and the Hitter alike.

Any self-respecting book about sales would not be complete without quotations from the ancient eastern logician Sun Tzu and his famous book, *The Art of War*. Sun Tzu was a Chinese general who lived over two and a half thousand years ago. Most likely, you have read the book or are familiar with passages from it. Probably the most popular and frequently quoted passage is the following: "If you know the enemy and know yourself, you need not fear the result of a hundred battles. If you know yourself but not the enemy, for every victory gained you will suffer a defeat. If you know neither the enemy nor yourself, you will succumb in every battle."[10]

Some lesser-known Sun Tzu quotes reiterate some of the important concepts presented in this chapter. "Once war is declared, he will not waste precious time . . . but cross the enemy's frontier without delay. The value of time, that is being a little ahead of your opponent, has counted for more than numerical superiority." Time is the ultimate enemy. Heavy Hitters protect their time above all else.

"He who exercises no forethought but makes light of his opponents is sure to be captured by them." Heavy Hitters think about every action strategically. In order to have the best battle plan, they are constantly triangulating information with others.

"The clever combatant will impose his will on the enemy, but does not allow the enemy's will to be imposed on him." Heavy Hitters know once they are in the collaborative quadrant, they have a clear path to win the business.

"He will win who knows when to fight and when not to fight." Heavy Hitters recognize when to attack and when to retreat from a deal.

"Knowledge of the enemy's position can only be obtained from other men. Hence, the use of spies."[11] Heavy Hitters understand they must have a coach to win. They need proprietary information that only a spy can provide. These words are as true today as they were two and a half thousand years ago.

7

Building Customer Rapport

As a woman in sales, Tracey faced many obstacles. The technology market segment she was selling in was completely dominated by men and all of her colleagues were men. Nevertheless, she was always one of the company's top sales reps and consistently closed the largest deals. Tracey was a person who was able to create "magic" when she was in front of a customer. She could put people at ease while still driving the deal to close. She could ask very tough questions in a very friendly way and persuade people to change their point of view using common-sense arguments. She had a presence that went way beyond her spoken words.

Heavy Hitters have several unique attributes. They are able to speak in the customer's language, they can decipher their incongruencies in communication, and they have a well-developed model for selecting the deals they pursue. One of the key differences from most salespeople is their ability to create a higher level of rapport with the important members of an evaluation team. In this chapter, we will review how Heavy Hitters determine who can help further their cause and how they build this unique level of rapport. Let's start by examining whom the Heavy Hitters target in their accounts.

Most high-technology products are sold directly into or are approved by the information technology (IT) department of a company. While many high-technology companies create products that require their sales efforts to focus on business line managers or end users, usually the IT department will have to bless the selection somewhere in the purchase process. At the very least, the selection of the product will have to conform to the standards set previously by the IT department. For example, most companies have standards regarding which desktop or laptop computers can be purchased.

The IT department's size is usually in proportion to the size of the company. The department's structure and organization will most likely reflect the complexity of the business and the complexity of the products it produces. For example, the IT organization of one of the "Big Three" automakers will reflect the nature and intricacy of the business. However, even a small IT organization can be very sophisticated in using technology.

Regardless of the size and complexity of the IT organization, you can classify people within the department into three basic categories of responsibility: product, management, and executive. Most likely, your solution is targeted at one of these categories. Your initial contact with the account and most frequent interactions with the customer will also be within one of these categories. Let's take a moment to define and understand the nuances of these categories.

PRODUCT CATEGORY

The product category includes those individuals who work hands-on with technology. This category includes programmers, system administrators, networking analysts, security engineers, and specialists of all kinds. Typically, people within this category will have "administrator," "analyst," or "engineer" in their titles. These people use a vendor's products to create a new product for their company. For example, the programmer is creating an application (product) by using programming tools and products provided by a vendor. The system operator is creating system availability (product) by managing the department's systems using hardware and software products that were provided by vendors. The security analyst safeguards IT assets (product) by using products from vendors.

MANAGEMENT CATEGORY

The management category provides direction to each of the various departments of the IT organization. The departments may include applications, systems, programming, networking, security, or Internet business. Departments also may be organized around initiatives or business practices. Typically, people at this level may have "director," "manager," or "leader" somewhere in their titles.

While many different management styles exist, there are two fundamental types of IT department managers: the "domain expert" and the "business expert." Domain expert managers achieved this position by being the most knowledgeable person within their department. For example, a network manager may have been promoted to a management position because of her troubleshooting expertise. Domain experts are the "alpha," or dominant, resource that all the other members of the group consult with for technical advice.

Meanwhile, business expert managers are responsible for representing their department to the other departments within the company. While they are still technical, they rely heavily on the technical opinions of a few key members of their team to make decisions.

EXECUTIVE CATEGORY

Probably the first instruction all new salespeople are given is to always "call high" when trying to penetrate an account and meet with the most senior executive. However, this is true only if the product you are selling is targeted at the executive category. The only products that will get executive-level attention are those major products that involve major pain for the company (whether in solving or creating a problem), major expenditures, major savings and revenue creation, or major company initiatives. For the sake of simplicity, you can define the term "major" as meaning someone will get fired or promoted over the event. This includes vendors too!

Companies experience different kinds of pain all the time. There are nuisances that create dull aching pains in every department, such as a temperamental copy machine. There are throbbing pains that may reappear occasionally, like Internet service providers that go down momentarily once or twice every few months. And there are stabbing pains that require immediate attention, for example, when the order-entry system is down and products can't be shipped and employees are sent home. Companies can live with dull aches and prioritize throbbing pains accordingly. It's the stabbing pains that receive immediate attention and dictate budgeting.

In larger companies, the executive IT level is composed of people who have the word "president" or "chief" in their titles, such as vice president, chief information officer (CIO), and chief technology officer (CTO). In smaller companies, the executive IT level may also include individuals with "director" or "manager" in their titles.

Each category of responsibility has a different orientation toward the operation of the department. The executive category ensures the IT department is coordinated with the business strategy and major initiatives. The management category leads ongoing projects, day-to-day operation of the departments, and supervision of the people responsible for "products." Meanwhile, the product category is focused on its microcosm of the IT department.

GENERALIZATIONS ABOUT REPRESENTATIONAL SYSTEMS

At the beginning of the book, you were introduced to the concept of general words through a discussion about pizza, horoscopes, and fortune cookies. General words require additional words called operators to make them meaningful. In a similar way, "generalizations" require additional investigation and analysis to ensure that they are correct.

Below, you will find some generalizations about the most common representational systems of the people that compose the executive, management, and product categories. These generalizations need to be validated for the particular market space you are selling your products into (whether it be networking, systems software, security, and so on). No category has an exclusive or definitive representational system. Rather, these generalizations are guidelines for you to use to explain your company's story and position your product until you have identified a person's representational system.

The executive category is most likely to contain individuals with strong visual systems. Let's assume you have been working a deal for some time and are in the collaborative quadrant. Your coach has arranged a presentation of your product to the CIO, whom you have never met. Present your information assuming that she has a strong visual system. As the presentation progresses, you will be able to further qualify the CIO's wiring and make any appropriate adjustments.

Another strategy is to present all of your ideas and thoughts in neutral wording without any reference to representational systems. Neutral wording enables listeners to apply the system of their choice to gain meaning. Here are some examples of representational usage (the first phrase in each pair) and the corresponding neutral wording usage (the second phrase):

- Instead of "I see what you mean," use "I agree with you."
- Instead of "I hear you," use "I understand."
- Instead of "Looks good," use "I think it will work."
- Instead of "I sense you don't like it," use "Do you doubt it will work?"

Those in the product category are more likely to have strong auditory systems, although this may vary by their area of focus. In particular, you will find an unusually high percentage of people in the programming areas to be Auditories. The nature of programming naturally attracts people who have an aptitude for words.

At the management level, the domain expert manager will have a representational system that resembles that of the product category people of that industry. In most cases, assume these IT people are Auditories. Business expert managers will most likely have strong visual and kinesthetic systems. They can see where their team fits into the needs of the company.

All of these generalizations are dependent upon the nature of the market space. For example, if you are selling an end-user application to the sales and marketing department, that is quite different from selling an application to the engineering department.

EXERCISE 9: GENERALIZATIONS

The above generalizations are fairly easy to validate by performing the following exercise:

1. While you are performing the VAK counts on customer calls, add a notation of whether the person is in the product, management, or executive category. When you have collected data during seven to ten sales calls, chart the VAK counts for each category.

2. During the next few days, make it a point to spend some time with product, management, and executive category people within your organization. Perform a VAK count for each person you meet and total the VAK counts for each category.

Here's the most important point. You need to identify the category of responsibility your product is targeted to with precision. This is the main group of people within the IT department you are trying to sell to (executive, management, or product). For your target category, you need to determine if there is a single pervasive representational system. If there is, you need to take this into account in the development of your sales strategies, messages, customer collateral, and staffing decisions.

During my career, I have sold four basic types of technology: enterprise applications, systems software, application development tools, and networking/security software. One of the groups I managed sold products into the security department. The product was specifically targeted at firewall administrators and security analysts, and I was chartered to build the sales team of this start-up business. As I was interviewing, I noticed that I was hiring a large number of auditory salespeople and managers. This began to make me curious.

My previous position involved selling to IT management. These people were more likely to have stronger visual and kinesthetic systems, so I hired accordingly. However, as I went on more and more of these security product sales calls, I began to realize that the percentage of Auditories within the security industry is very high. Without being conscious of it, my intuition had already begun the process of selecting people that matched the pervasive representational system of this target audience. In hindsight, it shouldn't have been surprising to find a high number of Auditories in the security area. After all, these product people are responsible for writing and coding the security policies associated with firewalls.

Another interesting characterization of the various people who are involved in the product selection process is displayed in the following graph, which represents four different characteristics that a person can be measured against.

The left axis is the degree to which a person insists that things be done her way. This is called being a "bully." A bully will get her way at any and all costs. Being a bully is not necessarily a negative term, nor does it mean that the person is physically intimidating. It is simply the description of people who will tenaciously fight for their cause. Also, people are more likely to be bullies when they have an elevated status

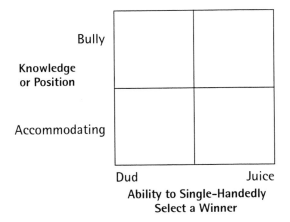

Figure 7.1 Characteristics of Evaluators

within the evaluation team. The status could be the result of their domain expertise or their title and the authority it commands.

At the other end of the spectrum are people who are accommodating. Typically, people with lower-level positions in an organization or low levels of knowledge or experience in a particular area of the company will be more accommodating to decisions being made. They are apathetic to whatever solution is purchased. The degree to which people are bullies or accommodating depends on the effect the purchase decision has on their span of control, position in the company, or ability to perform their job.

On the horizontal axis, is the concept of "juice" and the "dud." Simply put, juice is charisma. But even this definition is too simple. Some people are natural-born leaders. They have an aura that can motivate and instill confidence. That's juice. Juice is fairly hard to describe, but you know it when you see it.

Having juice does not mean that these people act like John Wayne, nor are they necessarily the highest-ranking people involved in an evaluation. Instead, they are the ones who always seem to be on the winning side. Only one member of the customer's evaluation team is the bully who has the juice. She imparts her own will on the selection process by single-handedly selecting the vendor and pushing the purchase through the procurement process. She can either finalize the purchase terms or instruct the procurement team on the terms that are considered acceptable.

"Duds" are named after the ineffective firework they represent. Sometimes the fuse of a firework will burn down but nothing will happen. Some fireworks may be very big but produce disappointing results. Duds have a lot of big talk but little action. "Accommodating duds" are people who do not take an active role in the sales process. Even worse are "dud bullies," who try to pretend they have juice but don't. For a salesperson, the realization of this may not come until too late.

For all of the people involved in the sales selection process, Heavy Hitters calculate their amount of juice and their propensity to be a bully. In the following example, John, Jim, Karl, and Rich are plotted according to the Hitter's assessment.

In the chart below, John is a dud bully, Jim is an accommodating dud, and Rich has juice. Hitters naturally gravitate to people with juice. However, a person with juice may be apathetic to the purchase of your product, such as Karl in the diagram. For example, a CIO who has juice probably doesn't care what toner cartridges

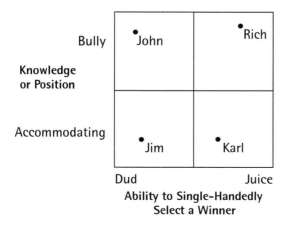

Figure 7.2 Plotting Individual Assessments

are purchased for the laser printers. He will be accommodating and support the decision of the people who make that decision. Someone else has the juice for the procurement of toner cartridges. Many people have juice (charisma and authority), but only one person has the juice to single-handedly select the vendor.

Let's assume the same company was making a decision about an enterprise resource planning system. You can assume the evaluation team's decision will match the CIO's preference. She may have imposed her will on the evaluation process through brute force or by finesse. Either way, her preference was "bullied" into the decision. The most powerful position in all of sales is when your coach has juice. If your coach has juice, you win! The next best scenario is when your coach can influence the person with juice.

I want to share with you a memorable, personal story about a bully who definitely had juice.

The local account team had been working with a prestigious financial brokerage firm in New York for five months. During that time, the potential customer had completed a thorough technical product evaluation in its IT lab. The sales team had invested a lot of presales engineering resources in this account. By doing so, the person (product category level) in charge of the technical evaluation had developed into a strong coach. He even approached the sales team to discuss the possibility of joining our company.

Our coach had warned us that the vice president of information services was a micromanager. He personally had to approve all new technology that was brought into "his" organization. Therefore, in order to receive his blessing, a company presentation was scheduled. The sales team can laugh about it now, but the presentation was much more of an interrogation than a business meeting.

From a personal standpoint, the vice president was combative and condescending. For example, as part of the presentation about the company, the sales team explained the patents that we had applied for and been awarded. To this point, he replied, "How do I know that these patents aren't just red herrings [false or nonexistent] to throw off your competition!" The entire meeting felt like we were appearing on *60 Minutes,* being asked by Mike Wallace, "Is it true you beat your wife?" Even though you answer no to the question, you are assumed to be guilty.

Given this set of circumstances, we had limited options to build rapport. First, we maintained our composure and did our best not to take the attack personally. Second, we agreed (profusely at times) with the VP's point of view when it was applicable. And finally, in the most professional, nonpersonal way we could muster, we countered on certain issues by offering other potential solutions. You do not want to directly contradict a bully who has juice.

As we left the meeting, I told the local salesperson that based on the beating we received, I thought it was a long shot the company would move forward with us. However, we had a secret weapon. Our coach would later tell us that our performance was deemed "acceptable" by the vice president. More importantly, our coach continued to lobby on our behalf. Several weeks later, we received our first purchase order from our new customer. It was through the coach's persistent promotion of our solution that we won the deal.

Heavy Hitters understand that they must deal with duds and bullies while they are in hot pursuit of the person who has juice. Heavy Hitters also have their own juice—their ability to create rapport. In order to win the deal, Hitters know how to communicate their message and influence others in the process, building a more intense level of rapport with their customers. The best way to illustrate this is to recount a recent sales presentation and explain the various techniques that helped create rapport.

My company was invited to participate in a seminar with four much larger and more well-known high-technology companies. The seminar's target audience was the product category people within the networking and security area. The audience consisted mainly of network analysts and security administrators. Most likely, the audience members were using one of the other vendors' products, and this was a great opportunity for my company to reach these target customers. However, we knew a lot of information would be covered because all the other vendors would be presenting their products. This created a problem because it would be easy for my company's story to be overpowered by all the other vendors' noise.

Our presentation was third and would last about thirty minutes. The two presentations preceding ours were from one of the largest computer hardware companies and a leading software company. Overall, the audience of about fifty people did not seem engaged. When the presenters asked questions of the audience, there was very little participation. Also, few questions were asked of the vendors following their presentations. A high level of "audience rapport" wasn't established.

I formulated my presentation strategy while watching the tepid reception given to the first two presenters. First, I was going to build a special level of rapport with the audience so that my presentation would have the greatest impact. In one sense, I considered the other presenters as my competitors—not from a product or company point of view but because they were all competing for the audience's mind share and to have their message valued as something important.

Second, I determined that my main benefaction of the meeting was to have the attendees remember who my company was and the problem our technology solved. I specifically wanted to see the audience members sitting "on the edge of their seats" and hear them ask questions at the end of my presentation. Ideally, someone in the audience needed my product today. Regardless, I knew my sales force would be following up personally with every attendee. In anticipation of their calling, I wanted to lay the foundation of credibility by utilizing the attachment theory of relationships, whereby a new relationship inherits positive qualities from a respected preexisting association.

Here are the first few sentences of my presentation. For illustration purposes, I am substituting "ABC Company" for the actual name of my company.

> Hello, I'm Steve Martin with ABC Company. Now, I would like to ask each of you for some help today. During the presentation, when I ask you a question, I would like you to honestly raise your hand. [You'll discover why I used this odd phrase later.]
>
> I know you are familiar with the other companies presenting today. I'd like to know, how many of you are not familiar with ABC Company?
>
> Thank you.
>
> Since you are not familiar with ABC Company, I only want you to remember one thing from today's presentation: ABC Company provides high availability and load balancing software for firewalls.

Let's analyze this communication event. I opened my presentation with, "Hello, I'm Steve Martin with ABC Company." Behind and to my left was the logo and name of my company projected onto a large screen. Usually, the announcement of my name elicits some soft laughter or at least a smile. With the exception of a handful of people, the audience remained emotionless. My internal dialogue told me it was time to do something drastic to get this audience engaged. It was time to interrupt their pattern of lethargic behavior.

For the past two hours, the audience members had been in the same state of apathetic or weak participation. Frankly, I didn't blame them since the previous presenters were poor speakers. Incidentally, the first presenter to any group greatly influences the demeanor and sets the standard of audience behavior. Unfortunately, the lead-off presentation was flat and unexciting, and as a result, the audience's behavior was similar. This pattern had been established and was now the accepted behavior of the group. To change this, I planned to perform a behavior interruption that would leave the audience members with no choice but to change their demeanor.

"Now, I would like to ask each of you for some help today," I said. The majority of the audience was composed of very technical, product category people. As we generalized earlier, product category people are more likely to be Auditories. Since I have been working with this particular market space for some time, I was fairly certain this was true for most of the attendees.

Asking someone for help is a great tool for Hitters. First, it is a natural human characteristic to want to help others. Within the business environment, the concept of helping others is even more accepted and expected. If you were to make ten telephone calls to others in your company, the most frequent response following "Hello" would be "How can I help you?"

Asking for help also starts the behavior interruption because people are naturally curious. When I asked "each of you for some help," I knew that all the audience members would become curious and ask themselves, "I wonder what he wants?" In a way, I was leading the way the audience was thinking by limiting what they could think about. I was getting their attention and forcing them to pay attention to my words.

I followed this statement with "During the presentation, when I ask you a question, I would like you to honestly raise your hand." As I said this, I raised my right hand. Once again, the statement was made in an auditory style. If the audience consisted mostly of visual managers, it would have been more appropriate to say, "Honestly show me you hands." [Again, you'll see why I used this phrase later.]

I also used a different tone in my voice when I said the words "ask" and "honestly." This is known as "marking." I specifically marked those words to call the audience's internal dialogues to attention. Marking has two purposes: it alerts the listener's conscious mind to highlight a specific thought, and it tells the subconscious mind to remember what might otherwise have been ignored. You can use all aspects of body language including hand gestures, facial expressions, posture, and speech to mark words. Words can be marked by varying their pronunciation with inflection, volume, pitch, speed, or accent.

The most common way to mark is to increase the volume. However, decreasing volume, even whispering, is just as effective in business meetings. Even words and phrases can be used to mark other words. If I say, "Listen up!" "Here comes the important part," or "If you're wondering what's next," your awareness and anticipation are heightened.

What does it mean to "honestly raise your hands"? How did you interpret this request? Did I mean for audience members to honestly raise their hands or honestly answer the question? This confusion may have caused a brief internal debate since an attempt had to be made to define what I meant. I actually meant both. Regardless, they still had to pay attention to me and by making this request in a certain way, I was again leading their thought process.

In conjunction with this request, I raised my right hand very slowly in a very specific way. I positioned it very close to my chest, much like the president would do when taking the oath of office. I could have raised my hand as high as possible, but this would be uncomfortable for Auditories. I was trying to engage their internal dialogue by keeping it very busy and attentive to me. By raising my hand slowly, they naturally had to follow it. Again, I was leading their behavior by showing them the "comfortable" or suggested way to raise their hand. If I had been presenting to a predominantly visual group, I would have held my hand higher and moved it faster.

"I know you are familiar with the other companies presenting today," I started. This was a verifiable statement. I was certain that everybody knew the two companies that presented before me. Therefore, as each of the audience members verified this statement with their internal dialogue, it would be true. They had no choice but to agree with my verifiable statement. Verifiable statements help build credibility and extend rapport with the presenter. Now, if I had opened up the presentation by stating that my company had the hottest new technology, there would be no way for the audience members to verify the statement. This unverifiable statement would naturally elicit skepticism and actually hinder creating rapport. Unverifiable statements must be proven true to be accepted.

"I'd like to know, how many of you are not familiar with ABC Company?" I continued. Normally, someone would ask, "How many people are familiar with ABC Company?" I knew my company was much less known than the other, larger companies. Before the seminar started, I even had casual conversations with a few of the attendees and validated they hadn't heard of my company. I marked the word "not" with tone inflection and held my hands chest high, open palmed, to the audience. I asked the question in a negative form and held my palms out to emphasize this. I wanted them to stop and think about the question so I paused momentarily. Their internal dialogue had to repeat the question to themselves to make sure they heard and answered it correctly.

One of my benefactions was to interrupt their noninvolvement in the presentation and get them all to raise their hands, instead of just a few attendees. The response to the question was perfect. With the exception of just a couple of people, all the audience members in the room raised their hands. The manner in which they raised their hands was also important. No one shot a hand in the air like Horshack on *Welcome Back, Kotter.* Rather, they comfortably raised their right hands as I did. "Thank you," I replied. It is very important to show respect and reward the appropriate response.

"Since you are not familiar with ABC Company, I only want you to remember one thing from today's presentation." This sentence has two separate parts that are linked together. The first part of the sentence is another verifiable statement. They had previously raised their hands and acknowledged that they weren't familiar with my company.

The second part of the sentence is a direct instruction on what I wanted them to do. Through "linkage," you can tie together two completely different messages. Since the first part is known to be true, the second part will have a higher likelihood of being accepted as the truth.

Let's interrupt this story for a brief experiment. As you finish reading this sentence, you will become aware of your breathing. The first part of the sentence is a verifiable statement. You are reading the words that compose the sentence and, undoubtedly, you will finish reading it. By linking it to the second part of the sentence, you have little choice but to think about your breathing (even if you didn't want to). Because breathing is an automatic process, you may have had to stop reading or breathing for a moment to check how you were breathing. If the sentence had only said, "Become aware of your breathing," it wouldn't have had the same impact and effect. Linkage is a very powerful sales tool, and Heavy Hitters continually link true statements to theoretical arguments in order to best argue their case.

As I said, "I only want you to remember one thing from today's presentation," I executed three different types of marking. I inflected my speech by increasing volume and adding urgency to the tone on the words "only" and "one." Physically, I held my right hand up chest high, forming the number one with my hand. Then, I paused for a moment to survey the crowd. I wanted to make sure they were looking at my finger. Everyone I could see was. I also took one step sidewise to the right as I said the word "one." This ensured that they would have to maintain a strong focal point of attention. I watched the audience members' heads move as they followed me.

I continued, "ABC Company provides high availability and load balancing software for firewalls." Using my speech, I marked "high availability and load balancing." I also changed my hand position from forming the number one to separating my index finger and thumb, as if I was measuring the words "high availability and load balancing." The audience followed the change in hand movement. I was creating an anchor.

As we learned earlier, an anchor is the process of associating a certain feeling or meaning to an object. That morning, the members of the audience were going to hear presentations from four different companies and I wanted to ensure my message wasn't lost. I wanted to ensure it was remembered in their mind's eye.

You may have noticed another aspect of what I said. I purposely created some confusion by intentionally contradicting myself. The meaning of the words I said was detached from the physical message my body was sending. "Detaching" refers to the process of dividing the listener's reality by separating pre-existing meanings from the words being spoken. I said the word "one" and formed the number one with my hand. However, I gave the audience two things to remember, "high availability" and "load balancing." A portion of the audience didn't notice I actually said two things. They considered it one statement and I was well on my way to developing rapport with these people. For the portion of the audience that considered these two items, this was not in alignment with their reality. It caused them to do an additional quick internal assessment about what was happening.

Up to that point in the presentation, I had been smoothly leading the audience where I wanted them to go. I had been marking key thoughts and linking messages together. The detaching of information completed the behavior interruption. It was another layer of information that had to be assessed and internalized, causing an additional level of information processing to occur. While this entire series of communication took less than a minute, audience members' state of engagement had changed from apathetic to interested. Their posture even changed and they sat more upright. Their facial expressions changed. It was as if they woke up. Now they were in an appropriate state of receptivity to hear my company's presentation.

Detaching can be an effective tool in situations where you want to change behaviors quickly. For example, when you greet someone, you will typically cheerfully say, "How are you doing?" The automatic response is "Fine" or "Okay." It is the expected and anticipated response attached to that particular question. Let's pretend you respond, "My dog just died." This answer is completely opposite from the expected response. Immediately, the person who asked the question would be detached from being cheerful and become somber or apologetic.

Salespeople are constantly detaching meanings. For example, since almost all customers have dealt with high-pressure salespeople in the past, they have attached a negative meaning to "salespeople" in general. In every sales call, the Heavy Hitter is trying to detach herself from this stereotype through her behavior and actions.

Within my sales organization, I have a favorite phrase that replaces "How are you doing?" I will say in a friendly voice, "Are you helping us?" Basically, I am trying to elicit honest, unedited information from my staff. "Are you helping us?" doesn't have an attached response. If there is good news or bad news, I want to know about it as early as possible. I have found that by changing this small greeting, I can get a very quick, current assessment of someone's recent accomplishments and the important issues they are facing.

STATES OF RAPPORT AND ENGAGEMENT

During the seminar presentation, I was able to change the state of rapport with the audience members in a very short time. I needed their state to change in order to create the best circumstance to have my message accepted and remembered. People experience many different types of states, ranging from fear and hate to love and trust. In the business world, we are typically operating in a very narrow range of states.

"State" also applies to engagement at work. Normal daily business is done in the awake or alert state. You're constantly alert for information, whether it comes from personal conversations, e-mail, or the telephone. And you're performing your duties as a participant of the company.

Figure 7.3 States of Consciousness

At the extreme ends of the scale are the avoidance state and the trance state. For example, you will go to a great deal of effort to avoid someone or something that is feared or hated. I dislike going to the dentist. As a result, I try to avoid it as much as possible and procrastinate about scheduling an appointment.

At the other end of the spectrum is being in a "trance." A trance is not necessarily equivalent to being comatose. A trance is entering a state where you are aware of your environment and the stimuli surrounding you but are intently focused on your internal dialogue. For example, my wife and I will read together in bed at night. We are very aware of each other and cognizant of noises coming from other parts of our home. However, since we are concentrating on reading, repeating, and interpreting words, we are very self-centered on our internal dialogues. When I am with my wife, I am very comfortable so it's easy for me to relax and enter a state of trance. Perhaps just by reading these last few sentences you may have felt yourself drifting off a bit.

Heavy Hitters are constantly trying to differentiate themselves from their competitors. While the rest of the competitors are operating in the "normal" range of business rapport, Hitters are trying to change the rules of the game and develop a more intense rapport that is outside the range of normal, where the customer is comfortable and at ease.

At the seminar, I was trying to achieve an intense state of rapport with the audience members. Since my product can help their businesses succeed, I felt it was important they heard my message. In order to ensure they were listening, I was marking specific words, making verifiable statements, and linking actions I wanted them to perform throughout the entire presentation. As a result, I was heavily exercising their internal dialogues and engaging all of their representational systems. By doing so, their pattern of behavior was interrupted, and I was able to lead them to the desired state of business rapport.

You may have been wondering how I knew I had achieved my goal. Through the years, I have developed a model for determining what state an audience is in. During any meeting or presentation, I am constantly sensing each individual's state of rapport. However, this is only practical in groups up to a certain size. With over fifty people at this seminar, this presented a different challenge. In order to validate the group's state of rapport, I had to create an easily observable cue to allow me to make the determination if what I was doing was, in fact, working. By asking the group to raise their hands, I was able to identify a "group pattern." Group patterns are presentation checkpoints used to measure rapport. Since almost all the audience members raised their hands, it was okay to proceed.

Another question you may have is whether I planned the entire introduction. Did I choreograph the physical movements, tone inflections, and the specific questions I asked? The answer is "Not really." It just happened. Through repetitive experience, I have developed the skill to do this. Like learning anything new, I started with small steps, such as marking words verbally and physically. Then I incorporated the concept of linking messages. Finally, I began to tie them together to form behavior interruptions. It takes practice, but it's well worth the effort.

CONCLUSION

One of the biggest challenges salespeople face is establishing a sufficient level of customer rapport to ensure their message is received in an open and honest manner. In this chapter, we reviewed the executive, management, and product categories of IT responsibility and discussed generalizations about their pervasive representational systems. Heavy Hitters adapt their communication and sales strategies depending on the category their product is targeted at.

Heavy Hitters know that the members of the customer's evaluation team do not share an equal vote or the same level of interest in the decision being made. Some members are apathetic while others are more insistent they get their way. However, one individual has the juice to single-handedly make the decision, and it is this individual that Hitters strive to build rapport with.

Finally, salespeople are constantly placed into situations where they must differentiate themselves and their product from other attention-getting solutions. In order to stand out and be remembered, they engage listeners' internal dialogue by linking messages together and marking specific words. Like the story about Tracey at the beginning of the chapter, they create "magic" in front of the customer.

To finish the story about the seminar, my presentation was very well received. A short question-and-answer session immediately followed the presentation. Unlike the other presenters, we were asked so many questions that we ran out of time. Perhaps the most interesting event occurred about an hour and a half later.

The final presenter of the day wrapped up the seminar. He thanked everyone for attending and summarized each vendor's presentation. As he summarized my company's product, he did the most complimentary impression. He moved to the exact position on stage where I had spoken earlier, held up his right hand with the index finger and thumb spread, and said, "and the one thing to remember about ABC Company is 'high availability' and 'load balancing' for firewalls." I was sitting in the back of the room with my local salesperson. She leaned over to me and said, "He got it!" I winked at her and said, "They all got it!"

8

The Complete Hitter

> The mood was somber. The vice president of sales had just begun
> to address the worldwide sales team that had been assembled. The
> previous quarter had been a disaster. Following fifteen straight
> quarters of unprecedented growth and incredible stock appreci-
> ation, the company announced it would miss its revenue targets
> by over 30 percent. In addition, articles in the press were criticiz-
> ing the company's aggressive accounting practices and unusual
> revenue recognition policies. Under these circumstances, the vice
> president began to speak, "We're just going to have to sell our way
> out of this thing."

In the previous chapters, we have discussed how to model Heavy
Hitters by reviewing how Heavy Hitters determine the "wiring"
of their customers, how they identify incongruencies to find the
truth, and how they select, qualify, and close deals. Because Heavy
Hitters are people worthy of imitation, we strive to emulate every behavioral characteristic completely. In this chapter, we continue our
modeling exercise by examining their relationship with their managers and reviewing the psychological drives that explain their motivations. For newer salespeople, this section will be a form of
mentoring, a discussion of how Heavy Hitters view themselves and
their career in sales. Experienced salespeople are likely to have a few
"aha" moments while reading this chapter when elements of their
own behavior are explained.

We'll start by reviewing the strategies Heavy Hitters use to build rapport with their manager. This discussion will include a review of the relevant sales management styles Heavy Hitters encounter. In the second half of this chapter, we will review the complex needs that drive a Hitter's actions. The psychological framework we will use to describe Hitter behavior is based on Abraham Maslow's "hierarchy of needs." Over the years, I have found the theory a useful and intuitively logical frame of reference to explain the complex issues that drive all human behavior. Not surprisingly, once we understand this universal model, we can also apply it directly to customers.

As I was walking the hallway at my office, I overheard a conversation between two managers. One said, "A players hire A players, B players hire B players, and so on." This quote refers to the popular axiom that the best managers will hire the best employees. In sales, this is extraordinarily true. Through the repetitive process of hiring salespeople and observing which ones succeed or fail, "A" quality sales managers have developed a keen sense for identifying top sales talent and a methodology for selecting the individual who has the right skills, attitude, and personality. Therefore, they are continually upgrading their sales teams with the "arrival of the fittest."

Conversely, "A" quality salespeople recognize their manager will influence their ability to succeed and the atmosphere of their day-to-day environment. Therefore, they want to work for "A" quality managers who add value to their sales efforts. This value may range from the managers' charisma to help close business to their proficiency in working on the salesperson's behalf within the company. Ultimately, the success of this relationship is dependent upon the personal "fit" between two people. Heavy Hitters know their sales manager can make their life enjoyable, tolerable, or miserable, and that their mental condition will be determined by this relationship.

UNDERSTANDING YOUR SALES MANAGER

Throughout the course of a career, every salesperson will work with a variety of sales managers. "Sales manager" means the person you directly report to, the individual who gives you guidance and ultimately evaluates your performance. A sales representative in a large company may report to the district manager. Meanwhile, the district manager's sales manager is the regional director, who in turn is led by the vice president of sales. Finally, the vice president reports to the president. Even a president answers to sales managers—the board of directors. Everyone has a sales manager!

Maybe your sales manager was one of the key reasons you joined your company. Perhaps your sales manager was thrust upon you during a reorganization. During my career, I have worked for at least twenty different sales managers. Some were very good and a few were just plain horrible. But I can honestly say I learned as much from the bad ones as from the good ones. It is equally important to understand what you shouldn't model as well as what you should!

A Heavy Hitter knows he can't successfully complete the entire sales cycle alone. He is not Superman. He counts on other people to help him. Just as the Lone Ranger needed Tonto and Batman had Robin, Heavy Hitters need a support team to help them defeat the bad guys, their competitors. The sales manager is a key member of this valiant team.

Rapport was not meant only for the customer. It's just as critical for Heavy Hitters to establish rapport with their sales manager. Heavy Hitters and their manager synergistically "click" together—sharing similar feelings and viewpoints about sales. While this relationship has probably developed naturally over time, here are three steps that anyone can use to build rapport with sales managers.

1. Identify the sales managers' representational system wiring.

2. Understand their style.

3. Always operate in their world, according to their wiring and style.

The prerequisite to establishing rapport is the identification of the person's primary, secondary, and recessive representational systems. Heavy Hitters have a complete and thorough understanding of their manager's representational wiring. And while Heavy Hitters may do this intuitively, it is helpful to use a formal process to ensure accuracy.

Review the last ten to twenty e-mails your manager sent you and perform a VAK keyword count. In addition, keep a precise VAK count during each of the next three times you speak with your manager (whether in person or over the telephone). The results of the e-mail VAK count should match the VAK counts from your conversations. If not, keep investigating and performing VAK counts until you are 100 percent certain you understand the manager's wiring.

After mapping his wiring, make a conscious commitment to always communicate with him on his terms using his systems, regardless of how you are wired. Remember, flexibility is the hallmark of a Hitter. In essence, you are going to treat your manager exactly as if he was your customer—because he is! If he is a Visual and you are an Auditory, adopt a Visual-based system when communicating with him. Similarly, if he is a Kinesthetic and you are an Auditory, change to his system. Also, adopt his entire spectrum of the human communication model, including the phonetic and physical layers. When I had a manager who had an accent or particular mannerism, I found myself naturally adopting a similar idiosyncrasy. I would even subconsciously adjust my style of dress to resemble his and find myself repeating his clichés.

After you have your manager's wiring identified and internalized, you need to understand his management orientation. Once again, this is analogous to selling to the customer. However, instead of placing him into the product, management, or the executive categories, you will catalogue him by his individual sales management style.

SALES MANAGEMENT STYLES

Just as people have different levels of gregariousness, assertiveness, and action-oriented tendencies, they have different sales management styles. Seven management styles are most prevalent. Most likely, your manager will have one dominant style. However, he will probably share a few characteristics from other styles and may even move from style to style depending on the situation. The seven most common sales management styles are the mentor, expressive manager, sergeant, Teflon manager, amateur manager, micromanager, and overconfident manager.

In addition to establishing rapport with their managers, Heavy Hitters also devise a long-term strategy for interrelating with them. With the exception of the amateur manager, the goal of each of these long-term strategies is to create a symbiotic, or mutually advantageous, coexistence between two close associates. The approach Hitters use is based upon the seven different sales management styles and is listed below.

Before we begin this discussion about styles and strategies, it is important to put the conversation in perspective. Successful navigation through life is based upon a series of continual small adjustments

Management Style	Long-Term Strategy
Mentor	Scholarly Student
Expressive Manager	Empathetic Ego
Sergeant	Straightforward Sincerity
Teflon Manager	Patient Pollyanna
Amateur Manager	Release Relationship
Micromanager	Perfect Performance
Overconfident Manager	Clever Conqueror

Figure 8.1 Sales Management Styles and Strategies

to the circumstances surrounding you. It is not typically done with cataclysmic adjustments. Similarly, these styles and strategies are frameworks to be used while you are accomplishing your normal daily routine in relation to the unique situation surrounding your workplace.

Also, it is human nature to judge others' actions and behaviors using broad generalizations. We typically take a negative position when passing judgments on others as we are comparing them to ourselves and own our idea of perfection. Frequently, people are classified as bad sales managers without any understanding of why they act the way they do. For instance, I remember a group of workers bitterly complaining about the frequent absences and lackadaisical work habits of a particular colleague until they learned he was battling cancer.

Many learned books have been written about sales management philosophies, processes, and how to develop the individual attributes required to achieve success. The intent here is much simpler. You need to study your manager in detail in order to identify and predict his behavior. Based upon the information you gather, you need to create your own plan for working together. This section should cause you to think about your manager in new or different ways. More importantly, by developing and executing a proactive strategy to interrelate with your manager, you gain more control over your environment.

MENTORS

Mentors are charismatic leaders and sales experts who measure their success using three criteria: exceeding revenue goals, creating an environment where the entire team can succeed, and helping all team members realize their individual potential. Mentors are confident in their own abilities and possess the business insight to know what needs to be done and how to do it.

Even though they believe in accountability and a strict code of ethical conduct, they relate well with their team and motivate by positive encouragement rather than fear. They are comfortable with themselves and are able to keep perspective and a sense of resolution during tenuous times.

The mentors' philosophy is an extension of their personality. While their demeanor may range from gruff and cantankerous to friendly and personable, they are well liked and act as a unifying force to their sales team members. Although mentors tend to have a very hands-on management style, they don't meddle in their teams' daily duties. They lead by example.

Mentors' sales intuition has been honed by many years of customer calls; therefore, their judgment is respected and advice highly sought-after. Mentors are highly effective in presentations or one-on-one customer meetings because customers genuinely like them and appreciate their presence. Since mentors usually have strong kinesthetic (or visual) systems, they are able to charm customers.

Heavy Hitters want to learn everything they can from mentors, so they adopt a strategy based on being a "scholarly student." They invite their mentors on calls, quiz them about tactics over lunch, or chat with them after hours about their sales experiences. Heavy Hitters have great hope that perhaps one day they will be able to mentor their own sales team.

EXPRESSIVE MANAGERS

Expressive managers are people-oriented with a flair for sharing their emotions and amplifying the emotions of those around them. Most likely, expressive managers have strong kinesthetic representational systems. They have a natural ability to put people at ease. They are very charming and gregarious individuals who are always ready, willing, and able to discuss personal matters in addition to events at work. They will frequently be seen chatting with coworkers in other departments at the "water cooler."

Expressive managers create an environment where a considerable amount of energy is focused on how they are thought of and perceived within the company. They crave attention and tend to be over-dramatic, by either exaggerating their accomplishments or overstating the prevailing circumstances their team is facing. Because of their need for constant emotional approval, they may become jealous when others receive recognition.

Expressive managers are master motivators of their team, and since people are so comfortable with them, they are very effective on sales calls. Customers perceive them as genuinely nice people who will personally take care of their account. However, their mood swings can be intense, and they have a natural tendency to become bored with mundane tasks because they would rather be working spontaneously based on their emotions. It is their emotions that drive their daily tasks and agenda.

The long-term strategy Heavy Hitters employ to shape their relationships with expressive managers is called "empathetic ego." Empathizing with expressive managers requires sharing their experiences through unselfish listening and continual confirmation that the Heavy Hitter understands the situation or dilemma. Expressive managers experience tremendous highs and lows; participating in the celebration of the good times is just as important as commiserating during the bad.

A key aspect of the strategy involves protecting the expressive managers' ego by supporting their position and validating their worth to others within and outside the sales group. This means only presenting information that supports their beliefs. Obviously this requires knowing where they stand on issues beforehand. One of the biggest insults to any manager, and expressive ones in particular, is being contradicted in public. Conversely, announcing their successes and broadcasting compliments will definitely yield relationship rewards.

SERGEANTS

The sergeant is named after the field sergeant in a military organization. Sergeants develop an intense loyalty to their team, perhaps even greater than their personal loyalty to their company. They are hard workers who are constantly worrying about their "troops." They will even sacrifice their own best interests and tolerate personal hardships if they feel it will benefit their team. Sergeants will usually have strong kinesthetic and visual systems.

Sergeants are strong performers on customer sales calls. Since they have participated in so many sales calls, they possess highly developed sales intuitions. As a result, they are excellent mentors to their team. And it is through their direct interaction with their team members that they draw satisfaction from their job.

Sergeants are likable, reliable people who have an intense pride in their work. They have a humble demeanor and will unselfishly pass any praise they receive directly to the team. They wear their emotions on their sleeves, and their team members always know where they stand.

While they understand their place in the organization and are confident of their own ability, they still feel somewhat expendable and may suffer from self-doubt. They do not accept criticism easily and will take faultfinding to heart. However, sergeants are typically some of the last people to leave a failing company and may have a history of staying with companies long after the good times have passed.

The strategy for building a successful relationship with a sergeant is based upon "straightforward sincerity." Since sergeants are "tell it like it is" people, Heavy Hitters' communication with them is open, honest, and candid. For example, sergeants want to know the bad news as soon as possible and don't appreciate it being sugarcoated.

Sergeants expect a sincere relationship in terms of words and actions. When they confide in their trusted team, it is imperative the team members maintain confidentiality. Since sergeants defend their team's honor, it is expected they will do the same. As opposed to editing oneself to suit the expressive manager's ego, building rapport with a sergeant involves supporting the person by honoring the friendship. Not surprisingly, Heavy Hitters' maxim for working with sergeants is the same motto used by the Marines: *semper fidelis,* "always faithful."

TEFLON MANAGERS

Teflon managers are pleasant, agreeable, and polite people who have strong visual systems. However, unlike sergeants, you may never really get to know Teflon managers, even after working with them for years. They avoid disclosing personal information or give just enough to be thought of as friendly. From this standpoint, some people will consider them superficial. Another characteristic of Teflon managers is their ability to stay above the daily fray of politics. Yet while they seem cooperative, they are usually very stubborn when it comes to their personal agenda.

Regardless of the situation, Teflon managers are even keeled and rarely frazzled. They always seem to be in control of their emotions and relate to others mainly in an edited, business demeanor. You will not find these people yelling in the office, and they rarely socialize or develop personal friendships with coworkers. They will share their honest feelings only when there is little personal risk and if sharing this information benefits their business position.

Nothing sticks to Teflon managers. Bad news that would devastate sergeants or expressive managers bounces off them. Teflon managers just keep moving forward and never seem to be depressed or give up. They enjoy prestige and title and act the role accordingly.

Working for Teflon managers creates an interesting dichotomy because of their personal nonattachment, comfort with solitude, idealized self-image, and desire to remain safe from criticism. Heavy Hitters employ a "patient Pollyanna" strategy to dovetail with these Teflon manager characteristics. First and foremost, Heavy Hitters will go to great lengths to ensure they do not make their manager look foolish but, instead, wise and proficient at all times. Therefore, Hitters always exude a cheerful, pleasant disposition to communicate everything is okay, even under the most dire circumstances.

To help keep themselves immune to criticism, Heavy Hitters adopt a "politically correct" demeanor, rarely making cynical statements and repressing any open display of anger or disrespect to others. Patience and temperance are virtues Teflon managers appreciate. Perhaps during their upbringing Teflon managers were taught "If you have nothing nice to say, then say nothing at all." Regardless, this becomes the Heavy Hitter's new mantra.

Teflon managers expect a high degree of loyalty and perfection from their staff, and Heavy Hitters try to achieve these standards. Most interestingly, no news is considered good news, so Heavy Hitters do not bombard Teflon managers with information. However, Heavy Hitters take advice from Machiavelli's *The Prince,* when he said that it is better to give bad news all at once and leak good news patiently over time.[12]

AMATEUR MANAGERS

Amateur managers are the toughest of all the types to work for. While they may make a great first impression, analogous to a great first date, each subsequent date becomes more painful and frustrating. Amateur managers may have any representational system, but most likely they have a stronger auditory system and weaker kinesthetic system.

Amateur managers most likely do not have an extensive background in sales, are very new to sales management, or lack the ability to manage a sales force. Since they lack practical experience, their management style suffers from an identity crisis. As a result, plans continually change and the sales organization suffers from a lack of focus.

Their shortage of sales experience also renders their advice on deals unreliable and their participation in sales calls ineffective.

Amateur managers fear being judged negatively by their superiors and peers, as well as their subordinates. As a result, they may perceive the company as unfriendly or hostile. Their fears may also play an interesting part in their decision process. Under stress they become worried and indecisive, or they propose so many different solutions that nothing ever happens. Or they may create outlandish plans and elaborate schemes that can't possibly be implemented in the real world.

Amateur managers may have a misconception of their own strengths and an incorrect perception of how the organization views them. They also have a demonstrated history of broken relationships and a tendency to try to fix business problems by anointing a new "hero of the day." This person is expected to fix the organization's problem and receives great initial support. Soon thereafter, the support wanes and amateur managers start to blame the hero for the department's problems.

The long-term strategy for working with amateur managers is directly opposite from strategies for all of the other management styles. Instead of investing in and building the relationship, you actually search for a way to be released or escape from it. The strategy for liberation from the amateur manager is called "release relationship."

Several different methods can be used to be released from the relationship. Heavy Hitters could ask for a transfer or reassignment, seek a promotion, quit, or be fired. Each of these is perfectly acceptable. "Being fired is acceptable?" you may be asking yourself. Absolutely. Heavy Hitters know time is short and they do not want to waste their lives making incompetent people money. They want to surround themselves with successful people they respect. They have the confidence to stand up for themselves and what they believe in.

Another more daring way to release the relationship is by "firing" the amateur manager. When a disgruntled sales team bands together, unemotionally documents their grievances over time, and presents them logically to the amateur's boss, the wheels of justice will start turning.

Executing the release relationship strategy is postponed in two situations: (1) when the Heavy Hitter's income level is not being affected and the working environment is acceptable and (2) when the Heavy Hitter is able to ignore the manager's authority and become self-governing. However, in both cases, the eventual solution is to end the relationship.

MICROMANAGERS

Micromanagers are the most organized and methodical of all the management types. They have a strong sense of responsibility to their company and they pride themselves on achieving their revenue goals. They tend to be black-and-white, all-or-nothing thinkers who want things done their way. They may have laboriously created methodical processes for every aspect of their job, most likely having used these same processes at previous companies.

They may be well known for their temper and are not considered people-oriented. In fact, they dislike human resource issues and are not regarded as great recruiters. They tend to hire people who they know will carry out their instructions to the letter, and even though one of the team members may achieve success, they will criticize that person if it wasn't done their way.

Micromanagers will have a long list of tasks on their white boards and keep records of all top accounts there in plain view. Micromanagers are a good fit for a company that needs to bring order to a sales environment that is transitioning from a start-up to a more mature organizational phase. They will usually have strong auditory and visual systems.

Heavy Hitters adopt a long-term strategy based upon their concept of the "perfect performance" of an efficient, industrious, and competent salesperson. Working efficiently equals being organized in the mind of a micromanager. Industriousness is akin to a single-minded, business-only attitude toward the job as evidenced by working long hours. Finally, the competent salesperson will complete tasks using the established processes.

To micromanagers, work and play are two entirely different matters. Therefore a sober disposition and attention to daily routines are necessary to function in a micromanager's world. In addition, the constant flow of information is critical to ensure a smoothly functioning world, and Heavy Hitters will overcommunicate by staying in constant touch.

OVERCONFIDENT MANAGERS

Overconfident managers are on the opposite end of the humility spectrum from sergeants. They tend to be self-centered and self-absorbed. While charming and gregarious in public, they rarely have deep relationships in private. When they do take an active interest in developing a relationship, it is because they believe it will benefit their cause—having orchestrated strong relationships with their superiors.

Overconfident managers usually have strong auditory and visual systems. They just love to talk about themselves and don't exhibit a great depth of feeling for others. They may boast of past successes and frequently recount stories about these achievements, regardless of whether someone may have heard them before. They also enjoy being the life of the party and know how to make any party an unforgettable event. They are typically flashier dressers and very concerned with their appearance.

They will receive strong reactions when they participate in sales situations. Some customers will absolutely love them while others will have an equally strong, opposite reaction. Similarly, they will not relate equally with all members of the team. Rather, they will have a few favorites that resemble them.

They are not open to feedback and are known to get quite defensive when criticized. They will get the job done their way and succeed at any cost. Although they are not exemplary planners, their sheer drive and tenacity make them well suited for roles where they have to launch a new product line or a new company.

Overconfident managers build a sales team of fighting gladiators who possess extraordinary will power, mental toughness, animated spirit, and intelligence. To be included in this team, Heavy Hitters adopt the "clever conqueror" long-term strategy.

Since Heavy Hitters regularly sell to people who are better educated and more technically proficient than they are, they know there's a difference between a smart person and a clever person. A smart person knows how something works, while a clever person knows how to get something done. The clever salesperson is skillfully talented and tactically shrewd in finding a way to win.

To be a conqueror, you must attack your enemies, be comfortable fighting for the cause, and not be afraid of rankling people in the process because the end justifies the means. It also means not exposing any weakness, such as fear, self-doubt, sadness, or embarrassment. As Julius Caesar said, *"Veni, vidi, vici"* (I came, I saw, I conquered").[13] Only the attacker can be victorious; at best, the defender will merely survive.

APPLYING SALES MANAGEMENT STYLES

In order to build rapport, Heavy Hitters understand their manager. They know their manager's primary, secondary, and recessive representational systems and understand his management style. Essentially, Heavy Hitters want to not only mirror the manager's communication but also understand and correctly mirror his behavioral style. To ensure success, they create and execute a long-term strategy based upon the manager's style and designed to create rapport or occasionally intentionally break rapport, as is the case with the amateur manager.

You probably noticed that each word of the long-term strategies' names begins with the same letter (release relationship, empathetic ego, and so on). These are called alliterations. Alliterations are repetitions of the same letter or sound at the beginning of adjacent words. Alliterations help the mind to remember by creating an association or "key" for easier storage. For example, "clever conqueror" is definitely easier to remember than if the strategy had been called "smart warrior." We will be exploring memory and how it relates to intuition in much more detail in the next chapter.

The vice president of sales who said, "We're just going to have to sell our way out of this thing" at the beginning of this chapter is a classic example of an overconfident manager. He was so full of his past achievements that he was not in touch with his current situation. It's also an example of a manager who destroyed the faith of his sales force. Given the magnitude of the problems facing the sales organization and the growing publicity surrounding the company, the salespeople should have been presented with a plan to reestablish the company's image. When they weren't, the sales team's faith in the company was lost.

The result was predictable: a mass exodus of people from the company. After many years with this company, I also left. Within a few months of the speech, the vice president was out of a job. He was out of touch with his sales force, and understanding the needs of the sales force starts with knowing the individual needs of the Hitter.

SALESPEOPLE THEN AND NOW

When I started my career in the early 1980s, I worked as a programmer in a computer firm. Throughout this company, salespeople were held in low esteem. They were thought of as egotistical, expendable equivocators. While other departments (engineering, IT, and accounting) included many people with advanced degrees, the sales organization didn't have this quantifiable measuring stick of intelligence. Nor were salespeople thought of as being particularly creative, like those in the marketing department. The role of the salesperson was anything but prestigious. Thinking back, I can't remember going to any party and hearing anyone proudly exclaim, "I'm in sales and I'm proud of it!" Rather, people would sheepishly explain they were in sales.

Until recently, the structure of most sales departments mirrored these perceptions and most were based upon a militaristic, centralized chain of command. Today, salespeople are looked upon in an entirely different light. The impetus for this change was the realization that some of the most talented leaders in a company are in the sales department. More importantly, salespeople are trusted with the company's most valuable asset—customers! While the job they perform and skill set they possess are quite different from those in any other area of the company, it could be argued their job is the most important one in the company. To validate this statement, you only need to ask any employee of a company that missed its last quarterly revenue goal.

Companies that may have previously considered salespeople a "necessary evil" now go to great lengths to understand their needs and requirements. Consequently, the structure of today's sales organization more closely resembles an interactive democracy. While the priority still remains on individual enterprise (the ability to make lots of money), salespeople's right to express their opinion has been emancipated in recent times.

Sales management philosophy of the past was that behavior was primarily motivated by a compensation plan. And while a compensation plan plays a fundamental role, truly understanding what motivates salespeople is a much more complex issue. In particular, what drives Heavy Hitters to succeed is different from what drives the average salesperson. Probably the best way to describe a Hitter's behavior is to introduce it in context of Maslow's hierarchy of needs. While the model is not new, it is a concise way to easily explain the actions and attitude of Heavy Hitters. However, it is not solely limited to them. The model applies universally to all people, including customers.

HIERARCHY OF NEEDS

Abraham Maslow is the father of humanistic psychology who published his theory of a hierarchy of needs in the '50s.[14] The theory explains that human beings need to satisfy an ever-escalating set of needs, which begin with biological deficiencies, ascend through social requirements, and ultimately culminate in the fulfillment of deeper spiritual needs. Before an individual can climb the ladder to fulfill a sophisticated need, the preceding lower-level need must have been met.

Maslow's theory was revolutionary during its time. His contemporaries focused only on abnormal personalities (Freudians) and animal research (Pavlovian behaviorists), thus reducing the human experience to instinctual impulses or simple mechanical concepts. Until Maslow, little focus had been put on the "humanity" of humans and their potential for excellence. Maslow felt people were basically trustworthy, self-protecting, and self-governing. It's an optimistic view of the human spirit compared to the pessimistic theories of that time. The basic premise is that humans want growth and love.

Just as we study Heavy Hitters to comprehend how they accomplish their sales achievements, Maslow studied exceptional individuals to try to understand the upper limits of human capability. Through his analysis, he defined four levels of needs: physiological, safety, belonging, and esteem. Only when all of these needs are met can people maximize their potential. Much like the popular army recruiting jingle, "Be all that you can be," Maslow referred to this highest level of achievement as "self-actualization." In order to become self-actualized, all of the preceding needs must be met in Maslow's specific order. The following diagram depicts the hierarchy of needs with the higher-level needs ascending the pyramid.

Salespeople are constantly traversing up and down the pyramid. At the end of closing a record quarter or year, a Hitter will be at the top of the pyramid. However, as the new quarter or year starts, the

Figure 8.2 Maslow's Hierarchy of Needs
Source: Toward a Psychology of Being, 2nd Edition, Abraham Maslow

sales numbers are reset to zero, and he quickly drops to the lowest level of need.

All Hitters have a distinct personality, an individual capability to understand technical concepts, and a certain amount of sales experience. Therefore, they have their own particular, unique needs. Heavy Hitters want managers to recognize their individuality and exhibit a genuine inquisitiveness about what makes them "tick." They want their managers to motivate them and to see that their needs are met.

Let's assume for a moment that you are Shaquille O'Neal's basketball coach. You would not motivate him by threatening to throw him off the team if he didn't score forty points in a game. This would not be the best way to get his best effort. More likely, you would motivate him by having him understand that his legacy and reputation are on the line in every game.

Heavy Hitters want a manager who knows where they are on their personal hierarchy of needs. Sometimes, they may simply want to be left alone. At other times, they may want reassurance. If a particular competitor is a problem, they want their manager to help find a way to win the deal and rally other departments to contribute to this cause.

Heavy Hitters need their managers to build a sales infrastructure that satisfies their lower-level needs so that they can get to the top of the pyramid as quickly as possible. As Shaq's coach, you would not spend a great deal of time teaching him how to slam dunk. He already has this physiological need mastered. Rather, you would make sure that he had the best medical care available to handle his physical needs. You would ensure that the other members of the team were a complementary fit. You would guarantee that the game plan was well thought out and communicated to everyone. Heavy Hitters want managers that create the best opportunities to succeed. Let's take a deeper look at each level of the hierarchy of needs from the Hitters' standpoint.

Physiological Needs of the Hitter

In Maslow's model, physiological needs are the basic needs for food, water, air, sleep, and shelter. Maslow's premise is that we are all consumed with satisfying each of these needs. However, once they are satisfied, we quickly reorient ourselves toward the next set of needs. If I had been wandering the desert for several days, my main goal would be to find water. Once my thirst was quenched, I would focus on food, sleep, sex, and so on.

For Hitters, physiological needs include the stability of their company, the competitiveness of the product, and the soundness of the marketplace. Successful sales without these three physical needs being met is tremendously difficult. After the quarter closes, the Hitters begin again with the most rudimentary need—finding new opportunities. Being part of a stable well-known company with a leading product will naturally help resolve this need. The time frame in which Hitters are able to build their pipeline will be determined by how well their physiological needs are being met.

Even if your company position is stable and you have a product that is competitive, you still have to be selling to a viable target market. Although Heavy Hitters could sell for a great company and have the best possible solution, they may be competing with a new technology paradigm. For example, selling word processor systems when the market has shifted to personal computers or selling external modems when the market has shifted to internal cards is an ill-fated position to be in.

Safety Needs of the Hitter

Maslow stated that after your physiological needs are met, you will begin the pursuit of safety needs, or needs that establish stability, such as home, family, and religion. Within sales, safety needs include information on how to compete with other vendors. While a company provides theoretical arguments on how to sell its product, it is the sales manager and the Heavy Hitter that convert them into real-world reasons that persuade a customer to buy. The composition of a Hitter's sales territory is also a critical safety need. A depleted, barren sales territory will force a Heavy Hitter back to the physiological need level.

One of the most important security needs is the sales management style and competency of the Hitter's manager. After interviewing hundreds of salespeople, I have found that the overwhelming reason they left a position was not because of the company but because of their sales manager. Conversely, Heavy Hitters will endure great hardships and work tirelessly if they have faith in their manager and company. Heavy Hitters will tolerate an inferior manager as long as their income isn't hindered. They'll start to search for a better environment as soon as the commission checks shrink or the bureaucracy becomes unmanageable.

Belonging Needs of the Hitter

People have a natural disposition to belong to groups. Through our involvement in groups, we are able to share similar interests and values, search for a sense of community, and seek affectionate relationships. Take a moment to think about all the groups you belong to. First are the more obvious ones, such as family, friends, hobby clubs, religious groups, and political party affiliations. You can even be grouped by your membership in frequent-flier programs, the neighborhood you live in, and the college you attended.

Sales is the most group-oriented department within a company, and this is not a coincidence. For example, most Heavy Hitters participated in team sports. In casual surveys I have conducted throughout the years, I have found that 90 percent of Hitters played organized sports in high school, and over 40 percent continued to play in college.

Being in sales takes a single-minded drive to achieve a goal. It requires an intensely competitive personality and the willingness to make a commitment and personal sacrifice to winning. The habit of putting in long hours, whether on a baseball diamond, on a football field, on a tennis court, or in a swimming pool, parallels the habits of successful salespeople.

In addition, salespeople do not expect to win every single deal they go after, and people who played sports know how to lose. They are able to handle emotional disappointments, bounce back from a loss, and get themselves ready for the next game. Also, through sports one learns how to accept criticism and perform under duress or difficult circumstances.

Most importantly, playing sports teaches independent thinking. Wrestlers or fencers are in a one-on-one battle with an opponent. They must take advantage of the opponent's weaknesses while executing countermoves to the opponent's attacks. Meanwhile, a football team does not consist of robots who are preprogrammed before every play. While thinking about their specific assignment, players must react and make instant adjustments to the circumstances in front of them as a play develops. All of these attributes inherent to playing sports are applicable to sales.

Heavy Hitters are comfortable with being part of a team and consider camaraderie a benefit of the job. Consider a typical Hitter based in the New York office of a medium-sized company. He is a member of at least six different groups that can be segmented by geography as well as by function:

- Local groups—These include his immediate sales team, other reps in his office, and all employees in the office.

- District groups—These include other Heavy Hitters in the offices that compose the district as well as all the employees in each of the offices.

- Regional groups—These include other Hitters in the districts that compose the region, as well as all the employees in each of the districts.

- North American sales groups—These include regional groups that comprise the North America sales group.

- Worldwide sales group—He's a member of the worldwide sales organization.

- Company—The company itself is a group.

Although Heavy Hitters are competitive individuals by nature, they are also team players who support their colleagues. An anonymous Middle Eastern saying is "Me against my brother, my brother and I against the world." This is analogous and applicable to sales groups. For example, the Eastern region group is competitive with the Western region group. When these groups combine to form the North American sales group, they compete against the European sales group. Together, they form the Worldwide sales group, which competes against other vendors.

Groups provide a place where Heavy Hitters can be appreciated and accepted and find a platform to rally around a cause. Groups provide Heavy Hitters with the opportunity to be needed and the opportunity to be acknowledged. However, Heavy Hitters want to be more than just members of a group, they want to be leaders. Which brings us to the next level of Maslow's hierarchy of needs, esteem-based needs.

Esteem Needs of the Hitter

The two main categories of esteem-based needs are the need to be deemed an expert and the need for power or position. The only way for a Heavy Hitter to fulfill these needs is to become a top sales producer. It could be argued that some Hitters are solely focused on money. In fact, one of the reasons for the intense preoccupation on the accumulation of money is that it serves as undisputed validation that the Heavy Hitter is a "sales expert."

Heavy Hitters feel their opinion matters and always want to be heard. They truly believe they are experts in the field of sales and know exactly how it should be done. They seek to achieve the alpha (or dominant) position within their group to ensure they are heard. They desire to see their actions emulated by others, and the only way to achieve the alpha position is by becoming a top salesperson.

For this reason, awards are extremely important to Hitters. Personally, I have experienced more motivation and harder work from my sales team by handing out a $45 trophy than would be achieved by increasing the compensation plan by one hundred times that amount. Heavy Hitters enjoy the acclaim and the public identification as a group role model. Thus, when I present an award to a Heavy Hitter, it is always done in full view of the entire group. The leadership position Heavy Hitters seek is not necessarily reflected in their title—it is a position of prominence based upon their knowledge and the recognition that comes along with being thought of as an expert.

The second type of esteem need is power or position. Interestingly, I have noticed two different behaviors once Heavy Hitters have achieved the alpha position. The first behavior involves Heavy Hitters becoming intensely focused on remaining in the alpha position. They will tolerate little, if any, distractions from this goal. The second behavior involves Heavy Hitters exercising their newly found prominence in an attempt to advance their career. They will be frequently involved in conversations regarding strategy, planning, and even the performance of other group members with the sales management. Other departments, such as marketing, accounting, and product management, will solicit their opinions on new programs and policies. The entire company considers the alpha Heavy Hitter a success (at least for this quarter!).

Up to this point, the entire discussion about needs has been focused on achieving the practical interests of Hitters, from the physiological needs of the sales environment to the need for power and position. Maslow described the final step in satisfying personal development as self-actualization, or the desire to be everything that one is capable of being.

Hitter Self-Actualization

For Hitters, achieving self-actualization is directly linked to leaving a legacy that will be remembered within the company. Life is about achieving significance more than success. While success is a fleeting, quarter-by-quarter, year-by-year proposition, a legacy can never be taken away. By achieving this maturity level, Heavy Hitters gain peace of mind.

Several years ago, one of my colleagues, a Hitter *extraordinaire,* closed a $28 million sale. This was quite an accomplishment given that within his company, the average deal size was $200,000. In celebration of this achievement, every employee, from the CEO to the receptionist, received a $1,000 check. Over a thousand people received this bonus. Clearly, this person left a legacy with everyone in the company.

Over the years, I have informally and formally surveyed various Heavy Hitters. When asked, "What is the most important criterion of job satisfaction?" the most frequently mentioned answers are the same. Here they are listed in order of frequency:

1. Making an impact

2. Learning new skills (sales and technical)

3. Compensation

4. The quality of the management team

5. Career advancement

6. The quality of the product

7. The culture of the company

8. The stability of the company

These results are interesting. The number one response, "making an impact," can be directly associated with the desire to achieve self-actualization. Heavy Hitters want to be remembered in perpetuity. They want to know they made a difference.

Learning new sales and technical skills is an esteem-based need. This need is associated with mastering particular tasks and becoming an expert. Compensation is both an esteem and a safety need. If salespeople are successful, they are well paid. Their compensation will also greatly influence their status and ranking in their local group. Since safety needs are directly related to the consistency and stability of the environment, their compensation must enable them to have a secure personal life for themselves and their families. Similarly, career advancement can be thought of as an esteem need.

Ultimately, the yardstick by which Heavy Hitters measure their success is revenue. While Heavy Hitters always exceed their overall revenue targets, they are not immune from losing. In fact, they will frequently fail on individual accounts. However, baseball players who safely hit four out of ten times at bat are considered great ball-players. People do not measure them as 60 percent failures. Rather, they are called four-hundred hitters. Heavy Hitters measure their own performance similarly. Most importantly, they know that true self-actualization is having those that know them best—their manager, colleagues, and family—respect them most.

If you were to ask a Hitter, "What is the most important sales management quality?" the answer would be, "Being treated as an individual." Every Hitter wants to be treated as an MVP. In sports, MVP stands for "most valuable player." For management, in the context of a Heavy Hitter, MVP has a different meaning: "motivate, value, and praise."

Relationships are not automatic; they require investments in terms of time and energy. Heavy Hitters wants their manager to understand how to motivate them since they are different from all the other members of the team. The A-quality manager knows that the different members of a team have different styles and viewpoints and that people should be valued for their diversity. Praise should be showered on all people generously. Great managers implement personal MVP plans for each member of their team.

CONCLUSION

One of Heavy Hitters' most important relationships is with their sales manager who creates the environment to succeed, motivates them to achieve, and counsels them with advice. The success of their relationship is dependent upon their rapport, and Heavy Hitters mold themselves to fit with their manager. Heavy Hitters will communicate with their manager using his representational system and implement a strategy corresponding to his management style. Conversely, an A-quality manager is aware of the unique needs of Heavy Hitters. The manager will develop the sales plan and environment that enable Hitters to succeed and inspire Hitters to achieve. To finish this chapter, here's a story that greatly influenced my own management style.

When I was a salesperson, I arranged for the vice president of sales to fly into town to participate in some important sales calls with me. The vice president was my boss's boss's boss, and I had several meetings scheduled that day all across town. I thought it would be a great opportunity to show him examples of our accounts, and hopefully we could close one of them. I also wanted to start a relationship with him, and driving him from meeting to meeting would give us plenty of time to get to know each other.

Well, the day didn't work out as expected. From the moment I picked him up at the airport, he was talking on his cell phone. I interpreted this to mean he had more important people to talk to than me. The only interruptions to his stream of telephone calls were the actual sales calls, and he didn't seem very interested in the customers either!

Up until that point, I was completely and totally committed to this company. I had prioritized my life around work, and I was working long hours and expending an immense amount of off-hour energy thinking about my job. That day changed me. I would never again be as committed to the company.

This was an important personal lesson. When I am on the road with my salespeople, I rarely take telephone calls. I am completely and totally with them. I want to make sure that we have rapport and that their commitment to the company and the sales organization is complete.

9

Finding Your Coach

For the past six months, the salesperson had been working non-stop selling his computer solution to a major retailing chain headquartered in New Jersey. Within the next couple of weeks, the retailer would make its final application vendor selection and start the negotiation process of what would surely be a multimillion-dollar deal. Although the salesperson felt he had developed strong relationships with key members within the information technology department, he was still nervous, as he had yet to meet the president, who was also the company's founder. This angst continued to build until one day, the salesperson saw the president and drummed up enough nerve to approach him. "Hello, I'm with National Computer Company. We've been working with the Information Tech—" the salesperson was immediately interrupted by the president, "Computers! I *hate* computers!" With that said, he walked away.

Throughout this book, the importance of establishing rapport and finding a coach have been reiterated as necessary steps to closing the deal. Coaches are individuals who provide accurate information about the sales cycle and competition to you. Coaches want you to win; they're your friends and allies.

Think about all the relationships you have in your life—deep, close relationships with friends you have known most of your life, casual relationships with colleagues and coworkers, and new relationships with customers. Regardless of how they were formed, all relationships share similar underlying characteristics. In order to find and recruit a coach, it is first necessary to understand the nature of friendships.

A big difference exists between a friend and an acquaintance. An acquaintance is someone with whom you have a cordial relationship. While the relationship is friendly, the unspoken understanding is that neither person will demand significant time of the other to maintain the relationship. Conversely, a friend is someone who unselfishly invests time to maintain the relationship and derives enjoyment from doing so. An acquaintance is someone you know slightly, a well-wisher with whom you may have pleasant lunches and other social get-togethers. A friend is a trusted sympathizer and, more importantly, an active helper. A friend is someone whom you can call at midnight to help fix your flat tire.

Time is a finite resource. Just as companies protect their time by limiting their number of vendor relationships, people limit the time they spend on relationships. They can have a few deeper relationships or many less time-demanding acquaintances.

A friend of mine has maintained contact with literally everyone he has ever worked with. While he doesn't spend extended periods of time with any one person, he expends considerable energy keeping up with his former coworkers. It's been more than fifteen years since I have worked with him, but I know if I wanted to reach someone from that company, he would have current contact information. Another friend maintains a small number of very close friends. These are mostly people he has known since childhood. In total, I estimate they both spend the same amount of time on maintaining their relationships.

Salespeople sometimes believe they have a coach when in reality they don't. Heavy Hitters know they have a coach when the person not only provides them with accurate information but also helps them by fighting for their cause. A true coach will represent and promote the Hitter's solution publicly with the Hitter and, even better, when the Heavy Hitter isn't present.

Unfortunately, two major obstacles stand in the way of establishing a coaching relationship with someone. First, finding a person qualified to be a coach is not easy. Within the customer's organization is a pool of candidates, many of whom may develop into a coach. However, it is difficult and too time consuming to court everyone. Heavy Hitters have a process for ranking and targeting the strongest candidate. Second, time to build the relationship is limited. While most personal relationships have the luxury of growing naturally over months and years, Heavy Hitters must accelerate this bonding process in a matter of days or weeks.

In order to find a coach, Heavy Hitters will identify all potential candidates. First, they will attempt to develop a relationship with the person who has the most juice and is the biggest bully. For example, let's assume that a Hitter is selling to a selection committee consisting of Jim, Karl, John, and Rich. She prioritizes her recruiting efforts in the following order.

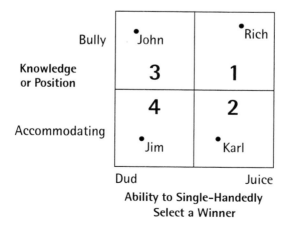

Figure 9.1 Selecting a Coach

Since Rich is a bully with juice, the Hitter knows if she can sway him to become her coach, she has won the deal. In addition, she will vigilantly monitor whether Rich has become a coach for another vendor. In case this happens, she knows the deal is lost and she should stop working on the account.

Assuming Rich is not a coach for any specific vendor, Karl is in the next most desirable quadrant because Karl has juice. However, he is apathetic to the decision that is being made. In this situation, the Heavy Hitter has an opportunity to explain the merits of her solution and why Karl should care more about the decision.

Let's assume Karl is the manager in charge of the application development team and Rich, who reports to Karl, is the programmer in charge of selecting new development tools. Assuming Rich isn't any vendor's coach, the Heavy Hitter could meet with Karl to explain how her product improves the ability to reuse code, therefore requiring less programming time to create applications. If Karl is very concerned with his application backlog, this could cause Karl's demeanor to change from accommodating his team's decision to bullying the decision. Then Karl will become the bully with juice and Rich will be accommodating to his decision.

As potential coaches, both John and Jim are in less desirable quadrants. However, if the Heavy Hitter determines that neither Rich nor Karl is coaching the competition, they can play an important role in providing another point of reference to triangulate information. However, if either Rich or Karl is coaching the competition, the Heavy Hitter knows she will not win the deal. Just as in poker, a pair of twos cannot beat four aces.

PARTICIPATION PIE

Group dynamics are very complex and often revealing. One way to identify which quadrant a person belongs to is by observing her behavior during presentations and meetings. Earlier, we reviewed how a pecking order is communicated by where people sit during meetings. Whether at a round table or in a classroom setting, the person with the most juice and greatest ability to bully will usually take the dominant seating position.

This dominating behavior is also evidenced in meeting interactions. To explain this, we need to introduce the concept of the "participation pie." The participation pie illustrates the amount of time each person interacts in a meeting or presentation.

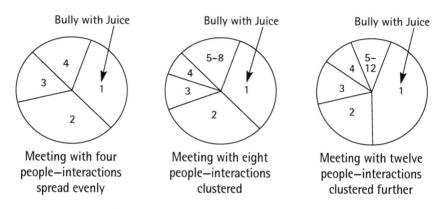

Figure 9.2 Participation Pie Charts

Usually, the person who interacts the most will be the bully who has the most juice. Bullies with juice are in charge and they want everyone to know it. And although dud bullies will be very active participants, the more they participate, the more it becomes obvious that they do not have the stature or expertise they think they do. We have all been in meetings where people like this are contradicted or even publicly chastised by members of their own team. Dud bullies didn't listen to Grandma when she said, "It is better to keep your mouth shut and be suspected of being a fool rather than open it and confirm suspicions."

Another key aspect of the participation pie is how the number of attendees affects the level of participation. In meetings with up to four members, the amount of time each person spends interacting and asking questions is relatively equal. As the group grows to eight people, the interactions become clustered around several people. Usually, these people are in the first or third quadrants. In larger groups, up to twelve people, the majority of interactions are usually among a few individuals. These people are most likely in the first or second quadrants.

Once Heavy Hitters have determined and ranked their potential coaching candidates, how do they actually proceed? The simple answer is, just as they develop a personal friendship, they develop a coach.

FRIENDSHIPS

Who are your friends? Most of my friends are in my same age group. I was introduced to most of them through an activity, whether it was work, school, or a hobby. We share similar backgrounds, live in the same geographic area, and have complementary personalities. Interestingly enough, most of my friends' representational systems mirror mine. They are wired as I am. Their stronger systems are the same as mine. In fact, I cannot think of a single close friend whose primary system is the same as my recessive system. Maybe opposites don't actually attract.

Also, we share similar values and motivations. We are striving to be successful, we are raising children, and we want meaningful lives. Certainly, we have diverse tastes and interests. However, we have far more in common than we have differences.

My friends' personalities are also similar to mine. The term "personality" refers to all aspects of a person's individuality. While everyone's personality is as distinct as a fingerprint, some traits of behavior can be classified to help understand a person's attitude, habits, and conduct.

Finally, my friends know that I will always act with their best interests in mind. I would help them, just as they would help me, fix that flat tire at midnight.

EXERCISE 10: LONG-TERM RELATIONSHIPS

Take a minute to do the following exercise. On a piece of paper write down the names of your closest friends and how many years you have known them. Then calculate the average time you have known your friends by adding all the years together and dividing by the total number of friends. What was your average? In my case, the average is over fifteen years.

Fifteen years is a long time, and that's the point. Friends think in context of long-term relationships just as customers do. The behavior of both parties in a long-term relationship is very different than in a fleeting short-term relationship. Honesty, integrity, and selflessness are the bonds that create long-term relationships with your friends, as well as your customers.

DEVELOPING FRIENDSHIPS

Basically, it is human nature to associate with people similar to oneself. Like animals in the wild, we tend to herd together with our own kind. Most likely, your friends share your interests. You were probably introduced to them through a mutual activity and over time an enduring connection formed.

The process for developing friendships has four major characteristics, and these characteristics can also be utilized to develop a coach. First, two people have an "intersecting activity." Second, a "kinship in communication" is established. Third, they have similar motivations and value systems. Finally, they have agreeable personalities that understand and appreciate each other. Let's examine each of these characteristics further to understand how Heavy Hitters develop a coach.

Intersecting Activities

Going into a first sales call with a new customer, Heavy Hitters don't know who their coach will be. Fortunately, through intersecting activities, circumstances are created that allow people to get to know each other and exchange dialogue. The first intersecting activity is the sales call itself. The customer is interested in the product and the Heavy Hitter is interested in selling it. Since this mutual interest has brought together two people who most likely would not have met otherwise, it is the most important intersecting activity.

Through intersecting activities, people display their personality types, representational system wiring, and value systems. Since the Heavy Hitter in our example sells high-technology products and the customer is employed in high technology, they probably share many other intersecting activities. They each follow the industry, use the same products (PCs, Windows, and cellular phones, for example), and perform many of the same activities (compose e-mails, write reports, and create spreadsheets). They read the same publications and know many of the same people. Even though they haven't yet met, they have a lot in common!

The Heavy Hitter uses this initial intersecting activity to begin building a personal relationship. For example, I know one salesperson who has developed a unique way to create personal friendships. On a first call, he will describe how his product works technically and answer questions, as you might expect. Because he has a technical background and brings authority to the interchange, his credibility builds. Also, he is a computer game expert and at the end of the call he will always ask if anyone plays computer games. In almost every call, one or more members of the customer's team is just as passionate about games as he is. They'll launch into a discussion about Everquest, StarCraft, or Quake 3. Immediately, the roles of customer and vendor are changed and he is bonding with the person. This mutual interest sets the stage for developing a personal relationship and ultimately a coach.

You may not be an expert at computer games, but think about all the potential subjects you can discuss:

raising kids	the cost of living	home ownership
cars	computers	dating and marriage
college	food	professional sports
traveling	dieting	music
movies	airplanes	toys
humor	astronomy	clothes
pets	poetry	religion
art	gardening	the economy
antiques	body piercing	billiards
investments	horses	karaoke
books	beer	firearms
television	origami	cigars

The Hitters' strategy is to use the first intersecting activity (the sales call) to find additional personal intersecting activities. By doing so, the Hitter is developing rapport with the *entire* person, not just the *business* person—building a personal friendship.

Kinship in Communication

One of the main objectives of this book is to identify and improve how people communicate. At the content level, the particular words people choose to use are directly related to their activities. For example, people in the high-technology industry use the technical specification language to communicate about computers. "Two phase commit" and "EJB" mean something important to a software programmer. Similarly, the terms "Everquest" and "StarCraft" are significant to a computer game expert. They are part of the language of game users. Each intersecting activity topic listed above also has a unique content language.

In order to have a meaningful conversation about an intersecting activity, you need to understand its language. For example, a conversation about stock investing requires an understanding of terms such as "price earnings ratio," "market cap," and "stock shorting." If you are talking with someone about dieting, being able to discuss the Atkins or Zone diet makes your participation in the conversation credible. Through the use and understanding of these common terms, rapport is established.

We also know that meaning comes not only from what you say but how you say it. Heavy Hitters are continually building rapport by mirroring the representational systems of the people with whom they converse. They know their customer's primary, secondary, and recessive representational systems. They adjust their vocabulary to resemble, sound like, and feel like the customer's. They coordinate their posture, speech, breathing, and movements, becoming Ginger Rogers to the customer's Fred Astaire. The flow of communication becomes enjoyable, natural, and comfortable—the goal of every Heavy Hitter's customer friendships.

Motivation and Values

Heavy Hitters always delve beneath the surface, the technical and business criteria, to uncover individual motivations. Customers may have their "official" reasons for purchase decisions; however, Heavy Hitters know there is also an "off the record" truth. The final decision is really driven by the desire to achieve a personal benefaction on the part of a few individuals. Therefore, like a psychologist, Heavy Hitters concentrate on eliciting the deep feelings and desires from the "patient." In this case, the Hitter is trying to determine the principles, standards, incentives, and priorities of the key decision makers. Always in the back of the Hitter's mind is the question, "What is this person's benefaction?" In other words, what is driving this person's behavior and how will my product help achieve it? And how do the various individual benefactions mesh? Even though a wide range of benefactions is possible, each benefaction is individually personal and self-centered.

Maslow's hierarchy of needs—physiological, safety, belonging, and esteem—applies to the customer as well as the Hitter. Here are two examples of how the customer's behavior is explained using the hierarchy of needs:

> Peggy wants to select a product with new, cutting-edge technology. By adding a valuable skill set to her resume, she will be able to command more money in the marketplace.
>
> - Physiological. She wants more money in order to buy a home for her family.
> - Safety. By knowing this new technology, she has the security of having a marketable skill.
> - Belonging. The industry periodicals and her friends are enamored with this new technology, and she's tired of feeling left out.
> - Esteem. There's power in knowledge. Knowing something her colleagues don't puts her in a superior position.
>
> Matt is a project leader who wants to select a particular vendor's product because it is successfully used by so many other local companies.
>
> - Physiological. A successful project is an opportunity to demonstrate his value to the company. He wants to keep his job during these difficult economic times.
> - Safety. He's risk averse and feels that by controlling the selection of the technology, the project will be successful.
> - Belonging. He can share tips with and leverage the experience of other local users of the product.
> - Esteem. If the project is successful, he'll earn the promotion he's always wanted.

Heavy Hitters intuitively map out the needs of every person involved in the selection of their product. They are searching for confidants who have a vested interest in selecting their product because it will help them attain their physiological, safety, belonging, or esteem needs.

Heavy Hitters will frame their conversations and product in terms of fulfilling these needs. In the first example the Hitter's strategy is to reiterate that her product is cutting-edge. She will provide collateral materials such as industry articles, press announcements, and technical documentation that confirm its technological advantage. She will capitalize on belonging needs by introducing Peggy to her other customers and the local user group. She will provide access to the technical individuals within her company to re-emphasize the innovation and uniqueness of the technology and accelerate Peggy's learning of it. She wants to help Peggy become knowledgeable and powerful.

In the second example, the Heavy Hitter will try to demonstrate to Matt that her solution is the least risky by providing thorough product demonstrations, an on-site evaluation, and ongoing implementation meetings. Customer references and site visits will also provide independent validation. If Matt feels confident the solution will work, he will support the Heavy Hitter's against solutions he believes are dangerous or unsafe.

The following form can help you identify benefactions and define courses of action for each individual in the sales process.

Complete a form for each member of the customer's selection team. Enter the name and title. Then, after you have identified his or her representational wiring, circle the corresponding system. The remainder of the form is used to plot a course of action based upon the person's physiological, safety, belonging, and esteem needs. Once a form is completed for each person, compare all the team members' forms. Do they share the same wiring? Do they have different benefactions? What sales tactics (or actions) would have the greatest impact? Which ones must be executed first or have a sense of urgency?

Name	Title
Representational Wiring	Primary V A K (CIRCLE ONE Secondary V A K IN EACH Recessive V A K ROW)

Need	*Personal Benefaction*	*Action*
Physiological Safety Belonging Esteem		

Figure 9.3 Customer Benefaction Form

These forms help discipline busy salespeople to stop and consider the customers' orientation before executing account strategies.

Heavy Hitters always align their strategy with the personal needs of an individual. By doing so, the individual will support them and their product. People who have a vested interest in having the Heavy Hitter win naturally evolve into coaches. But even with a coach firmly ensconced at their side, Hitters are constantly aware of the personal benefactions of each of the individuals involved in the decision and work to solve potential conflicts before they arise.

Agreeable Personalities

Remember the last time you made a very important personal decision? Perhaps it was a major purchase such as a house, a car, or stocks. Maybe it was a personal decision to get married, start a family, or change jobs. Whatever the case, many different factors influenced the decision you made. Ultimately, your decision was based upon logic, feelings, and the characteristics of your personality.

Early in my career, I made the transition from a technical position into sales. My new employer sent me to several well-known sales training programs. Each of these programs taught some form of personality training using a variation of Carl Jung's philosophy of psychological types. Most frequently, it was the Myers-Briggs Type Indicator (MBTI). The MBTI uses four measurements classify a personality into one of sixteen different types.[15] These measurements include your level of extraversion, whether you use intuition or physical observation to make decisions, how much you trust logic versus feelings, and finally, whether you perform detailed analysis or make instantaneous decisions.

Armed with this newly learned information, I eagerly went about trying to apply it to my sales opportunities. However, it didn't match what I was experiencing. I quickly realized that classifying my prospect's personality into one of sixteen types didn't help my sales efforts. However, over time I began to realize what was important. I started to identify my prospect's dominant personality traits and link them to the sales cycle experience. Essentially, I created a practical knowledge base of sales cycles that was indexed by the prospect's major personality traits and my success or failure.

PERSONALITY TYPES

During the past twenty years, I estimate that I have met over ten thousand people. While I believe each person has a unique personality, I have found that key personality attributes can be classified, measured, and used to predict behavior during the sales cycle. By building a similar knowledge base, you can determine which strategy will provide the highest probability of winning. Heavy Hitters do this intuitively.

The best formal model for classifying personality types is the five-factor model. This model has five personality factors (or dimensions): negative emotionality, extraversion, openness, agreeableness, and conscientiousness.[16] Each of these factors has six facets, and each facet has a low, medium, and high measurement. The facets describe the major characteristics of the factor.

Each individual's personality is a mixture of all five factors, and obviously many different combinations are possible. Rather than try to classify each personality type, Heavy Hitters have a different strategy. First, they sense the strength of each factor to determine which ones are more prominent. Heavy Hitters know that people with higher measurements of agreeableness, extraversion, and openness are more easily developed into a coach than someone who exhibits low measurements of these factors.

As they are working an account and becoming familiar with the customer, Heavy Hitters are judging certain personality factors based upon the strength of the dominant facets. (Remember, each factor is composed of individual facets.) They are also on the lookout for particular facets that have extreme measurements. For example, if someone has a very low measurement of the activity facet (extraversion factor), a Hitter knows the sales cycle will proceed at a leisurely pace. Therefore, it makes little sense to push the customer to move forward. However, if the customer has a very high activity facet, the Hitter can predict the sales cycle will be swift and vigorous and adjust her strategy and the pace of activity with this in mind. Essentially, the Hitter is mirroring the customer's dominant personality factors and facets and adjusting the strategy in order to be perceived by the customer as a match.

Once a prominent factor and facet is recognized, Heavy Hitters will select their course of action based upon previous experiences with people who had the same attributes. They are always adding to their knowledge base of individual behavior patterns. They continuously classify personalities, associate them with the success or failure of the relationship, and link them to the characteristics of the sales cycle. They will draw upon these past personal experiences in order to choose the appropriate behavior and select the optimum strategy to develop a coach. Heavy Hitters are lifelong, full-time, professional students of people.

For each of the five factors, the following examples of sales processes will help you learn specific tactics for selling to a customer with a prominent factor. In these examples, I will also identify the customer's primary representational system. Identifying their systems is important, as people's wiring directly influences their decision-making process.

FACTOR 1—NEGATIVE EMOTIONALITY

People have different tolerances for stress, anger, and worry. At one end of the spectrum is the person who is always experiencing a crisis. At the other end is the calm, collected individual who is unshakable, even under immense pressure. From low to high, here are the six facets of negative emotionality:

Facets	Low	Medium	High
Worry	More calm	Worried/calm	More worried
Anger	Slow to anger	Not too quick to anger	Quick to anger
Discouragement	Seldom sad	Occasionally sad	Often sad
Self-Consciousness	Seldom embarrassed	Sometimes embarrassed	Easily embarrassed
Impulsiveness	Seldom yielding	Sometimes yielding	Often yielding
Vulnerability to Stress	Resists stress	Handles some stress	Is prone to stress

Figure 9.4 Facets of Negative Emotionality

If a customer is an even-keeled person with low negative emotionality facets, Heavy Hitters will mirror that behavior during the sales cycle. Heavy Hitters know the sales process will be logical, unhurried, and sedate. They will adjust their style and tactics accordingly.

Kurt had worked in the same local government agency for over twenty years. During this time, he had risen to the position of director. The agency was migrating from antiquated mainframe systems to state-of-the-art computers and software. Kurt was in charge of selecting the new technology. Kurt's environment was structured around order and predictability. He had strong auditory and kinesthetic systems. Everything, including his appearance, his office, and the process to select the new solution, reflected this.

Susan, the Heavy Hitter, had to make an important decision early in the sales cycle. She had to decide whether to pursue the business. Based on Kurt's personality, she knew that she would not be able to accelerate or change the selection process. Kurt's orientation was long-term, and there would be no quick decisions. The evaluation process would be well thought out and lengthy. The winner would be the last vendor standing, the one who exhibited the attributes necessary to have a long-term partnership with the agency. In essence, the sales cycle was a miniature dry run of the long-term relationship.

To develop Kurt into a coach, the Heavy Hitter's strategy was to prove that she and her company were "like" Kurt. She had to adopt Kurt's calm, unimpulsive traits (not an easy task for a high-energy salesperson). First, she adopted his personal demeanor. Every communication with Kurt was structured and well documented. When meeting with Kurt, she consciously slowed down her speech, breathing, and mannerisms from her normal hyperactive pace.

Part of the Hitter's strategy was also to introduce herself to Kurt's other long-time business partners, the members of Kurt's staff. Through these meetings, she gathered more information about Kurt. She was told about a past incident when a vendor tried unsuccessfully to go around Kurt to sell his solution. She met with other vendors with whom Kurt had existing relationships. From these vendors, she hoped to uncover any potential preexisting relationships that might work against her. She was also demonstrating to Kurt her desire to enter Kurt's world and his network of relationships.

As the sales cycle progressed, the other vendors' patience and commitment to the opportunity waned. They had miscalculated their ability to shorten or subvert Kurt's process. As this happened, Kurt spent more time with the Heavy Hitter, which gave her the chance to build a personal relationship. The Heavy Hitter learned Kurt rode horses, had served in the military, and, surprisingly, had been married twice. Kurt ultimately became her coach and shepherded the purchase through the bureaucratic sales process of the agency.

While an aggressive, high-energy strategy might be appropriate in certain sales situations, the decision to model Kurt in a complementary reactive manner was an equally effective strategy.

At the other end of the spectrum from Kurt is a person who is impulsive, doesn't handle stress well, and is a constant worrier. He would have a high negative emotionality factor. This type of person is orientated around crises.

Larry was worried. There had been talk about outsourcing his group's application development function. Since he had been with the transportation company for over thirteen years, he was also angry with his employer and somewhat discouraged with his current predicament.

One project that he had unsuccessfully tried to get funding for in the past was a new online reporting application to replace their paper reports. He had ulterior motives for completing this project. He knew that once the flexibility of online reports was introduced, it would be well received, and perhaps a more positive view of his group's value would be adopted. Also, the reporting system would become irreplaceable, requiring continual enhancements and maintenance from his team. Larry asked all the leading reporting tools vendors to present their technology to his team. Of course, none of the vendors had any background information about Larry's dilemma.

However, the Heavy Hitter had a different strategy for the meeting. Prior to the technology presentation, he met with Larry to further understand his needs. From this meeting, he determined that Larry had three problems. First, there wasn't enough time for his team to learn the new tools and build the application to meet Larry's schedule. Second, Larry was concerned that his team was not technically capable of completing the project. Finally, Larry didn't have a defined budget approved for the purchase! This information makes any salesperson nervous. Was Larry serious about the purchase or just "kicking tires"? Was there even a project?

Then the Heavy Hitter decided to do something to separate himself from the other vendors. While the other vendors would tell Larry how much easier their product was to use, the Heavy Hitter would build a prototype of the reporting system. He wanted to show Larry (a strong Visual) that his project could be completed successfully within Larry's constraints. However, prior to committing the resources to execute this strategy, he completed a background check of Larry. He wanted to know if Larry had juice. By understanding the past projects Larry had successfully managed, he was able to satisfy himself that Larry was not a dud. The Heavy Hitter decided that the strategy had an acceptable risk and committed the resources to build the prototype.

All the other vendors gave Larry and his team a presentation of their company, their product's feature set, and a short product demonstration. It seemed to Larry that any of the vendor's products would meet his requirements. To add to Larry's confusion, all of the products were priced similarly.

However, the Hitter's presentation was different. He showed the completed prototype application. Following this, he dissected the prototype, displaying the unique features that had made the prototype so easy to create. Larry's team was excited! The Heavy Hitter was invited back the following week to show the application directly to the nontechnical employees who would ultimately use the reports.

Building the prototype had other benefits. In order to create it, the Hitter's technical team met with Larry's team to define basic functionality. This is a much more desirable intersecting activity (or pretense) for them to build relationships than the duress of a sales presentation.

While the technical relationship was being developed, the relationship between the Heavy Hitter and Larry changed dramatically. Larry asked for a detailed proposal for training his team and a bid to build the entire application. To do this required constant communication between Larry and his team and the Heavy Hitter and his. The other vendors were locked out of the opportunity.

The presentation to the users the following week was a success. They wanted the application—the sooner the better. Money was allocated, terms were finalized, and the project was completed successfully ninety days later. Larry was extremely happy—until the next crisis.

Heavy Hitters know there is a path to every piece of business. They understand that they must walk the path in the shoes of their customer.

FACTOR 2—EXTRAVERSION

People have different capabilities to build and manage relationships. Extroverts are comfortable with lots of relationships, while introverts tend to be reserved and more comfortable being alone. Obviously, extraverts are one of the most preferred of the five factors to sell to while introverts are more challenging. Here are the six facets of extraversion:

Facets	Low	Medium	High
Warmth	Aloof	Attentive	Cordial
Gregariousness	Prefers to be alone	Likes being alone or with others	Prefers company
Assertiveness	Stays in background	Stays in foreground	Is a leader
Activity	Leisurely pace	Average pace	Vigorous pace
Excitement Seeking	Low need for thrills	Occasional need for thrills	Craving for thrills
Positive Emotions	Seldom exuberant	Sometimes exuberant	Usually cheerful

Figure 9.5 Facets of Extraversion

An introvert, or a person with a low level of extraversion, is generally thought of as being shy. However, a more appropriate way to think of an introvert is as a person who is predominantly concerned with her own thoughts or internal dialogue. In addition, introverts are usually independent, and this presents an additional challenge for a Hitter.

Gary is a network engineer for a large bank who works on complex low-level networking issues. He is on call by pager around the clock in case the network goes down. Gary's opinion on networking technology and products is highly valued throughout his department. A new product would not be purchased without his explicit approval. Yet in several meetings with Gary, the Heavy Hitter had been unable to develop any significant relationship with him. It seemed that Gary (a strong Auditory) couldn't relate to salespeople.

But the Heavy Hitter had a secret weapon. She introduced her system engineer to Gary. While the two technicians' relationship started off slowly, it ultimately turned into a friendship. One of the key turning points was when they installed an evaluation copy of the software on Gary's network. Because of the operations environment, this work had to be done at two in the morning and took several hours to complete. Through this early-morning intersecting activity, their relationship became personal—as relationships often do when people are working side by side under difficult or unusual circumstances. Gary recommended the purchase of the Hitter's product.

Although the Heavy Hitter tried, she never developed more than a congenial relationship with Gary. But in the end, she didn't need to as she was able to "draft," or ride the wind of another relationship, to find her coach.

The extravert, on the other hand is a friendly, outgoing person who is usually more verbally dominant in social settings. The extravert enjoys giving as well as receiving attention.

Bob is the director of information technology for a small division of a multibillion-dollar conglomerate. Bob wanted to make his mark, not only within his organization but also within the parent company. Bob's vision was to create the ultimate IT operation. His organization would become the model to be emulated by all the other IT organizations affiliated with the parent company. As a result, he deployed the latest products in his attempt to build his technology "showcase."

Bob was a high-energy person who moved at a fast pace. In order to drive his agenda, he was constantly meeting with his own team, as well as the other departments within the organization. His demeanor was friendly and optimistic. Bob had strong visual and kinesthetic systems.

The Heavy Hitter frequently met with Bob. Through these meetings, the Heavy Hitter truly understood the depth of Bob's conviction to accomplish his goal. Bob had a fantasy. The Heavy Hitter determined the best way for Bob to become her coach was to match fantasies. Instead of focusing on product features and functionality as Heavy Hitters may do with an introvert, the sale to Bob would be at a higher, more strategic level. The Heavy Hitter offered Bob a way of achieving his vision.

The Heavy Hitter used her manager extensively during the sales cycle. These customer meetings were more like conversations between friends who daydreamed about their future plans. Bob needed comrades who believed in him and would shower him with support. While this strategy would have little impact on an introvert, Bob viewed the Hitter's company as an integral component for achieving his dream.

FACTOR 3—OPENNESS

Some people are happiest when they are in a familiar environment with defined daily routines. They seek structure and are focused on the task immediately at hand. They would be classified as having a low openness factor. Others seek variety and are open to new experiences. They may dream about the future, seek deeper meanings for their emotions, and be genuinely curious. They would be classified as having a high openness factor. Here are the facets of the openness factor:

Facets	Low	Medium	High
Fantasy	In the here and now	Occasionally imaginative	A dreamer
Aesthetics	Uninterested in art	Moderate interest in art	Major interest in art
Feelings	Ignores feelings	Accepts feelings	Values all emotions
Actions	Likes familiar	Likes a mixture of new and familiar	Prefers variety
Ideas	Narrow focus	Moderate curiosity	Broad curiosity
Philosophy	Conservative	Moderate	Open to new values

Figure 9.6 Facets of Openness

A person with low openness will concentrate on a vendor's "here and now" characteristics, including vendor stability, technical support, product features, and the quality of the product.

John was an extremely difficult person to sell to. He was the vice president of information services for an outsourcer of computer applications. John had been a product person who had worked his way up to the executive level. His technical expertise made him even more intimidating to vendors.

He was a realist who based his decisions on facts rather than ideas or emotions. He was a strong Auditory who was only interested in discussing the "here and now." With every topic, he carefully selected his words to reflect their accuracy. Like Joe Friday from the *Dragnet* television show, he wanted nothing but the facts.

With John there wouldn't be any detailed discussions about the company's vision or any deep personal conversations. The topic would always be the product—how it worked, what features it lacked, and details about the underlying technology that most customers would consider minutiae. However, John needed to hear all the particulars.

Developing John into a coach involved several critical steps. First, the Heavy Hitter never went to a meeting with John alone. She always had her system engineer or other technical team members on hand to help answer John's questions.

Second, the Heavy Hitter and her team gave only definitive, truthful answers to John's questions. They answered his questions with the same precision as they were asked. They wanted to maintain their credibility. They edited their usual extravagant product claims to mirror John's conservative demeanor.

Third, they always worked with John's best interests in mind. They wanted him to know both the features and limitations of their product. It made no sense to sell John a product that didn't meet his requirements. Rather, it was important that his expectations were set correctly during the sales process. They arranged for a detailed on-site technical evaluation of their product and provided technical resources to assist him.

During this evaluation process, an interesting change in John began to occur. He began to openly criticize the other vendor's sales tactics and honesty. Also, he uncovered many flaws in the Heavy Hitter's product. However, instead of criticizing the product and declaring it unsuitable, he worked with the Heavy Hitter's team to find workarounds for these limitations. John was now the Hitter's coach.

Heavy Hitters wear many sales hats. In some situations, they are the customer's friends. In others, they are the promoters of the company's vision. In this situation, the Heavy Hitter became the human "dictionary" of all the facts about her company's products.

As opposed to John's narrow focus, people with high openness prefer variety and are much more in touch with their own feelings.

Tom was the manager of the information technology department for a small college. Tom was an engaging, interesting person. He was friendly, outgoing, and easy to talk to. He was even a part-time actor and member of the Screen Actors Guild. Since he was a strong Kinesthetic, acting came naturally. Tom's background didn't include any formalized computer training, yet somehow in his past he had become involved with computers.

Tom's world was more political than technical. He spent the majority of his time meeting with the various deans and placating them. His department was staffed with young graduates who didn't have any previous business experience. While Tom did not get deeply involved in the detailed technical issues, he clearly had juice and approved every decision within the department.

When the Heavy Hitter met Tom, her first impression was that Tom was bored and unfulfilled by his job. When she tried to talk about her products, Tom kept changing the subject back to the Hitter by asking personal questions about her family and where she grew up. This was not a typical sales call!

However, what many salespeople would have viewed as small talk was actually a key part of Tom's decision process. Tom was trying to determine if there was a personal fit between him and the Hitter. For Tom, this was an important business prerequisite. The Heavy Hitter mirrored Tom and asked him the same type of personal questions. Tom described his childhood in the Midwest, his affinity for the Chicago Cubs, and his desire to retire in a few years. As a result, a meeting that should have taken forty-five minutes lasted over two hours.

Many additional meetings would follow where product features and functionality would be discussed in addition to lunches and happy hours where they discussed personal life. But the most important aspect of Tom's sales selection process was already decided; he liked the Hitter, and they became friends.

If you are unsure whether a customer is your friend or a business acquaintance, apply the barbecue test. Would you invite the person to your home on a Sunday afternoon for a barbecue with your family and close friends? If you would and the customer would accept your invitation, then you are most likely friends, or there is enough compatibility for a friendship to develop. The more important question is whether your customers would invite you to *their* barbecues?

FACTOR 4—AGREEABLENESS

Some people get along better in groups than others. They have a high level of agreeableness. These people take direction and seek the approval of others. Conversely, people with a low level of agreeableness are more independent, interested in their own well-being, and concerned with either acquiring individual power or remaining autonomous. Here are the six facets of agreeableness:

Facets	Low	Medium	High
Trust	Skeptical	Cautious	Trusting
Straightforwardness	Guarded	Tactful	Frank
Altruism	Uninvolved	Willing to help others	Eager to help
Compliance	Aggressive	Approachable	Deferential
Modesty	Superior	Equal	Humble
Tender-Mindedness	Hardheaded	Responsive	Easily moved

Figure 9.7 Facets of Agreeableness

Paul was the manager in charge of information systems security in a well-known financial services company. He would be accurately described as someone with a low agreeableness factor. His main responsibility was to ensure customers' data was safe and secure. The position held a lot of responsibility and commanded equal authority. A breach in a customer's data could have significant financial implications. In addition to the legal liability, the unfavorable press would impact the company greatly.

Paul was a tough-minded authoritarian. He didn't meet vendors, rather he verbally abused them in front of his staff! These staged events were designed to showcase his considerable knowledge and the extent of his authority. Paul didn't trust anybody. He spoke negatively about other divisions of his company and how he would manage them differently. Paul had strong auditory and visual systems.

Developing Paul into a coach was critical. He was the bully who had all the juice. If the Heavy Hitter didn't win him over, she wouldn't win the deal. She knew it was pointless to argue with Paul, as there was nothing to be gained by doing so. He would not be swayed by any vendor's logic or reason. Paul marched to his own drumbeat.

Paul would choose the solution he believed was in his own best interest. So what did Paul want? He wanted to be a hero. He wanted to prove he was a smart businessman. He was seeking the recognition he felt he was entitled to. The Heavy Hitter's mission was to ensure that the selection of her product helped Paul achieve his needs.

Paul was considering replacing the company's existing security vendor because of continual product stability problems and the quality of its support. The product was originally purchased before Paul was hired, and the company had spent a significant amount of money purchasing and implementing it. Knowing this, the Heavy Hitter worked with her management to package a very compelling proposal that included a full product trade-in credit and free implementation services. This excited Paul! He would take great pride in boasting to his managers how he not only fixed the problem but essentially got their money back too.

The Heavy Hitter continually sold to Paul's ego. At every opportunity, she elicited Paul's feedback, not so much for its own merits but rather so Paul could hear himself talk about the Heavy Hitter's solution. She arranged for Paul to meet with others from the Hitter's company—the technical support manager, the product management team, and various members of the executive staff. By doing this, the Hitter's colleagues were subjected to Paul's pontificating, and the Heavy Hitter was freed for other tasks. The Heavy Hitter even arranged for Paul to be invited to join her company's customer advisory committee.

Paul would ultimately become a fantastic coach and an incredible champion. He was sold on the Hitter's company as well as the product. Finally, someone was treating him with the respect he deserved. Later, he even met with the president about the possibility of joining the Hitter's company. Paul wasn't such a tough guy after all.

Heavy Hitters know you must understand your customers' desired benefactions in order to lead them to your solution.

FACTOR 5—CONSCIENTIOUSNESS

Conscientiousness can be defined as a person's degree of diligence and ability to complete tasks. People with a low level of conscientiousness will procrastinate and put in the minimal effort to get the job done. Meanwhile, people with a high level of conscientiousness will go to great lengths to ensure their duties are completed correctly. Here are the facets of conscientiousness:

Facets	Low	Medium	High
Competence	Unprepared	Prepared	Capable
Order	Unorganized	Half organized	Well organized
Dutifulness	Covers obligations	Is casual about priorities	Has strong conscience
Achievement	Casual about success	Serious about success	Driven to succeed
Self-Discipline	Distractible	Mix of work and play	Focused on work
Deliberation	Spontaneous	Thoughtful	Careful

Figure 9.8 Facets of Conscientiousness

For the past five years, Lou had worked as the system administrator responsible for the database operations at a medium-sized electronics manufacturer. Lou was not the type of person who was intensely focused on his career. He was a happy-go-lucky guy who did the minimum to get by. This also applied to his interest in technology. While he understood concepts, he did not seem particularly interested in mastering the details. Lou would be classified as having low conscientiousness.

Although he was part of the evaluation team, he was not a key influencer of the group. In team meetings, his only contribution was an occasional wisecrack courtesy of his dry sense of humor. In short, Lou was an accommodating dud. In spite of this, the Heavy Hitter made a special effort to get to know Lou.

Acknowledging Lou's traits, the Heavy Hitter arranged unusual activities that were outside the work environment. To become better acquainted, the Heavy Hitter took Lou to lunch at eclectic restaurants, to the local pub, and even miniature cart racing at the nearby mall. The Heavy Hitter was normally an intense person with a very high conscientiousness factor. However, she had to suspend this personality characteristic when she was around Lou. Over time this "odd couple" actually found they enjoyed each other's company.

None of the other vendors paid any attention to Lou, as they considered him trivial to the decision process. In addition, none of the vendors (including the Heavy Hitter) was able to develop a coach out of anyone else on the selection team. Lou was the only coach to be found. For the Hitter, Lou developed into a great source of information about the company's political environment and how the sales process was progressing. While the other vendors were flying blind, the Heavy Hitter knew who was for and against her product and what objections she had to overcome. She knew the prices bid by her competitors. Lou even told the Heavy Hitter she had won the deal before it was publicly announced.

A person with a high level of conscientiousness will most likely be in a leadership position or a key player in the product selection process.

Mr. Johnson was the chief information officer of a multibillion-dollar publicly held medical device manufacturer. He was the prototypical executive: confident, capable, and successful. However, one huge problem in selling to Mr. Johnson was that it was impossible to meet with him personally. For purchase decisions, he had several trusted lieutenants who did most of the data gathering and analysis.

Mr. Johnson would become involved only very late in the sales cycle, after the preliminary recommendation had been made for his review. Until that time, the Heavy Hitter would have to work within the established process and find a coach elsewhere. In the Hitter's case, she was able to accomplish this with one of Mr. Johnson's direct reports, Michelle, the vice president of applications development.

Michelle made every vendor complete an immense RFP and laborious spreadsheets. Each product feature and operation had to be fully documented. Following the responses, Michelle performed a meticulous hands-on evaluation of each product and painstakingly documented her findings. It was clear that Michelle felt the decision process was a direct reflection of her competency. It wasn't until Michelle was completely satisfied with the Hitter's product that her demeanor completely changed from cross-examiner to collaborator. Suddenly, Michelle was strategizing with the Hitter about presenting her recommendation to Mr. Johnson.

Michelle scheduled the meeting with Mr. Johnson to present her decision and asked the Heavy Hitter to attend. The Hitter knew the deal was won if they made it successfully past this final hurdle.

Michelle planned and rehearsed every detail of the presentation. The Heavy Hitter was fearful that Michelle's decision could be overruled, and Michelle was fearful the Heavy Hitter would somehow embarrass her. The demeanor of the participants was also rehearsed. Both Hitter and coach had to display confidence and professionalism, along with the etiquette expected when meeting a person of Mr. Johnson's stature.

The Heavy Hitter and her manager arrived early to meet Michelle at Mr. Johnson's office. The Heavy Hitter was nervous, and while the meeting seemed like life or death to her, it was just a small item on Mr. Johnson's daily calendar. They had been allotted forty-five minutes of his time. Unfortunately, Mr. Johnson was running late and their meeting would be pushed back a half-hour and shortened to twenty minutes.

Mr. Johnson opened the meeting with an overview of his expectations. He then asked a series of high-level questions about the Heavy Hitter's company, product, competitors, and customers that Michelle and the Hitter answered together. However, rather than the grueling interrogation that had been expected, the

Heavy Hitter felt this meeting was more ceremonial. Michelle's attention to detail had already won the deal!

Sometimes not losing the deal is a key part of winning the business.

There are five different personality factors. Each factor has six facets that are each measured as low, medium, or high. Together, these factors help the Heavy Hitter categorize the individuals she encounters. The Hitter's goal is to build a memory bank of previous experiences with dominant factors and prominent facets. From this storehouse of knowledge, the Heavy Hitter determines the best course of action to win the deal by winning over the decision makers.

SALES CALL MEMORY

While the examples given for each of the factors are valuable, it is more important that you build your personal knowledge base with your own experiences. Obviously, taking insightful notes during sales calls will help you recall the meeting. However, during the next sales call you won't have time to search through your notes to find the "right" answer to a customer's question (nor would it be considered appropriate). Information must be available instantaneously by committing it to memory. Heavy Hitters have the ability to precisely recall events. Here are six principles to help improve your sales call memory:

1. *Sensory information.* During the sales call, consciously gather as much information as possible from your sight, sound, and touch senses. A vivid event is more likely to be memorized than a dull one, and the more sensory information that is incorporated into your memories, the higher your likelihood of recording it.

2. *Association.* Thoughts and experiences are more readily recalled when they are linked to a specific association. A very simple association would be the success or failure of the call. The association may be further defined by the customers' technical and business requirements, their objections to purchasing your product, their prominent personality factors and facets, their representational wiring, and so on. Movement or action can also be used to add a third dimension to the memory and help ensure the event's retention—for example, imprinting in your mind that you were writing on a white board when the customer presented a significant objection. How something is remembered will determine how much is remembered.

3. *Specificity.* The persistence of a memory is directly related to the precision of details that are input at the time of the experience. During a sales call, you may even want to tell your internal dialogue that some information is important and is not to be forgotten.

4. *Unique events.* Many sales calls are free-flowing events that lack a strict organization of facts. Therefore, it is easier to remember any unusual and unique aspects of a sales call that stand out from the ordinary and mundane.

5. *First and last.* Most salespeople are quick to remember how a sales call began (the grand opening) and how it ended (the big close). This is a natural characteristic of memory, whereby we tend to remember the information that is presented first and last more than the details in between. This particularly applies to longer sales calls, more than an hour. One way to help remember all of the in-between information is to mentally break the sales call into smaller segments (or chunks) either by time, presenter, or topic of discussion.

6. *The good, the bad, and the ugly.* Be forewarned, your brain has been trained to block out unpleasant images. However, it is crit-

ical that all information during a sales call, both good and bad, be stored.

Memory plays a fundamental role in determining the strength of a salesperson's intuition. As salespeople, we spend most of our time trying to predict the behavior, intentions, attitudes, and feelings of our customers. To accomplish this, our senses gather information from the words they speak, their gestures, and other sensory perceptive signals.

SALES INTUITION

Sales intuition is the ability to read and anticipate a customer's action beforehand. Four components of sales intuition are recognizing all the elements of a message using representational systems, decoding the meaning, storing the experience and linking like experiences, and finally, retrieving and comparing information.

The first component of sales intuition is recognizing all the verbal and nonverbal communication during a sales call. It is being aware of phonetic, content, purpose, representational system, and physical layers of the human communication model. After the information is distinguished, it must be decoded (the second component of intuition). Language is the medium used for interpreting the definitions of words, identifying their value, and finding out their purpose.

Recognizing all sensory-related information	Decoding the meaning	Storing the experience	Retrieving and comparing

Figure 9.9 Components of Intuition

People have their own personal dictionaries or lexicons of words. In fact, the average person's vocabulary is about fifty thousand words. However, the definitions or semantics of the words vary between people. People who have been blind all of their lives can say "light" exactly the same as people with sight. Not unexpectedly, their lexical definitions of what light is will be very different. Correctly ascertaining the meaning people are actually trying to communicate by the words they select, the order of the words, and the way they are said is necessary for proper decoding. "Does the customer's dictionary definition of a particular word match mine?"

Decoding also requires determining the congruency of people's communication. It's not only making sure the speaker's and listener's dictionaries are the same but also checking if the speaker's verbal and nonverbal communications are in agreement.

Once decoded, the next component of sales intuition is storing the experience. An analogy of how computers operate helps us understand how our memory works. One of the simplest ways to store information on a computer is in a key access file.

	Key	Attributes		
Record #1	Anderson	123 Elm	Mayberry	555-1212
Record #2	Andrews	456 Maple	Petticoat Junction	123-4567
Record N	Zigler	689 Fig	Springfield	555-4111

Figure 9.10 A Key Access File

Let's suppose you had to enter a thousand names, addresses, and telephone numbers into your computer. The most logical way to enter and access this data is by name. Therefore, you would use each person's name as the key to access the attributes (address and telephone number) that are associated with it. By using a key, you are able to directly access that record instead of performing a time-consuming sequential search of all the records for a match.

In this example, we would expect numbers in the telephone column, a combination of numbers and letters in the address column, and letters arranged in a certain way for the names and addresses. You wouldn't expect to see a town named "Bob" or see "Petticoat Junction" as someone's last name.

The mind's ability to store information is much more sophisticated and structurally complex than this rudimentary representation. The attributes that are stored in the mind are unstructured objects. The objects are pictures, sounds, feelings, or actions that represent experiences or stored information. In addition, each object has the potential to be a key. Here's how sales calls would be stored into memory:

Attributes—Pictures/Sounds/Feelings/Action

	Data	Data	Experience	Data
Sales Call #1	Data	Data	Experience	Data
Sales Call #2	Data	Experience	Data	Data
	Key	Key	Key	Key

Figure 9.11 Sales Calls Stored in Memory

The next component of intuition is linking like experiences and similar data. These relations combine attributes from completely different sales calls and help create intuition. In the example below are two different sales calls with customers who are strong Visuals stored in memory. You will notice that the customers have different attributes of personality. However, unlike a key access file where there is only a single key, every attribute has the potential to be a key.

Attributes—Pictures/Sounds/Feelings/Action

Sales Call #1	Joe Smith	Visual primary	Sales call successful	Open
Sales Call #2	Jane Doe	Rejected trial close	Visual primary	Skeptical
	Key	Key	Key	Key

Figure 9.12 Two Sales Calls and Their Attributes

Retrieving and comparing the individual entries within memory is the final component of intuition. Let's pretend the salesperson from above is on a new sales call and recognizes the person she is meeting with is a Visual. By recalling past sales calls that contain a visual key, she is able to access the other attributes from these sales calls, which enables her to determine the best course of action for this account. By linking attributes, you are able to search your memory and retrieve one or more records containing information that satisfies your query.

Learning continually occurs through the ongoing accumulation and consolidation of information from sales calls and interactions with people. When the model of intuition is finally assembled, it is a three-dimensional cube that enables instant matching of previous experiences to the current situation. From this knowledge base, salespeople can predict what will happen and what they should do in light of what they have done in the past.

INTUITION AND THE SALES CALL

How do the components of intuition actually work during a sales call? In order to answer this question we need to revisit the concept of vignettes from chapter 2. Vignettes are short interactions between a customer and salesperson about a topic or one conversational

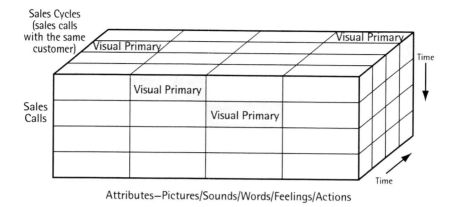

Figure 9.13 Sales Intuition Cube

theme. Each vignette is composed of a series of actions the Heavy Hitter or the customer may execute.

The decision about which response Heavy Hitters will give during a vignette is largely the result of their sales intuition. During a vignette, when they are asked a question or make a statement, they will provide either an "instantaneous answer" or a "calculated answer." The instantaneous answer is available immediately since it is either the recall of a logical fact or the recollection of a "flashbulb episode." Logical facts include details committed to rote memory, such as product specifications, features, and performance details. Flashbulb episodes are emotional, physical, or cerebral experiences that were so overpowering that they are permanently imprinted in short-term memory. The story at the beginning of this chapter where the salesperson was told by the president of the company that he hates computers is an example of a flashbulb episode.

Meanwhile, the calculated answer is akin to solving a mathematical equation within your mind by searching and selecting the right answer or creating an appropriate answer based upon a set of rules learned from prior experiences. The vignette answer retrieval diagram below helps illustrate these concepts.

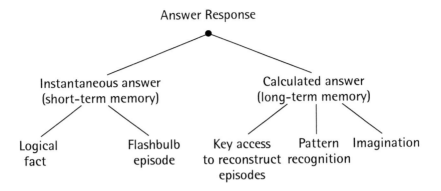

Figure 9.14 Vignette Answer Retrieval

Three types of calculated answers are constructed in long-term memory. The first type uses a key attribute of the call to search previous experiences, for example, recalling previous meetings with Visuals to help answer a question asked by a Visual.

Pattern recognition requires a more complex calculation involving multiple attributes. Let's say you were asked by an Auditory with a skeptical, detail-oriented personality how your product is different from your major competitor's. The creation of your answer would be based on previous encounters with this particular circumstance. Pattern recognition can be thought of as trying to find the what, when, where response—what you should do, when you are in this circumstance, where you need to respond to a question or execute a sales-related action.

Finally, in some instances Heavy Hitters are presented with situations they have never encountered before and they will have to use their imagination to create an answer. Making a best-guess answer requires a pattern recognition search to find closely resembling experiences plus additional hypothetical reasoning to create a new model. Obviously, this process takes the most time.

Since all types of calculated answers require processing in long-term memory, they take longer to produce. Recalling a logical fact that is resident in short-term memory is much easier than figuring out what to do next based on imagination. However, a customer expects you to respond to a question within a certain time frame. If you are face to face, this time is measured in seconds and there is a penalty for delay. The customer will perceive your answer as untruthful if the expected length of time is exceeded. This results in "selection pressure" on Heavy Hitters to produce an answer promptly. Quite often, when salespeople lie to a customer it is more likely because of the pressure to produce an instantaneous answer rather than a conscious decision to mislead.

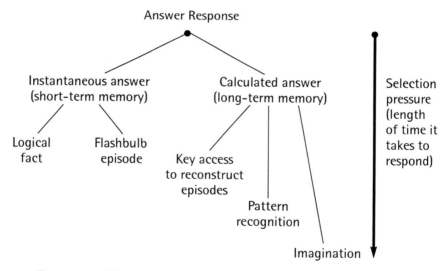

Figure 9.15 Vignette Selection Pressure

Unfortunately, many high-technology companies today are making two common mistakes. First, the majority of sales training time is spent only on memorizing logical facts about the company, product, and competitors. Little or no training is given on the development of sales intuition, when in fact a person's intuition is responsible for saying or doing the right thing at the right time. Sales intuition is responsible for all answers that are calculated from long-term memory and flashbulb episodes from short-term memory.

The second mistake is made during the hiring process. Most companies make previous experience in the same industry their main criterion for hiring. Since experienced people command the logical facts, they are assumed to be qualified candidates. I refer to this as the "trained simian" approach to hiring since even monkeys are capable of simple learning, such as distinguishing colors. A more important hiring criterion is how candidates respond to selection pressure. In other words, how quick-witted or fast on their feet are they, and are they able to solve complex problems in real time?

THE CUSTOMER PUZZLE

Every person involved in the selection process presents the Heavy Hitter with a "customer puzzle." The pieces of the puzzle include finding intersecting activities, determining personal motivations, understanding the customer's dominant personality characteristics, and building a kinship in communication. The glue that holds the puzzle together is sales intuition.

In order to solve the puzzle, the Heavy Hitter must accumulate data. While the information is sometimes obvious, most often it is hard to uncover. Learning how to find and interpret, store, and recall valuable information is a skill that Hitters must develop over time.

In a meeting with two new members of my sales organization, as an exercise about paying attention to details, I asked one to describe the lamp directly behind him without looking at it. He gave an elaborate description of the size of the lamp, the texture and color of the lampshade, and the shape of the base. However, when asked whether the lamp was turned on using a switch on the base, a knob near the bulb, or a chain, he didn't know. He had collected a lot of data but missed one of the most important pieces of information—how to turn the lamp on!

The second salesperson had been intently listening to the discussion. I asked him the same question, "Without looking, describe the lamp behind you." He started to repeat almost word for word what the first salesperson said. I interrupted him, "There are two lamps behind you. How did you know which one I meant?" He had incorrectly assumed that I was asking about the same lamp.

Heavy Hitters always pay attention to the details, never make assumptions about data, and triangulate to ensure the data's correctness. Heavy Hitters are students of people. Being a student means paying attention to the details.

The kinship-in-communication piece of the customer puzzle requires recognizing a person's representational system and anticipating its effect on the decision-making process. Since Visuals, Auditories, and Kinesthetics process information differently, they also approach the decision process distinctively.

For example, choosing a spouse is one of life's most important decisions. A colleague of mine who is a strong Auditory recently told me how he met his wife. They were seated next to each other on a long plane flight. While neither thought the other was particularly interesting, out of boredom they started a conversation. Even though there was not a great deal of physical attraction, by the end of the flight they had exchanged telephone numbers. Since they lived in separate cities, they started talking on the telephone regularly. Through these long conversations they fell in love, and they eventually married.

A close friend of mine with a strong visual orientation has a completely different story about how he met his wife. One night at a party, he saw a beautiful girl walk into the room. He said to himself, "This is exactly who I have been looking for!" He introduced himself to her and even told her that night that he was going to marry her. A year later, they did exactly that.

CONCLUSION

Let's take another look at the story from the beginning of this chapter about the president who hates computers. The salesperson went on to close a multimillion dollar deal with that company. His coach was the director of information technology, who represented and sold the solution to the president. Neither the salesperson nor any member of his company ever met with the president.

Following the successful implementation six months later, the director of information technology was promoted to vice president. A full year after his first conversation with the president, the salesperson saw him at a trade show and gathered enough nerve to approach him again. He started to introduce himself. "Hello, I'm Steve with National Computer Company—" Once again, the president startled him by interrupting him in midsentence. However, this time there was a much different demeanor. The president shrugged his shoulders and held his hands up. "User-friendly computers!" he said, then turned and walked away. I know that story very well, because I was that salesperson.

10

The Deeper Meaning of Language

The presentation to the customer's selection team had lasted about an hour and a half. During that time, the salesperson had explained the origins and background of his company. He provided examples of successful customers and spoke of the underlying technology that separated his solution from the competition's. He detailed product features and showed how they would benefit the customer. Finally, he closed the meeting with a discussion about pricing and the resources required for successful implementation.

Although the presentation was filled with facts, figures, and technical information, it was far from boring. The salesperson's presentation style, while professional, was not stuffy or overly rehearsed. He held each person's interest and kept everyone involved by drawing out questions and seeking individual comments. He illustrated the conversation by using descriptive words, animating his speech, and making occasional humorous remarks. The presentation reflected his confidence in the solution and the personal attention he would give the customer following the sale.

After he finished, the selection team members gathered around him as if they were supporters of a political candidate who had just heard an electrifying campaign speech. They wanted to spend more time with him and to get to know him personally. Most importantly, they would ask him to come back the following week with a price quote and implementation plan.

The goal of this book is to help you determine the different languages your customers speak and how to structure your message in language that persuades them to buy. This chapter presents the idea that there is a deeper meaning of language, an additional dimension that will ensure your message is accepted, remembered, and acted upon.

You communicate thousands of different messages on any given day. During the average business phone call you deliver hundreds of unique thoughts. These thoughts are manufactured on the internal assembly line of your mind that starts with a purpose and ends with words being enunciated in the optimum manner. The receiver of your message has to disassemble your package of words to interpret them. Situated below this automatic process is the underlying deeper meaning of language.

Whatever your age and experience in life, you have already mastered how to use language. As a child, you learned the complex process of conveying your thoughts, how to tell the truth, and how to lie. You have become an expert on the nuances of how to say something with maximum impact, and you understand that sometimes what's important isn't necessarily what you say as much as how you say it. You already know how to create a message with a clear and a compelling sense of urgency. Heavy Hitters are no different from the average person in this regard.

However, Heavy Hitters amplify their use of language by adding an additional dimension of meaning and structure within their usual conversations with the customers. By doing so, they instill their suggestions into the customer's thought process with what seems like telepathy. The common term for this is "persuasion." Persuasion is not solely a recital of logical arguments or factual information to a customer. Instead, it is the process of projecting your entire set of beliefs and convictions on another human being.

THE FIVE STEPS OF THE DEEPER MEANING OF LANGUAGE

Heavy Hitters employ five steps intuitively to create the deeper meaning of language. By understanding and utilizing these steps you will be able to deliver the same compelling communication.

1. Delivering your message with conviction and congruence.

2. Knowing your listener's benefaction and delivering your message in different languages.

3. Establishing and maintaining a receptive state of uninterrupted rapport with your listener.

4. Guiding your listener's internal dialogue.

5. Delivering your message directly to your listener's subconscious mind using a highly developed form of intuitive persuasion.

At the beginning of the book, I mentioned my interest in hypnosis. I believe the dictionary's definition of hypnosis—"A state like sleep in which the subject acts only on external suggestions"[17]—is actually wrong or at best only half true. In addition, the association of hypnosis to the pocket watch or the staged nightclub spectacle is irrelevant. Rather, hypnosis is about the structure and use of language.

From the perspective of Heavy Hitters, every communication event has the potential to have suggestive hypnotic qualities. If you understand how listeners process language, then you can help manage this process for them. This ensures your message will be successfully received and the action you suggest will be taken. This is a more definitive description of hypnosis. Once you have mastered the following five steps, your ability to communicate will become even more powerful. You will be able to deliver a message that effectively influences your listener with your suggestion.

Step 1. Delivering Your Message with Conviction and Congruence

During recent times, we have had two presidents that were extraordinary Hitters who understood and employed the deeper meaning of language. Presidents Bill Clinton and Ronald Reagan were both prolific speakers with unique talents. In terms of their accomplishments, history will ultimately decide how each of these men is regarded. However, they each enjoyed a unique talent for communication and building rapport.

From a management-style perspective, they both exhibited strong Teflon styles. Both men had juice, and they were both bullies but in very different ways. You could argue that the scandal President Clinton brought upon himself greatly limited his ability to accomplish his agenda. Surely, this was an act of overconfidence. And as with an overconfident sales manager, people either love Bill Clinton or hate him.

As president, he was a master of projecting congruence. Whatever the topic and regardless of who had written the speech, he was able to align his *entire* body to deliver a spoken message. He had a natural ability to mark words with voice inflections and physical mannerisms, for example, when he clinched his jaw. He seemed to do it consciously to further emphasize his conviction about a topic. Whether he was mad or sad, it became his facial exclamation point.

President Reagan had a natural ability to create rapport with a wide spectrum of people. He was able to obtain support from both major political parties and from people from all walks of life. Although his political enemies may have heartily disagreed with his agenda, they found it hard, if not impossible, to hate him personally. For this reason, he was able to accomplish (bully) more of his agenda.

Recently, a book of Ronald Reagan's personal writings was published. *Reagan, in His Own Hand* offers some unique insights into the president who was also known as "The Great Communicator."

In the book's foreword, Secretary of State George Schultz recounts the following story about the Geneva Summit in 1985.[18]

> Mikhail Gorbachev suddenly began to harangue us about our Strategic Defense Initiative, our plans for missile defense. President Reagan exploded. The two leaders went back and forth, interrupting each other and expressing their views with vehemence.
>
> Then Ronald Reagan got the floor. He spoke passionately about how much better the world would be if we were able to defend ourselves against nuclear warheads and ballistic missiles. He was intense as he expressed his abhorrence at having to rely on the ability to "wipe each other out" as the only means of keeping peace.
>
> The depth of President Reagan's belief was vividly apparent. Ronald Reagan was talking from the inside out. Translation was simultaneous. Gorbachev could connect what Reagan was saying with his facial expressions and body language.
>
> When the President finished, there was total silence. After what seemed an interminable time, Gorbachev said, "Mr. President, I don't agree with you, but I can see that you really mean what you say."

The congruence and conviction with which President Reagan spoke made an immense impression on Mr. Gorbachev. These two men went on to develop a very personal relationship, and the rapport they built literally changed the world.

Although this meeting didn't result in any breakthrough agreements, George Schultz credited this conversation with establishing the foundation from which many future successful negotiations resulted. And this is an important point to remember. Not every sales call results in a sale. But every sales call is a chance to use rapport to build a relationship.

For example, a Hitter and his system engineer arranged a meeting with a potential customer. Initially, they were very excited about the opportunity. Unfortunately, the company was located in another state, and they would have to spend a full day just traveling there. Once at the meeting, it became apparent that this company was not going to buy their product in the near term. The Heavy Hitter was embarrassed. Both he and the system engineer felt bad that they wasted an entire day.

A couple of months later, the Heavy Hitter received a surprise telephone call. One of the people attending the previous meeting had moved to a new company. His new company was much larger, and he was recommending it purchase the Hitter's product. He specifically mentioned that he was impressed with their conviction about their product's capability and belief in their company. Hitters garner many new customers from past sales efforts because customers believe in them. Heavy Hitters internalize their message so their bodies, demeanor, and words exude conviction.

Step 2. Knowing Your Listener's Benefaction and Delivering Your Message in Different Languages

If selling is about speaking the language of a customer, then there are as many varieties of languages as there are customers. By speaking a customer's unique dialect or language, Heavy Hitters are able to create rapport. Let's review the different types of language Heavy Hitters mirror when they speak with a customer.

- Representational system language. Heavy Hitters consciously use the same representational terms as the customer. They paint a picture of their solution to a Visual, tell the product's story to an Auditory, and get a grasp of a Kinesthetic's problem.

- Physical communication language. Hand in hand with the customer's representational system is the language of the body. Heavy Hitters reflect their customer's dialect using their speech, breathing, hand movements, facial expressions, and body posture.

- Technical specification language. This language is the content-level trade language of the customer. Each industry has its own language and slang with unique terms and nomenclature.

- Intersecting activity language. In order to facilitate the building of a personal relationship, Heavy Hitters are constantly searching for intersecting activities they have in common with customers. Each intersecting activity also has a unique dialect of terminology.

- Orientation language. Heavy Hitters know they need to understand the benefaction of everyone involved in the sale. This includes each decision maker along with recommenders who can influence the selection process. Hitters find a way to help them achieve their benefactions through the sale of his product.

Each customer's language is sophisticated and the dialect unique. In order to truly speak the language of the customer, the Heavy Hitter speaks many different languages that reflect a person's representational wiring, body language, jargon of the industry, intersecting activities, and benefaction. Like explorers who are making their first contact with a primitive tribe, Heavy Hitters cautiously study their customers' languages before making any sudden movements. They know any misinterpretation can have catastrophic results.

Step 3. Establishing and Maintaining a Receptive State of Uninterrupted Rapport with Your Listener

In chapter 7, I recounted the story of the seminar where I performed a behavior interruption to change the audience's demeanor from apathetic and indifferent to engaged and involved. My goal was to create a "receptive state" with each audience member. A receptive state is the positive environment that enables a message to be accepted and remembered.

Creating a receptive state is like hosting a party. Imagine you have invited a group of people together to the intersecting activity of a celebration. Most likely, your guestlist includes people that have never met as well as friends. As the host, you want everyone to be comfortable so you make sure the location, facilities, food, beverages, and entertainment are conducive to having a good time. Like a party host, Heavy Hitters are responsible for creating the mental environment (message content) and the communication accommodations (message delivery) for a customer (the guest) during a sales call.

Heavy Hitters consciously create a receptive state at the beginning of every meeting in order to build rapport. As the meeting progresses, they continuously monitor the level of rapport of each attendee. The Hitters' goal is to create four different receptive states: personal, technical, business, and political. The first priority is to build a personal receptive state with each individual. To accomplish this, Hitters will try to determine people's unique language, search for intersecting activities they might have in common, and determine the traits of their personalities.

Once personal rapport is established, Heavy Hitters will execute a series of premeditated vignettes to qualify the customer's technical fit. The criteria to determine technical fit have been supplied by their company. However, they do not want to jeopardize the personal rapport they have established. Therefore, they take great care to build a technical receptive state through understanding the customer's problem. They want to ensure they understand the technical problem the customer is trying to solve and compare it against their company's definition of technical fit. Their line of questioning is not like a police officer interrogating the prime suspect in a crime case. Rather, it is interwoven as a natural part of the conversation without much fanfare. These vignettes are designed not only to qualify the technical fit but also to insert logical arguments that the Hitters' solution can solve the customer's technical problem.

As Heavy Hitters demonstrate their primary interest is in the customer's success, they begin to build a business receptive state. At this point, the customer starts to consider the Hitter more than a vendor. He becomes a business consultant who has the expertise to solve the customer's problem.

Finally, the political receptive state is established when the customer uses the Hitters' solution to achieve his personal benefaction based on his physiological, safety, belonging, and esteem needs. The graph below depicts the ideal progression of rapport and momentum during the sales cycle.

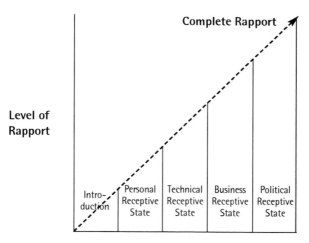

Figure 10.1 Receptive States during the Sales Cycle

At the bottom of the graph is the concept of time. The amount of time required to create rapport depends on the product you are selling. For example, it may take weeks or months to achieve "complete rapport" for a Heavy Hitter selling a million-dollar software application or just minutes for an inexpensive product.

The Foundation

In order to influence his customer, the Heavy Hitter must lay the foundation of successful communication using the deeper meaning of language. The first three steps of this process—delivering the message with conviction and congruence, speaking in the customer's different languages, and using receptive states to create rapport—must be completed before proceeding to the hypnotic delivery of the subliminal message. Taking the first three steps alone will help you enjoy more effective communication with customers and improve the odds of winning the deal. However, Heavy Hitters want more. They want their message to be instilled in the customer's thought process as if it were the customer's own idea. The ability to master the final two steps of the process ultimately determines the Hitters' persuasiveness.

Step 4. Guiding Your Listener's Internal Dialogue

Your internal dialogue is the never-ending, honest, unedited conversation within your mind that represents your deepest feelings. Basically, you are always talking to yourself. This discussion is the real you and the summation of your personality. However, we don't usually expose this dialogue to the outside world until we pass it through our own editing process. The editing process interprets and validates the information we receive and approves the messages we send. In essence, we use the editing process to protect ourselves.

However, it is possible to lead or manage another person's editing process. First, you have to establish that you are working in that person's best interest, using the previous steps of the deeper meaning of language. Then you have to be able to guide the person's internal dialogue. To help understand this concept, let's once again examine President Reagan's use of language.

President Reagan was an impressive politician. He utilized his communication talents to win over his customers—the American people, Congress, and foreign leaders. He possessed an extremely balanced communication style that he used effectively to create complete rapport. He spoke with conviction and had a natural command of language that amplified his sincerity. He was also a master at guiding his listeners' internal dialogue.

Before and during his presidency, he wrote over six hundred radio addresses by himself, in his own handwriting. They were not the work of a team of speechwriters. The structure and content of these addresses are well worth examining and understanding. "Looking Out the Window" was delivered on January 27, 1978. The text that follows is exactly as he wrote it, with his punctuation and spelling. For the sake of brevity, some cuts have been made. If you can, try to imagine yourself listening to his voice over the radio as you read it.

It's nightfall in a strange town a long way from home. I'm watching the lights come on from my hotel room window on the 35th floor.

I'm afraid you are in for a little bit of philosophizing if you don't mind. Some of these broadcasts have to be put together while I'm out on the road traveling what I call the mashed potato circuit. In a little while I'll be speaking to a group of very nice people in a banquet hall.

Right now however I'm looking down on a busy city at rush hour. The streets below are twin ribbons of sparkling red & white. Tail lights on the cars moving away from my vantage point provide the red and the headlights coming toward me the white.

Oh, but I wonder about the people in the cars, who they are, what they do, what are they thinking about as they head for the warmth of home. Come to think of it I've met them—oh—maybe not those particular individuals but still I feel I know them.

Someone very wise once wrote that if we were all told one day that the end was coming; that we were living our last day, every road, every street & all the telephone lines would be jammed with people trying to reach someone to whom we wanted simply to say, "I love You."

But doesn't it seem foolish to wait for such a final day and take the chance of not getting there in time? And speaking of time I'll have to stop now. OPERATOR I'D LIKE TO MAKE A PHONE CALL – LONG DISTANCE

This is Ronald Reagan. Thanks for listening.[19]

Here's a paragraph-by-paragraph analysis to help you understand how President Reagan guides the listeners' internal dialogue. I have highlighted the VAK keywords, as well as identified all of the different communication techniques he has interwoven into his message.

> It's nightfall in a strange town a long way from home. I'm *watching* the lights come on from my hotel room window on the 35th floor.

The first paragraph of all his radio addresses helps create a personal receptive state for the audience. The words, "nightfall," "strange town," "long way from home," provide the mental imagery that enable the listeners to be quickly transported to Reagan's place and mood (in an unfamiliar place a long way from home).

The second sentence is an operator on the first sentence. It further defines where he is physically and forces the listeners to adjust their viewpoint to the thirty-fifth floor of a hotel room. Both of these sentences are verifiable statements. Most everyone has experienced being a long way from home and feeling homesick. Most everyone has been in a high-rise building. As listeners receive information, they check with their internal dialogue to verify the statement's accuracy. Assuming the listeners have been homesick before, this statement is agreed to and considered truthful. The honesty of the statement is also passed on to the presenter. Verifiable statements enable the presenter to quickly gain credibility and rapport.

> I'm afraid you are in for a little bit of philosophizing if you don't mind. Some of these broadcasts have to be put together while I'm out on the road traveling what I call the mashed potato circuit. In a little while I'll be *speaking* to a group of very nice people in a banquet hall.

Preapologizing is one technique for developing a receptive state with an audience. This is one form of a "softener." A softener eases listeners into the next thought or can be used to set expectations. Usually, these radio addresses discussed the economy or issues of foreign and domestic interest. Here President Reagan is signaling that the intent of this week's message is different. He's adjusting the listeners' frame of mind from being issue based to being more reflective and introspective. Basically, he's telling their internal dialogue to relax a little.

He's on the road, about to give a speech on what he calls "the mashed potato circuit." How do you interpret that statement? Speaking to a group of people in the heartland of America is quite different from speaking to people from the East or West Coast. What would you have inferred if he had called it the "steak and wine circuit"? Perhaps that he considers these dinner speeches less than important and feels he should be performing his "real" job of leading the land. There's an underlying meaning that he is trying to communicate. However, the interpretation of the statement is dependent upon each listener's viewpoint, and there is no right or wrong answer. Regardless of the answer, the listeners' internal dialogue empathizes with the position he is in.

> Right now however I'm *looking* down on a busy city at rush
> hour. The streets below are twin ribbons of *sparkling* red &
> white. Tail lights on the cars moving away from my *vantage*
> point provide the red and the headlights coming toward me
> the white.

The paragraph visually leads the listeners to create more mental imagery. The words "Right now" grab the listeners' attention. The listeners' internal dialogue is quickly forced to look down with him at the street. Then he provides an unusual description of something seen nightly. This paragraph causes the listeners to create a lot of mental activity, which in turn forces the listeners' internal dialogue to become increasingly busy.

The metaphor of the car taillights as twin ribbons is another receptive state development technique using a verifiable statement. Although you probably have never thought of car lights as "twin ribbons" before, you have seen the taillights of cars as they are lined up on the highway.

This analogy also draws you closer into Reagan's world. What was the first thought that came to mind as you read the words "sparkling" and "ribbons"? Did you associate them with patriotic events such as "the rockets red glare" or the ribbons on the Medal of Honor? Did you link them to something highly valued, such as a first-place ribbon, or to the sparkle of a diamond or ruby? These words convey another level of meaning, which is transposed onto the content of the message. It's up to each individual's internal dialogue to discern the relevant meaning from all the possibilities.

> Oh, but I wonder about the people in the cars, who they are,
> what they do, what are they thinking about as they head for
> the *warmth* of home. Come to think of it I've met them—
> oh—maybe not those particular individuals but still I *feel*
> I know them.

When he "wonders" in the first sentence, this causes the listeners' internal dialogue to also wonder. Nearly everyone has driven a car and can relate to the intersecting activity of driving a car. You've also probably wondered who those people are in the cars next to you on the road. What do they do for a living and where are they going?

Driving is one of the few times during the day that is specifically dedicated to chatting with your internal dialogue. If a listener drives a car home from work, the reaction to this statement may have been, "I do that." If the listener was in his car while hearing this message, he would have definitely said, "Hey, that's me!"

The word "warmth" is a "double entendre." That is, it has two distinct meanings. Remember, this speech was given in January. Did Reagan mean the physical temperature of the home? Or did he mean the atmosphere of emotional affection inside the home? The listeners are left to interpret this sentence, and there isn't a wrong answer.

The final sentence is very important. Here Reagan is sharing his internal dialogue directly with the listeners. If you could view the transcripts of a person's unedited internal dialogue, you would see his "honest" thoughts. In this case we can actually do that as the original writings have been reproduced in the book. Reagan's handwriting shows his exact stream of consciousness, including corrections and amplifications. Therefore, he's speaking with congruence and conviction. He does seem to know the listeners. He's described activities they can relate to. He has been telling their internal dialogue what to think about. He has created a personal receptive state with each individual listener.

> Someone very wise once wrote that if we were all *told* one day that the end was coming; that we were living our last day, every road, every street & all the telephone lines would be *jammed* with people trying to *reach* someone to whom we wanted simply to *say*, "I love You."

Who is this "someone very wise" that he mentions? Depending on the deepness of the receptive state, the listeners may have performed a quick memory search of well-known wise people. Remember, he previously told you to "wonder."

Examine the second sentence again. What's the difference between a road and a street? The listener is forced to make a distinction between the two. Notice how he associates the word "jammed" to road, street, and telephone lines. He is using a single word with two completely different representational system interpretations. A jammed road is a kinesthetic event. A jammed telephone line is an auditory event. Also, "reaching" someone by road or street is a kinesthetic event; "reaching" someone by telephone is an auditory event. Once again, the listeners have to determine their own meaning from these general words.

> But doesn't it seem foolish to wait for such a final day and take the chance of not getting there in time? And *speaking* of time I'll have to stop now. OPERATOR I'D LIKE TO MAKE A PHONE *CALL*—LONG DISTANCE
> This is Ronald Reagan. Thanks for *listening*.

These two paragraphs are constructed entirely from the perspective of the auditory system. By asking a question, he is leading the listeners' internal dialogue and limiting what they can be thinking about. He gives you no choice. You have to answer the question in your mind. His suggestion is that it would be "foolish" not to. In addition, he uses the word "time" in the second sentence as a form of linkage. It links the discussion of your internal dialogue to the action of making a phone call.

The underlying complexity of this message is very sophisticated. Each paragraph is written entirely in one representational system. He's taking the listeners from system to system. Here's the pattern below:

Paragraph 1	Visual
Paragraph 2	Auditory
Paragraph 3	Visual
Paragraph 4	Kinesthetic
Paragraphs 5–7	Auditory

Throughout the example, Reagan has been guiding the listeners' internal dialogue, directing it to create certain images and specific feelings, and telling it to ask certain questions to limit what the listeners can think about. He's using words with multiple meanings and he's speaking with congruence and conviction. He's accomplished the first four steps of the deeper meaning of language and is now ready to move on to the final step.

Step 5. Delivering Your Message Directly to Your Listener's Subconscious Mind Using a Highly Developed Form of Intuitive Persuasion

Like every salesman, President Reagan had a product to sell. As a politician, his product was not only his policies but, equally important, himself. Each of his radio addresses had a political purpose, and this one was no different. He had a very powerful message that he wanted to deliver that was camouflaged beneath the content of the story. Now I doubt that Ronald Reagan sat down and said, "I'm going to create a message that interweaves all of the listeners' representational systems and instill subliminal thoughts in their minds." Rather, this message, like all the other ones he wrote, came naturally to him.

Here is the most fascinating part by far. Our subconscious minds are always receiving information that our conscious minds may not even recognize. More importantly, Hitters know that during the course of a normal conversation they can have direct communication with people's subconscious minds that can influence their opinions and points of view.

Recently, I had an interesting experience that illustrates the concept of intuitive persuasion and the perceptiveness of the subconscious mind. It happened while I was having surgery for a bothersome knee.

During the previous months, my knee had been a great source of pain and frustration. Instead of my knee healing over time, the discomfort intensified until even walking became a chore. After procrastinating as long as possible, I visited a knee specialist who recommended surgery. Although I dreaded having surgery, I looked forward to being pain free and active again.

While I was being anesthetized for knee surgery, I became quite talkative and animated. While my speech was sober and coherent, my thought process was inebriated. My wife was present, and she would later relish telling me of my somewhat embarrassing behavior.

I have no recollection of anything I said or did. The drugs had disconnected my ability to store any of the events in my short-term or long-term memory. However, my subconscious mind was still alert and gathering information. It was as if I were in a drug-induced state of intuitive persuasion.

I was later told I had a very rational conversation with the doctor in the recovery room where he told me the surgery had gone very well. However, I have absolutely no recollection of this conversation either. When I awoke a couple of hours later, I sat up and began speaking as if the doctor were still standing at the foot of my bed, although he had left hours earlier. "I'm fixed!" I said aloud.

Although I didn't consciously remember our conversation, I knew the operation had been a success. My subconscious mind had been present to receive my doctor's message on my conscious mind's behalf.

CONCLUSION

The content level of the words you speak is like your own anesthetic that you can learn to use to "knock out" your customer's *conscious* mind. It is the customer's conscious mind that is full of objections, doubt, and cynicism. If you can bypass it and speak directly to the subconscious mind, you can send the customer your message without interruption, offer suggestions on how the customer should behave, or explain why he should trust you.

The "knock out" I am referring to is not the same as that delivered by a boxer who uppercuts an opponent into unconsciousness. Rather, it is using the first four steps of the deeper meaning of language to get past a person's conscious mind. If you speak with conviction and congruence, know your listener's benefaction, deliver your message in "different languages," and establish and maintain a receptive state of rapport to guide the listener's internal dialogue, you will have set the stage to speak directly to your customer's subconscious mind. In the next chapter, we'll unlock the secrets of the final step of the process, intuitive persuasion.

11

Intuitive Persuasion

The vice president of sales was about to announce the top sales producer for the quarter at the awards ceremony. In the back row, two salespeople were talking to each other.

"Well, it isn't any surprise who gets this award," said the first salesperson sarcastically.

"Unbelievable. Three quarters in a row," responded the other.

"Yeah, last quarter she closed one big account and this quarter she closes ten small ones," said the envious first salesperson.

"How does she do it?"

"Yeah, how does she do it?"

In Ronald Reagan's message that we reviewed in the last chapter, he created an incredibly deep level of hypnotic, subconscious communication using each of the five steps of the deeper meaning of language. Below (in parentheses following each paraphrased sentence) is his real message to his listeners. This is the encoded message that the listeners' subconscious minds received. It is also a great example of intuitive persuasion.

- "In a little while, I'll be speaking to very nice people." (You are nice people.)
- "Although we haven't met, I feel I know them." (I know you.)
- "Reach you, to simply say I love you." (I love you.)

Why was this message interpreted in this way? On the surface, Reagan constructed a series of everyday thoughts that created the content-level story. He explained the circumstances surrounding his emotional state, talked about the speech he was about to give, and described the sights around him. However, underneath this visible story was an invisible message to his customers, the listeners. The message assured the listeners that Reagan knew them and cared for them. Undoubtedly, it was received by their subconscious minds and influenced those people who heard it.

In every conversation, both conscious and subconscious communication is being transmitted, assessed, and cataloged by each participant. And each layer of the human communication model is capable of sending observable (conscious) and unobservable (subconscious) messages simultaneously. Although each listener can receive only a finite amount of information at any one time, very little of the information that is transmitted across all layers is lost. What isn't consciously received is processed subconsciously.

If you overwhelm the conscious mind's capability to process information, reduce its ability to handle data, or turn it off completely (such as creating a trance state), you will be talking directly to the subconscious mind. Recently, *Scientific American* magazine described this experience in an article on hypnosis: "Over the past few years, researchers have found that hypnotized individuals actively respond to suggestions even though they sometimes perceive the dramatic changes in thought and behavior as happening 'by themselves.' During hypnosis, it is as though the brain temporarily suspends its attempts to authenticate incoming sensory information."[20] Later, we will review different techniques to accomplish this.

However, it is important to recognize the first step of the process, speaking with conviction and congruence, requires the presenter to be telling the truth. In fact, truth is the key ingredient of the entire process. If your fundamental message is not based upon truth, it will fail. Was Reagan telling the truth or was he just another slick politician manipulating the populace? The answer is that he was emphatically telling the truth. The speech was written in his own handwriting, and by examining it, you can witness his unedited internal dialogue being put onto paper. He was writing down the exact conversation he was having with himself at the time. The subconscious message he delivered was in complete congruence with his actual thoughts. Being a Heavy Hitter requires believing in your company, product, and yourself.

Both the conscious and subconscious dimensions of information are stored together in a person's short- or long-term memory. Once stored, the "complete experience" can be recalled. The complete experience is comprised of all the sights, sounds, and feelings gathered by the representational systems, along with information that has been collected by the subconscious mind.

For the Hitter, each sales call and every sales cycle results in an incredible amount of data to be stored. Once stored, this information can be accessed during the current sales situation to determine how the Heavy Hitter should behave personally or to select a course of action to win the deal.

INTUITION

This process is called "intuition"—comparing a series of past experiences against current circumstances. You can think of intuition as a highly developed model for making decisions and a powerful heuristic engine that is constantly learning from the past. When you invoke your intuition, you're accessing previous complete experiences in order to gather the widest range of information. Once your conscious and subconscious minds have gathered all the information about a current deal, it can be compared to previous sales cycles you have worked on. This results in the best possible decisions being made.

All salespeople store their conscious experiences. However, Heavy Hitters are able to see a wider spectrum of data, have a keener sense of the situation, and are more in tune with the customer. They have a more fully developed awareness of representational systems. In addition, they have more effective methodologies to store and retrieve all the visible and invisible layers of the human communication model. Since their intuition is far superior than that of average salespeople, they have a greater proficiency to win business. The formula for intuition can be summarized into the following equation:

Intuition   =   Cataloged experiences   ×   Representational system
                 (short and long term)   awareness

Figure 11.1 The Formula for Sales Intuition

The first half of this equation is the ability to store and retrieve experiences. The second half of the equation is the aptitude to recognize all the available information from an experience using all of the senses. How often have you attended a sales call with a colleague who had a different opinion of the success of the meeting or the quality of the opportunity? Most likely, the difference in "reading" the meeting is because one person collected more data than the other and had more experiences to compare it against.

All your life you have used intuition to make important personal and business decisions. Usually, we think of our intuition in a reactive state. You gather information, check with your intuition, then make a decision or take some action. However, another, even more powerful form of intuition is comparable to hypnosis. It's a proactive intuition called "intuitive persuasion."

Intuitive persuasion is a natural extension of intuition with two additional capabilities. The more important capability is that you can deliver your message directly into someone's mind, as President Reagan did with his radio message. Two key requirements must be in place in order to accomplish this successfully. Listeners have to be in an intense personal receptive state, and their internal dialogue has to be occupied. In other words, personal rapport must be established, and their internal dialogue must be immersed in an all-encompassing activity, even if that activity is resting.

How many times have you missed your freeway exit while you were driving and "woke up" afterward? Or have you gone through an intersection and later asked yourself if the light was green? In both cases, you were physically driving your car, but your internal dialogue was very busy talking to itself or someone else, listening to the radio, singing, or daydreaming. Meanwhile, you successfully turned over the driving duties to your subconscious mind. This is an example of your internal dialogue being overloaded and turning inward.

In Ronald Reagan's radio address, he was vigorously exercising all of the listeners' representational systems. Overwhelming people's representational systems causes their internal dialogue to start an intense conversation with itself and turn inward. In turning inward, the internal dialogue changes from being externally focused on the outside world to internally focused within the mind. The point of reference of the senses changes from outside the body to the exclusive conversation with oneself. This also happens when people pray, meditate, chant, or engage in activities that require intense concentration, such as painting or drawing.

When the internal dialogue becomes too busy keeping up with the conversation by managing the tasks of creating pictures, sounds, and feelings, it starts to turn inward and turns off the outside world. When bombarded with information, the internal dialogue may even declare itself "lost" and turn inward by having a separate conversation on a completely different topic. Or if a topic of conversation is very meaningful or pertinent to an individual, the internal dialogue discusses how it applies to the individual. I've been in many presentations where the customer is too busy implementing the product in her mind to listen to the presentation.

Once turned inward, the internal dialogue is not an active participant, as if the listener's conscious mind has been turned off (or the volume turned way down). Certain bands of information that were previously received consciously are shut down. However, the information is not lost. It is still being received by the person's representational systems, but it is processed and cataloged directly into the subconscious mind. It is at this time that the subconscious mind is open to receiving information and suggestions. For example, this is the precise moment when a hypnotist is able to tell the person who seems asleep (in a deep trance) to raise her arm.

EXERCISE 11: INTERNAL DIALOGUE AWARENESS

Try this exercise to explore how your internal dialogue can turn inward. Start counting backward from one hundred to one. As you are counting, try to sense the specific number where your mind starts to wander. At that point, try to sense when your internal dialogue starts another conversation or to turn inward. As it turns inward, you are still aware of your surroundings. However, information is being pushed into the background while you try to focus on the task at hand, counting backward.

Now try a slightly different experiment. Say the alphabet backward. You will notice it is harder to do since there isn't a sequential relationship or pattern among the letters. Therefore, you may have had to first say the alphabet forward in order to reverse it. This creates a more stimulating task for your internal dialogue so it cannot turn inward as quickly. When it does, it is more likely to be from frustration rather than the boredom associated with counting backward.

READING MINDS

The second capability of intuitive persuasion is that it provides Heavy Hitters with the ability to read minds. Of course, no one can read minds. Rather, Hitters can predict what will be in the listener's mind based upon the specific words they know they are going to deliver. For example, if I say, "Don't think about snakes," you have to think about snakes in order to "not" think about snakes. Therefore, I could have predicted two paragraphs ago that very shortly you would be thinking about snakes since I was guiding your internal dialogue to the idea of snakes.

Whether you thought of rattlesnakes, pythons, or sidewinders, you had to disassemble the sentence in order to interpret it and you had to think about snakes. In addition, most people don't like snakes and by inserting them into the dialogue I am actually breaking rapport. If the subject had been puppies instead of snakes, the effect would have been different.

Intuitive persuasion is an elegant and sophisticated strategy for talking to your customer's mind. By creating a deep receptive state and guiding the internal dialogue of your customers, you can deliver a message directly to their subconscious minds that will be acted upon. Instead of barraging customers solely with logical arguments, facts, and figures, you are finessing them to believe. While a challenge to execute, once you have mastered intuitive persuasion you will not only enjoy the satisfaction of accomplishment but sell more too. Here's the equation for intuitive persuasion.

$$\text{Intuitive persuasion} = \left(\begin{array}{c}\text{Cataloged experiences}\end{array} \times \begin{array}{c}\text{Representational system awareness}\end{array}\right) + \left(\begin{array}{c}\text{Personal receptive state creation or rapport}\end{array} \times \begin{array}{c}\text{Ability to guide listener's internal dialogue}\end{array}\right)$$

Figure 11.2 The Formula for Intuitive Persuasion

You'll notice the first half of the equation is the formula for intuition. This part of the equation enables Heavy Hitters to sense all the data emanating from the customer and, by comparing the scenario to past situations, correctly interpreting the situation. When intuition is combined with intense rapport and guiding the listener's internal dialogue, Heavy Hitters are capable of an entirely different level of superhuman persuasion.

First, Heavy Hitters create an extraordinarily intense personal receptive state by assuming the customer's representational wiring completely. They subtly mirror all aspects of the person's physical communication (breathing, speech, and body movements). They adopt the person's language and representational system orientation, using their VAK keywords. They will speak the same language and establish a complete kinship in communication.

Once intense rapport is established, Hitters add the final ingredient of guiding the listener's internal dialogue—by managing what it can think, keeping it extremely busy, telling it what to do, or even by lulling it into relaxation. Many different techniques can accomplish this, and Ronald Reagan's radio addresses show examples of the most prevalent methods.

TECHNIQUES FOR GUIDING A LISTENER'S INTERNAL DIALOGUE

Below you will find the title, date, and initial passages of a variety of Reagan's radio addresses along with a brief discussion of the technique being used. Keep in mind that these are small samples of various techniques to occupy the listener's internal dialogue. The techniques can be combined and interwoven into your presentation strategy.

Recessive System Access

> Day Care Centers—March 23, 1977
> It has been said a baby sitter is a teenager acting like a parent while the parent is out acting like a teenager. Government sees it as something much more grandiose.[21]

Here is the technique of recessive system access. Everyone has a primary, secondary, and recessive representational system. By constructing and communicating your message by speaking with words matching the listener's primary system, moving to her secondary system, and ending in her recessive system, you will have a profound impact on your listener. This technique requires that you understand your customer's representational wiring explicitly and are able to establish and maintain intense rapport. If you execute this technique correctly by patiently moving to the recessive system in a natural manner, you will ultimately put this person into a hypnotic trance.

The primary system is the system most frequently used by the conscious mind during daily conversation, while the recessive system is the least used and can be thought of as being "closer" to internal dialogue. Assuming rapport is present, as you access each progressively weaker system, the listener's internal dialogue becomes more relaxed. The consciousness of the internal dialogue starts to diminish, and it is lulled into an inward thought process as it disengages from the conversation.

Have you ever had conversations with people who mesmerized you? As they spoke, you could feel yourself slipping away, but you didn't fight it; in fact, it felt good. It wasn't so much the content of their words but their manner of speech that made you feel so relaxed and at ease. It was almost as if your ears were being tickled and your mind was being massaged. If this has ever happened to you, whether in person, over the phone, or even while watching television, most likely the speaker's representational wiring was the opposite of yours, and she was naturally accessing your recessive system.

In the day-care center example, President Reagan starts with the auditory system, moves to the kinesthetic system, and ends with the visual system. The sentence has a different impact on a listener who is wired with an auditory primary, a kinesthetic secondary, and visual recessive system than someone who is wired in the opposite manner. While this sentence alone will not induce a hypnotic trance, by organizing segments of your discussion or structuring sections of your presentation to work from people's primary to recessive systems, you will be able to speak directly to their subconscious minds.

When speaking to large groups, one way you can determine whether you have group rapport is through "sampling." It's best if you can meet a few members of the audience prior to the presentation to get an idea of their wiring, but it is not necessary. Pick five or six people who occupy easy-to-spot positions in the audience, either in the first couple of rows or at the end of an aisle.

From this sample of the audience, you can judge how your presentation is proceeding and determine what adjustments are needed as you progress. During the presentation, try to keep the majority of the sample members on the "edge of their seats," meaning their internal dialogues are very engaged. Since it is likely there will be a diverse variety of representational system wiring among the members in the sample, lead several of them into a trance by using the recessive system access technique.

Now most people assume that a speaker is boring if listeners seem to be sleeping when she is talking, and this is true if the speaker didn't intend for them to close their eyes. However, when it is done purposefully, it actually indicates the speaker is in complete control of rapport with the audience.

How do you know when someone is in a trance? It's more comfortable for most people to enter a trance by closing their eyes. So you literally want them to close their eyes or have to fight to keep their eyes open. When they're in the deepest trance, their eyes will slowly move back and forth, and you can watch the impression of the iris as it moves under the eyelid (like rapid eye movement during deep sleep). Other people will enter a trance with their eyes open. Their pupils will dilate and it's almost as if their eyes become "vacant."

The recessive system access technique is used most frequently because it naturally fits into the flow of a conversation. Let's examine some other ways to guide a listener's internal dialogue.

Contradiction and Confusion

> Chile—July 27, 1979
> Evidence continues to pile up that for some unexplained rea-
> son our diplomats have 20/20 vision with regard to the faults
> of our friends.[22]

Here the technique is contradiction and confusion. In this example, President Reagan layers different levels of "contradiction." First,
there is a contradiction between "evidence piling up" and "for some
unexplained reason." Logic dictates that if you have evidence, you
should be able to explain what's happening. There shouldn't be an
"unexplained reason." The usage of "20/20 vision" also contradicts
the rest of the sentence. Normally, you would expect the exact opposite statement, such as "our diplomats are blind with regard to the
faults of our friends."

These contradictions cause the listener's internal dialogue to
work harder to understand the meaning of what is actually being
said. While this internal debate is occurring, the speaker is delivering
more words. The resulting backup causes the internal dialogue to
become overwhelmed. The internal dialogue may even say, "I give
up." Assuming rapport is present, the customer's conscious mind
gently slips away, and at this point you can deliver the message you
desire.

However, without the credibility of rapport, you've only alien-
ated the listener. Therefore, this technique is risky and works best in
certain high rapport accounts.

Simulation

> Olympics—September 19, 1978
> A wave is beginning to roll, a worldwide wave and it may just
> break over the heads of the International Olympic Committee.

A great many people don't want the 1980 Olympics held in Moscow![23]

Here is the technique of simulation. Simulation is structuring language to provoke a particular emotional or physical response. For example, as you read about the wave rolling, you may have naturally increased the pace of your reading and the pitch of your internal voice (like a wave) until it broke in the second sentence. In this way, the structure of the communication simulates the wave.

Here's another example of simulation that illustrates how words can impact the body. You probably have never noticed it, but you breathe in a certain way, and as you breathe, you can feel your chest rising and falling. There's also a certain sensation in your nose when you breathe and you are able to feel the temperature of the air. As you become more aware of your breathing, it's harder to concentrate on other details. Reading this description about breathing may have even simulated a change in your breathing pattern.

Simulation exercises the senses, engages the personality, and occupies the internal dialogue. Salespeople want the customer to simulate the benefits and feelings of owning their product during the sales cycle. Car salespeople are experts at using simulation. The test drive is a way to get the buyer to simulate the fantasy of owning the car. They want you to enjoy the smoothness of the ride, experience the "new car" aroma, and feel the power of the acceleration. They know a customer who successfully simulates ownership during the test drive is a good prospect for a sale. The same principle applies to Hitters. If they can get the prospect to envision being a happy customer while still in the sales cycle, they are well on the road to winning the deal.

Imagination

Endangered Species—July 6, 1977
How much do you miss dinosaurs? Would your life be richer

if those giant prehistoric flying lizards occasionally settled on your front lawn?[24]

Here the technique is imagination, which entails making the listener form mental images, concepts, situations, and sensations that do not exist or have yet to be experienced. It's a very effective technique to guide the internal dialogue.

The first question in the example causes the listener to create the mental image of a dinosaur. Did you picture a *Tyrannosaurus rex?* a brontosaurus? a velociraptor? The creation of the first image is relatively easy. Just as soon as listeners have created their first image, however, they are forced to make another. The second question requires listeners to create an image of a specific type of "flying lizard" and then place it on their front lawn. This request requires much more effort, as listeners have been directed to create a picture of a creature they probably haven't experienced and combine it with something they see every day. Invoking imagination makes the internal dialogue very busy!

Metaphor

> Ocean Mining—October 10, 1978
> It may not be the shot around the world, but the US has finally told the U.N. to stop pushing us around.[25]

Metaphor is the technique here. The "shot heard round the world" is the phrase given to the first musket fire of the Revolutionary War. Metaphors deliver a lot of information quickly as they link to past receptive states. In this example, the skirmish on the Lexington Green was the start of the American fight for independence from an oppressive government. It's a source of national pride and patriotism. Transposing these feelings of independence onto a United Nations that is "pushing" us around is a very powerful transference of meaning.

Split Brain

> Seal Hunt—May 15, 1978
> It sometimes seems we can get more emotionally aroused over mistreatment of animals than we can if the victims are human. A few weeks ago a writer in the *Los Angeles Times,* did an article on the 1978 Canadian baby seal hunt. One line in the article was very thought provoking, "If seal pups were as ugly as lobsters, their harvest would go unnoticed." Accompanying his article was a photo that proved his point. It was a snow baby seal with its black nose and round eyes looking like something you'd put in the nursery for children to cuddle.[26]

The split brain technique here in essence involves separating the brain by making the listener carry on two concurrent internal conversations. One way to do this is to force the listener to follow separate streams of logic. For example, the first sentence about people becoming "more emotionally aroused over mistreatment of animals than people" is followed by a completely different stream of logic in the next sentence introducing the Canadian baby seal hunt. The listener holds the thought of the first sentence during the second sentence.

Another, more sophisticated example of the split brain technique is to have a factual conversation with the "logical" side of the brain while carrying on another stimulating discussion with the "creative" side of the brain. In the seal hunt example, the first and second sentences start unique streams of logic that are resolved by the side of the brain that solves problems. The third and fifth sentences, which include "ugly as lobsters" and "black nose and round eyes," would be handled by the opposite side of the brain, which is proficient in the arts and drawing.

The split brain technique works well in sales situations since most salespeople are trained, experienced, and comfortable presenting the logical reasons, arguments, and benefits of selecting their product. By adding an artistic dimension of dramatization to the humdrum of a logical dissertation, the entire brain is stimulated and the story is brought to life.

Belief System

> Vietnam I—November 30, 1976
> Government has no greater responsibility than to protect the least among us wherever he may be in the world if his right to life, liberty and the pursuit of happiness is being unjustly denied.[27]

Here the technique applies to belief systems. Over the years, your belief system is formed based on observation, experience, and faith. It may include a spiritual belief in the afterlife, a scientific belief in the big bang theory, or a hope in the Chicago Cubs winning the World Series.

The unique aspect of these philosophical frameworks is that all people consider their own belief system correct. Presenting a message that is in alignment with the listener's belief system adds credibility to a message. Natural defenses of skepticism are lowered since the message is concealed within the Trojan Horse of an existing belief system.

Broadcast-Unicast Messages

> The Hope of Mankind—September 21, 1976
> In a dinner at Mt. Vernon back in revolutionary times, Lafayette turned to his host and said, "General Washington,

you Americans even in war and desperate times have a superb spirit. You are happy and you are confident. Why is it?" Washington answered, "There is freedom, there is space for a man to be alone and think and there are friends who owe each other nothing but affection."[28]

This story is an example of the broadcast-unicast technique. Underneath the surface, these anecdotes, parables, and stories have layers of interpretations that convey moral and spiritual lessons.

From the story above, you could infer many different meanings. To a historian, it is an account of an intriguing conversation between two great statesmen. To a patriot, it is a story about the importance of freedom. To the insecure, it is a message to be confident. It's also about the importance of friendship, gratefulness, and the American spirit. From a single story, listeners derive their own personal meaning. Their internal dialogue turns inward because it believes the story is intended solely for them.

CONCLUSION

Whether they realize it or not, all salespeople are natural hypnotists who use the power of suggestion to persuade customers to buy. However, unlike professional practitioners of medical or therapeutic hypnosis, they do not place customers into a stuporous trance or deep sleep while the suggestions are instilled. Rather, they use sales hypnosis during the course of normal conversation by speaking with customers in their own terms and at all levels of their individual personality and needs.

Heavy Hitters use hypnosis to disarm customers' conscious defenses. Like therapeutic hypnotists who want to solve their clients' problems, they start by establishing relationships based upon mutual trust and rapport. Both Heavy Hitters and professional hypnotists adapt their use of language to provide individualized treatment, and they both guide their clients through the process of finding the correct solution. Finally, they both use the power of words to implant posthypnotic suggestions in order to create profound changes in attitudes and actions.

The customer's conscious mind acts like an emotion-suppressing system. It is full of doubt, cynicism, and distrust. It is the cautious skeptic that is continually protecting the buyer from making bad choices or forming ill-advised relationships. Therefore, even truthful, helpful information that is presented in the customer's best interest tends to be discounted or ignored.

Fortunately for Hitters, the conscious and subconscious minds can operate together or independently. Intuitive persuasion is a communication strategy for managing a customer's internal dialogue in order to talk directly to one's subconscious mind.

Since the subconscious mind has access to more information, it has ultimate approval in the decision-making process. As Dr. Milton Erickson wrote, "Your conscious mind is very intelligent, but your unconscious mind is a lot smarter."[29]

Dr. Erickson also believed that hypnosis does not really exist. Since hypnosis is nothing more than communication, his assessment is correct. Rather, hypnosis and intuitive persuasion are models for describing how thoughts can be structured and words communicated to produce desired responses. While hypnosis doesn't exist, the words spoken and their impact are quite real.

Over the years, I have conducted training classes with my sales teams about intuitive persuasion. During one of these sessions, I used the recessive system technique to place a cynical salesperson into a trance. While everyone else was unaware of any difference in my presentation style, the salesperson was fighting hard to keep his eyes open. After a few more minutes, he slipped into a deep trance. At that point, I interrupted his slumber and asked him to describe his experience to the surprised audience. He explained that although he could hear my words and understand their meaning, something else made him feel very comfortable and relaxed. He enjoyed it and didn't want it to end.

Whereupon I remarked, "I hope all of our sales calls are as satisfying."

Epilogue

THE ESSENCE and purpose of this entire book can be distilled into one analogy—"The Sales Iceberg." The visible portion of the iceberg above the water represents the logic of selling. All salespeople are aware of their products' features, benefits, and specifications. Their companies have identified processes to educate customers about their products and established procedures to determine customers' business qualifications and technical requirements.

However, underneath the waterline is the unseen, intangible part of the sales process that is ultimately responsible for the decision being made. The submerged portion symbolizes the influence of human nature during the sales process. Since most salespeople find the human element of selling to be more complex, unpredictable, and difficult to manage, they don't fully take advantage of customer behavior or they misinterpret and ignore it.

Unfortunately, most companies only train their salespeople on the logic of selecting a product. And like a ship on the Arctic Ocean, salespeople who aren't aware of the part of the iceberg that cannot be seen do not know whether they will survive or perish on the voyage. Meanwhile, Heavy Hitters successfully reach their destination by using intuition to plot a course based upon their customers' behavior.

At the foundation of all of sales is a relationship between people. Just as a submerged block of ice can sink a ship, misunderstanding human nature can wreck any business or personal relationship. Of course, many of the concepts covered in this book can also be applied to your personal relationships with your spouse, children, relatives, and friends. Even these relationships require time, effort, and rapport to succeed. You have to wonder how many marriages, friendships, and family relationships have failed because someone wouldn't listen, didn't stay in touch, or couldn't see the other person's point of view.

I have saved perhaps the most important point regarding Heavy Hitters for last. This final lesson about being a Heavy Hitter took me many years to learn. A very good friend of mine, who's made and lost millions of dollars during his lifetime, recently told me, "Never let your successes go to your head, and never let your failures go to your heart." He's right. You will have good quarters and bad ones. You will win large deals and lose them. Hopefully, you will succeed more often than you will fail.

I honestly cannot remember whether the third quarter of 1996 was a good or bad one. I can barely remember what happened just a few quarters ago. However, I do remember that at that moment in time it was the most important quarter ever and my drive to succeed dominated all my thoughts. I also remember that I worked with some very talented people whom I desperately wanted to impress.

As salespeople, our world is structured on a value system that is intimately tied to the production of a single revenue number. We post this number monthly, quarterly, and yearly. This number is how the rest of our world measures our contribution, and it is also how we tend to judge our own worth.

However, you will never be truly happy or satisfied if you measure your self-worth solely by the revenue you generate. You know you are not a good person because you make your number, just as you are not a bad person if you don't. Life is about being with your family and friends and, most importantly, having a relationship with your creator. These relationships are a true reflection of your life's significance.

And now I would like to have a final word with your subconscious mind.

Your genetics may explain your predispositions in life, such as your height and the color of your eyes, but they certainly don't decide your ability to learn something new. Understanding and using these new language models will make you not only a better salesperson but a better person.

Your brain has a limitless capability. It knows how to absorb seemingly disconnected happenings into meaningful structured experiences. It has been accumulating these experiences for decades and can create completely new ways to use this information to accomplish what you want so you can get more enjoyment from life.

While some people mistakenly believe they have only one chance to be a success, in fact life provides endless opportunities to those who allow their subconscious minds to be a positive force in their lives. All you have to do is pay attention to it, just as you would listen to your best friend. It can help you recognize an opportunity and tell you when to take a chance. And as your subconscious mind already knows, you are destined for great things.

Notes

1. *Advanced Techniques of Hypnosis and Therapy: Selected Papers of Milton H. Erickson, M.D.,* ed. Jay Haley (New York: Grune & Stratton, 1967).
2. Ibid.
3. Robert Lee Holtz, "NASA Failures Prompt Vow of Program Reform," *Los Angeles Times,* 8 December 1999, 1.
4. Victoria Neufeldt, ed., *Webster's New World College Dictionary,* 3d ed. (New York: Prentice Hall, 1996).
5. Bill Walsh with Brian Billick and James A. Peterson, *Finding the Winning Edge* (Champaign, Ill.: Sports Publishing Inc., 1998).
6. Elizabeth Knowles, ed., *Oxford Dictionary of Quotations,* 5th ed. (New York: Oxford University Press, 1999).
7. Johanna McGeary, "Odd Man Out," *Time* (10 September 2001): 22–32.
8. *Thomas Jefferson: Writings,* ed. Merrill D. Peterson (New York: Library of America, 1984).
9. Nathan Haskell Dole, ed. *John Bartlett's Familiar Quotations,* 16th ed. (Boston: Little, Brown and Company, 1992).
10. Sun Tzu, *The Art of War,* ed. James Clavell (New York: Delacorte Press, 1983).
11. Ibid.
12. Niccolò Machiavelli, *The Prince,* ed. Jean-Pierre Barricelli (New York: Barron's Educational Services, 1975).
13. Dole, *John Bartlett's Familiar Quotations.*

14. Andrea Gabor, *The Capitalist Philosophers: The Geniuses of Modern Business—Their Lives, Times, and Ideas* (New York: Crown Business, 2000).

15. Calvin S. Hall, Gardner Lindzey, and John B. Campbell, *Theories of Personality,* 4th ed. (New York: John Wiley and Sons, 1997).

16. Lawrence Pervin and Oliver John, eds., *Handbook of Personality: Theory and Research,* 2d ed. (New York: The Guilford Press, 1999).

17. Laurence Urdang, ed., *The American Century Dictionary* (New York: Warner Books, 1995).

18. *Reagan, in His Own Hand: The Writings of Ronald Reagan That Reveal His Revolutionary Vision for America,* ed. Kiron K. Skinner, Annelise Anderson, and Martin Anderson (New York: Free Press, 2001).

19. *Reagan, in His Own Hand.*

20. Michael Nash, "The Truth and the Hype of Hypnosis," *Scientific American,* July 2001, 47–55.

21. *Reagan, in His Own Hand.*

22. Ibid.

23. Ibid.

24. Ibid.

25. Ibid.

26. Ibid.

27. Ibid.

28. Ibid.

29. Kenneth S. Bowers, *Hypnosis for the Seriously Curious* (New York: W.W. Norton, 1983).

Bibliography

Andrews, Robert, Mary Briggs, and Michael Siedel, eds. *Columbia World of Quotations.* New York: Columbia University Press, 1996.

Bowers, Kenneth S. *Hypnosis for the Seriously Curious.* New York: W.W. Norton, 1983.

Dole, Nathan Haskell, ed. *John Bartlett's Familiar Quotations.* 16th ed. Boston: Little, Brown and Company, 1992.

Erickson, Milton H. *Advanced Techniques of Hypnosis and Therapy: Selected Papers of Milton H. Erickson.* Edited by Jay Haley. New York: Grune & Stratton, 1967.

Gabor, Andrea. *The Capitalist Philosophers: The Geniuses of Modern Business—Their Lives, Times, and Ideas.* New York: Crown Business, 2000.

Hall, Calvin S., Gardner Lindzey, and John B. Campbell. *Theories of Personality.* 4th ed. New York: John Wiley and Sons, 1997.

Holtz, Robert Lee. "NASA Failures Prompt Vow of Program Reform." *Los Angeles Times,* 8 December 1999, 1.

Knowles, Elizabeth, ed. *Oxford Dictionary of Quotations.* 5th ed. New York: Oxford University Press, 1999.

Machiavelli, Niccolò. *The Prince.* Edited by Jean-Pierre Barricelli. New York: Barron's Educational Services, 1975.

Maslow, Abraham. *Toward a Psychology of Being.* 2d ed. Princeton, N.J.: Van Nostrand Reinhold, 1968.

McGeary, Johanna. "Odd Man Out." *Time* (10 September 2001): 22–32.

Nash, Michael. "The Truth and the Hype of Hypnosis." *Scientific American,* July 2001, 47–55.

Neufeldt, Victoria, ed. *Webster's New World College Dictionary.* 3d ed. New York: Prentice Hall, 1996.

Pervin, Lawrence, and Oliver John, eds. *Handbook of Personality: Theory and Research.* 2d ed. New York: The Guilford Press, 1999.

Reagan, Ronald. *Reagan, in His Own Hand: The Writings of Ronald Reagan That Reveal His Revolutionary Vision for America.* Edited by Kiron K. Skinner, Annelise Anderson, and Martin Anderson. New York: Free Press, 2001.

Sun Tzu. *The Art of War.* Edited by James Clavell. New York: Delacorte Press, 1983.

Urdang, Laurence, ed. *The American Century Dictionary.* New York: Warner Books, 1995.

Walsh, Bill, with Brian Billick and James A. Peterson. *Finding the Winning Edge.* Champaign, Ill.: Sports Publishing Inc., 1998.

Glossary

Agreeableness One of the factors in the five-factor model; it describes how well people get along in group settings and their level of independence.

Anchor The conscious, premeditated association of a specific feeling to an object.

Auditory A person who processes information primarily using the auditory representational system.

Belonging needs People's natural disposition to want to be part of a group in order to share similar interests and values, a sense of community, and affectionate relationships.

Benefaction To derive an advantage that contributes to one's well-being, such as happiness, esteem, power, or wealth, that results in influencing the way the customer behaves during the sales cycle.

Coach A friend and ally within the customer's company who provides accurate information about the sales cycle and promotes the Heavy Hitter's solution.

Computer communication model The established standards, protocols, and methods that ensure disparate computers can transmit and receive information correctly.

Congruence Truthful communication defined when all layers of the human communication model are in agreement.

Conscientiousness One of the factors in the five-factor model; it describes a person's degree of diligence and ability to complete tasks.

Conscious mind The part of the mind that a person controls.

Content layer The actual words spoken during the course of a conversation.

Customer placebo Misleading information presented by the customer to nonfavored vendors, such as false buying signs and a display of more product interest than actually exists.

Esteem needs The need to be deemed an expert and the need for power or position.

Extraversion One of the factors in the five-factor model; it describes a person's capabilities to build and manage relationships.

Five-factor model A formal model for classifying personality types that includes five personality factors: negative emotionality, extraversion, openness, agreeableness, and conscientiousness. Each of these factors has six facets, and each facet has a low, medium, and high measurement.

Flashbulb episode An emotional, physical, or cerebral experience that is so overpowering that it is permanently imprinted in short-term memory.

General word A word that is nonspecific in meaning and requires the use of operators to achieve a specific interpretation.

Heavy Hitter A successful high-technology salesperson.

Human communication model The layers of verbal and nonverbal communication (including the phonetic, content, purpose, representational system, internal dialogue, and physical layers) used by people to convey and interpret thoughts, personality, and experiences.

Hypnosis A communication model for describing how thoughts can be structured and words communicated to produce desired responses.

Incongruence Misleading communication where layers of the human communication model contradict each other.

Internal dialogue The never-ending stream of communication inside the mind that represents honest, unedited, and deep feelings.

Intersecting activities Interests, hobbies, and personal pursuits by which people display their personality types, representational system wiring, and value systems.

Intuitive persuasion The strategy to instill a message in the customer's mind by sensing all the data emanating from the customer, comparing the current scenario to past situations, creating a deep receptive state, and guiding the customer's internal dialogue.

Kinesthetic A person who processes information primarily using the kinesthetic representational system.

Leading The process of influencing another person's actions by purposely changing yours.

Linkage The connection of two nonrelated messages together in order to have the second message more readily accepted by the listener.

Marking Using body language and speech to highlight spoken words so that they are remembered by the subconscious mind.

Maslow's hierarchy of needs The theory explaining that human beings want to satisfy an ever-escalating set of needs, which begin with biological deficiencies, ascend through social requirements, and ultimately culminate in the fulfillment of deeper spiritual needs.

Mirroring The conscious act of modifying your behavior to fit into your surroundings.

Models Descriptions and representations of how systems work.

Negative emotionality One of the factors in the five-factor model; it describes a person's tolerance for stress, anger, and worry.

Neurolinguistics The study of how the brain uses and interprets language.

Neutral wording The presentation of ideas and thoughts without any reference to representational systems.

Openness One of the factors in the five-factor model; it describes whether a person prefers a familiar environment with defined daily routines or seeks variety and is open to new experiences.

Operator An additional word that is added to a general word to more accurately convey meaning.

Pacing The natural process of adjusting your tempo to your environment.

Phonetic layer The enunciation and vocal sounds of the actual words being spoken.

Physical layer Also known as body language, the nonverbal communication emitted by a person's body posture.

Physiological needs Basic needs that are necessary for survival such as food, air, sleep, and shelter. For Hitters, physiological needs include the stability of their company, the competitiveness of their product, and the soundness of the marketplace.

Primary representational system The default or main mode of communication (either visual, auditory, or kinesthetic) that a person is most comfortable using and uses most often.

Purpose layer The intentional assembling of words to selfishly communicate an idea or experience.

Rapport A special relationship between two or more individuals based upon harmonious communication.

Receptive state The positive environment that enables a message to be accepted and remembered.

Representational system wiring The mind's ability to use a unique combination and amount of the visual, auditory, and kinesthetic representational systems.

Representational system/representational system layer The mind's method of gathering information, accumulating knowledge, and recording experiences based upon one of three senses—visual, auditory, or kinesthetic.

Safety needs Needs that establish stability, such as home, family, and religion. In sales, safety needs include information on how to compete with other vendors and the competency of the Hitter's manager.

Sales intuition The ability to read and anticipate a customer's actions beforehand.

Search loop A person's unsuccessful search for information by repeatedly accessing each of the representational systems.

Selection pressure The pressure on the salesperson to promptly answer the customer's question in order for the response to be perceived as truthful.

Self-actualization The personal maturity that is achieved after all physiological, safety, belonging, and esteem needs have been satisfied.

Subconscious mind The part of the mind that a person doesn't control but still collects information and is capable of influencing behavior. Also referred to as the unconscious mind.

Technical specification language   The androgynous, nonpersonal, and technical communication that is one of the primary languages the high-technology customer speaks.

Triangulation   The process of identifying and validating information by using different sources.

Unverifiable statement   A statement that elicits skepticism since the internal dialogue does not accept it as being true.

VAK count/VAK keyword count   Tally of a person's use of visual, auditory, and kinesthetic keywords in order to determine their representational system wiring.

Verifiable statement   A statement that the listener will accept as true after it is validated by the internal dialogue.

Vignette   Short interactions of dialogue between the Heavy Hitter and the customer, usually about one topic or conversational theme.

Visual   A person who processes information primarily using the visual representational system.

Index

A

accounts, qualifying, 145–148
Advanced Techniques of Hypnosis and Therapy: Selected Papers of Milton H. Erickson, M.D. (Haley, ed.), 3
agreeableness, 241–243
agreeable personalities, 227–228
alliterations, 202
alpha position, 211
amateur managers, 197–199
anchors, 74–76, 180
answer retrieval, 253–255
applying sales management styles, 201–202
Art of War, The (Sun Tzu), 161–162
assessments
  by customers, 32
  plotting individual, 171
  representational systems, 125–126
  types of, 36–37
association (for memory), 248
attachment theory of relationships, 158–159
attack/retreat strategy, 153–154
attention to details, 257
attributes of successful salespeople, x–xii
Auditories
  adjusting communication to, 38
  eye contact of, 89
  eye movements of, 88
  hand movements of, 110–111
  handshakes of, 109
  self-listening of, 69
  speaking characteristics of, 129–130
  See also representational systems
awards, 210

B

barbecue test, 241
baseball diamond analogy (triangulation diamond), 51–55
behavior
  interrupted patterns of, 183
  leading, 177
  passing judgments on, 192
  society's guidelines for, 108
belief system technique, 293
belonging needs of Hitters, 207–210
benefactions
  conscious mind and, 103
  customer benefaction form, 227
  customers', 59
  identifying others', 224, 226–227
  knowing your listener's, 264–265
  of listeners, 265–268
  mentioned, 8–9, 53–54, 55–58, 116
  rapport-building, 177–178
body language
  definition of, 102

body language, *continued*
eye movements, 86–89
and group meetings, 117–119
three-dimensionality of, 40–41
types of, 108–113
body posture, observing, 114–117
brain
capacity of, 299
compared to computers, 80–84, 86
logical/creative sides of, 292
split brain technique, 292–293
See also memory
breathing, 111–112, 122, 127
broadcast-unicast messages technique,
293–294
bullies, 169–170, 172–173
bush leaguers, characteristics of, 11–12

C
calibrating eye movements, 94–98
Callas, Constantine, 2
call to action, 159
categories of information technology
(IT) organizations, 164–169
characteristics
of bush leaguers, 11–12
of Heavy Hitters, 6–7
of high-technology sales, 10–11
of people involved in product selection, 169–172
speaking, 129–130, 130–132,
132–133
technical specification language,
28–29
clichés/sayings, 69–74
Clinton, Bill, 262
closed body posture, 118–119
coaches
developing, 239, 243
example of, 205–206
ideal, 144
importance of, 162
selecting, 215–218

coaching relationships, establishing, 7,
217–218
communication
adjusting, to Auditories, 38
alliterations, 202
biological factors in, 137
conscious/subconscious, 104, 280
content layer of, 20–29, 43–44
customer examples, 26–29
between different representational
systems, 135
events, 15–16
flexibility, 18
general versus specific words, 22, 24
Human Communication Model,
18–19, 119
hypnotic qualities, 4–5
internal dialogue layer, 38–39
kinship in, 223–224, 257
language skills, xi
marking, 173–174
meaningful conversations, 223–234
operators, 24–26
phonetic layer, 19–20
physical changes during, 106–107
physical layer, 39–43
purpose layer, 30–37
representational system layer, 37–38
seven-layer computer communication model, 17–18, 23
verbal/nonverbal, 3–4
See also deeper meaning of language
company fit, 148–149
compensation, 212
competence, 59
competition
attacking, 153–154
enemies in the sales cycle, 151, 201
time as, 106, 145
components of intuition, 249–252
computers, compared to brain, 80–84,
8. *See also* brain; memory
confusion, 289

congruence, 133–134, 262–264, 280
conscientiousness, 243–247
conscious mind, benefactions and, 103
consciousness, states of, 182
conscious/subconscious communication, 104, 280
content layer of communication, 20–29, 43–44
contradiction/confusion technique, 289
conversations, 119, 223–234, 287
conviction, 262–264, 280–281
credibility, 9
criteria for sales, 59
criticism, 197, 201, 239
culture, and handshakes, 110
customer examples, using, 26–29
customer interaction vignette, 31
customer puzzles, 256–257
customers, xiii
  conscious mind of, 277
  customer benefaction form, 227
  fit of, 148–149
  identifying wiring of, 76–77
  placebos for, 147
  relationships with, 16
  triangulation by, 143
  using language of, 264–265
  See also rapport
cycles. *See* sales cycles

D

deal qualification, 8, 145–148
decoding information, 250
deeper meaning of language
  establishing/maintaining rapport, 265–267
  five steps of (overview), 261
  guiding listeners' internal dialogue, 268–275
  message delivery, 262–265, 275–276
  See also communication; language
desires. *See* benefactions

details, attending to, 257
disagreements, 51
dominant representational systems, 61–62, 69, 92–93, 109
duds, 170–171

E

editing process for spoken words, 39
enemies in the sales cycle, 152, 201
engagement, and rapport, states of, 181–183
engineers, presales/system, 49
Erickson, Milton, 2–4, 5, 294
esteem needs of Hitters, 210–211
evolution of sales cycles, 147
executive category of IT organizations, 165–166, 167
experiences, cataloguing of, 78
expressive management style, 193–194
external assessments, 36–37
extraversion, 235–237
eye contact, 89
eye movements
  calibrating, 94–98
  meanings of different, 86–89
  memory and, 89–90
  and VAK counts, 98–99

F

facets of personality factors
  agreeableness, 241
  conscientiousness, 244
  extraversion, 235
  negative emotionality, 230
  openness, 238
facial expressions, 112–114
failure, results of, 44
fantasy theme of sales cycle, 5, 159–161
fear, uncertainty, and doubt (FUD), 153
feedback, 105, 201
first and last memories of sales calls, 248

fit, customer, 148–149
five-factor model of personality types.
   See personality factors
flashbulb episodes, 253
flexibility, 144–145, 190
formula for intuitive persuasion, 285
formula for sales intuition, 282
foundation-laying, 263, 268
Freudian slips, 39
friendships, 220–228, 241. *See also*
   relationships
FUD (fear, uncertainty, and doubt),
   153

G
gathering of information, 33–34
gestures, 110–111
glossary of terms, 305–310
goals
   of communication, 30
   of customers, 16
   of sales organizations, 9–10
   of triangulation, 143
   See also benefactions
Goldin, Daniel, 44
groups, 29, 117–119, 208–210,
   218–220, 288. *See also* meetings

H
Haley, Jay, 3
hand movements, 110–111
handshakes, 109–110, 122
Heavy Hitters/salespeople
   about, xii–xiii, 49
   attributes of, 163
   attributes of successful, x–xii
   as breed apart, 6–7
   challenges for, 184
   then and now, 202–203
   work areas of, 161
hierarchy of needs, 188, 203,
   204–213, 225–226
high-technology sales, 9–13

hiring process, 255
human communication model,
   18–19, 41–42, 119. *See also*
   representational systems
humor, 75–76
hypnosis, 4–5, 294–296

I
iceberg analogy, 297
identifying your position. *See* triangulation
imagery, 272
imagination technique, 290–291
influencing another person, 105–106,
   111, 275–276
information
   conveying, 80, 139
   detaching technique, 180–181
   interpreting/filtering, 140–142
   sources of inside, 144
   storage of, 251
   triangulating, 142–143
information technology (IT),
   163–165
inside team sales, 50
integrity, 9
internal assessments, 36–37
internal dialogue layer of communication, 38–39, 102, 128–129
internal dialogues
   awareness of, 284
   guiding listeners', 268–275, 285
   leading, 177–178
   observing, 85–86
   techniques for guiding listeners',
      286–294
   your, 84–85
interpreting information, 139
intersecting activities, 221–223, 265
introverts, 235
intuition
   in deal qualification, 147
   development of, 8

importance of, xi–xii
of mentors, 193
sales, 249–256
sales intuition cube, 253
using, 44
intuitive persuasion, 275–276, 281–
284, 284–286
investments during sales cycle, 156

J
job satisfaction, 212
juice, 170, 173

K
key access files, 250
keywords, VAK
auditory primary system, 63, 130
kinesthetic primary system, 63–64
VAK keyword count charts, 64–65
VAK keyword count patterns, 67–
69, 98–99
visual primary system, 62–63
See also "Looking Out the Window"
(Reagan); representational systems
kinesthetic representational system eye
movements, 88
Kinesthetics
adjusting communication to, 38
eye contact of, 89
hand movements of, 110–111
handshakes of, 109
speaking characteristics of, 131,
132–133
See also representational systems
kinship in communication, 221, 223–
224, 257

L
language
of activities, 223–234
alliterations, 202
editing process for spoken words, 39
simulation, 289–290

technical specification, 28–29
word selection, 37–38, 167
See also communication; deeper
meaning of language
layers of human communication,
42–43. *See also* human communication model
leading
behavior, 177
conversations, 120–123, 134
internal dialogues, 177–178
linkage, 179
listeners
benefaction of, 265–268
conscious mind of, 283–284
guiding inner dialogue of your,
268–275, 286–294
message delivery to subconscious
mind of, 275–276
long-term memory, 72, 95
long-term relationships, 216, 221–
228
"Looking Out the Window" (Reagan),
269–275, 279–280, 283

M
management
in the past, 203
of sales cycle, 138–139
styles of, 191–192, 201–202
See also strategies
management category of IT organizations, 163–164, 165
managers
amateur, 197–199
expressive, 193–194
micromanagers, 199–200
overconfident, 200–201
relationships with salespeople,
213–214
roles of, 13
sales, 50–51
sergeant, 195–196

managers, *continued*
  Teflon, 196–197
  understanding your, 189–190
marking, 173–174, 179
Martin, Steve, xiii–xv
Maslow, Abraham, 188, 204
Maslow's hierarchy of needs, 188, 203, 204–213, 225–226
meaning of language. *See* deeper meaning of language
meetings, 58–60, 124–129, 218–220. *See also* groups
memory
  and eye movements, 89–90
  improving sales call, 247–249
  short-term/long-term, 72, 93–94, 95
mental imagery, 272
mentors, 192–193
message delivery
  broadcast-unicast, 293–294
  conviction/congruence in, 262–264
  in different languages, 264–265
  using intuitive persuasion, 275–276
metaphor technique, 290–291
methodologies, established, 1–2
micromanagers, 199–200
mind-reading, 284–286
mirroring, 120–129, 134, 135
mistakes, 11–12, 157
model of personality types. *See* personality factors
motivation, 213, 224–227
MVP (motivate, value, and praise), 213
Myers-Briggs Type Inventory (MBTI), 227–228

N
name-dropping, 27
negative emotionality, 230–234
nervousness, indicators of, 110
neurolinguistics, 2–4, 5

O
observing internal dialogues, 85–86, 116–117

open body posture, 118–119
openness, 237–241
operators, 21, 24–26
organizations. *See* sales organizations
orientation language, 265
overconfident managers, 200–201

P
pacing conversations, 120–123
pain in organizations, 166
participation pie, 218–220
peer groups, 29
perceptive persuasion, 105
personal fit, 59, 148–149
personalities, 67, 227–228
personality factors
  agreeableness, 227–228, 241–243
  conscientiousness, 243–247
  extraversion, 235–237
  negative emotionality, 230–234
  openness, 237–241
persuasion, 7–8, 105, 260
phases of the sales cycle, 158–161
phonetic layer of communication, 19–20, 43, 102
phonetics, 102–103
physical changes, during communication, 106–107
physical communication language, 264–265
physical layer of communication, 39–43, 102
physiological needs of Hitters, 206–207
placebos, 147
politics theme of sales cycle, 159–161
posture, 114–117, 117–119. *See also* body language
Powell, Colin, 98–99
praise, 213
premises of the sales cycle, 139–145
presales engineers, 49
presentations, 173–181, 184–185
primary representational systems, 92–93, 287

product category of IT organizations, 164–165

product theme of sales cycle, 159–161

proposals, requests for, 151

protect strategy, 155

purpose layer of communication, 30–37

pyramid of meeting success, 58–60, 61

Q

quadrants of the sales cycle, 149–152, 153–155

qualifying an account, 8, 145–148

R

radio address examples, Reagan's
belief system, 293
broadcast-unicast messages, 293–294
contradiction and confusion, 289
imagination, 290–291
"Looking Out the Window" (Reagan), 269–275, 279–280, 283
metaphor, 291
recessive system access, 286–288
simulation, 289–290
split brain, 292–293

rapport
breaking, 285
building, 6
customer fit, 148–149
and engagement, states of, 181–183
establishing, 134–135, 151
example of, 115–116
gaining, 126
importance of, 7–9, 60
and internal dialogue, 282–283
nonexistent, 75
during presentations, 173–181
representational systems and, 60–64
for successful relationships, 105
testing by mirroring, 122–123
with your listener, 265–267

with your sales manager, 189–190
See also relationships

reading minds, 284–286

read of customers, 143

Reagan, in His Own Hand (Reagan), 262–263

Reagan, Ronald, 262–263, 269–275, 279–280

receptive states, creating, 265–267, 273

recessive representational systems, 73, 109

recessive system access, 286–288

references/referring, 27–28

relationships
attachment theory of, 158–159
building personal, xi
with customers, 16
establishing coaching, 217–218
as foundation of sales, 297–298
friendships, 220–228, 241
long-term, 216
mentors, 192–193
personal fit between people, 59
with sales managers, 213–214
strategies for building, 195
win-win, 8–9
See also customers; rapport

replies/responses of Heavy Hitters, 32–33, 34–35

representational system layer of communication, 37–38

representational systems
adapting to anothers', 190
assessing someone's, 125–126
communicating between different, 135–136
consciousness of others', 61
determining someone else's, 58, 62, 65–67
dominant, 61–62
exercises, generalization, 166–168
generalizations about, 168–181
identification of your sales manager's, 190

representational systems, *continued*
  and information processing, 77–78
  language of different, 264
  layers of, 102
  learning your, 64–65
  overview of, 46–48
  understanding your own, 134
  VAK keyword count patterns, 67–69, 98–99
  visual primary, 38
  See also Auditories; Kinesthetics; Visuals
requests for proposal (RFP), 151
retreat strategy, 153–154
revenues, 213
roles of managers, 13

S
safety needs of Hitters, 207
sales
  criteria for, 59
  formula for sales intuition, 282
  high-technology, 9–13
  inside team, 50
  intangible side of, 2–4
  mistakes of bush leaguers, 11–12
  relationships as foundation of, 297–298
sales calls
  first and last memories of, 248
  memory and, 247–249
  pyramid of meeting success, 58–60
  vignettes, 33
sales cycles
  enemies of, 152, 201
  evolution of, 147
  expertise with, xi
  management of, 138–139
  phases of, 158–161
  premises of, 139–145
  quadrants of, 149–152
  qualifying an account, 145–148
  stages of, 156–157
  strategies of, 152–157

sales department structures, 203
sales iceberg analogy, 297
sales intuition. *See* intuition
sales management. *See* management
sales managers. *See* managers
sales organizations
  categories of information technology (IT), 164–169
  goals of, 9–10
  pain in, 166
  typical, 11
salespeople. *See* Heavy Hitters/ salespeople
sales teams, 50
sampling, 288
satisfaction, job, 212
sayings/clichés, 69–74
Schultz, George, 263
search loops (memory), 92
secondary representational systems, 73
seek strategy, 154–155
selection pressure, 255
self-actualization of Hitters, 211–213
sensory information, 247
sergeant management style, 195–196
seven-layer computer communication model, 17–18, 23. *See also* communication
short-term memory, 72, 93–94
sign language, 40
simulation technique, 289–290
skin color/tone, 114
softeners, 271
specificity of memories, 248
speech/speaking characteristics
  of Auditories, 111, 129–134
  congruence of, 133–134
  of Kinesthetics, 131, 132–133
  marking technique, 173–174, 179
  of Visuals, 130–132
split brain technique, 292–293
stages of sales cycle, 156–157
standards of communication, 16–17
standing conversations, 119

states of rapport and engagement,
181–183
strategies
adjusting sales styles, 231–234
for building relationships, 195
forming, 137
intuitive persuasion, 285
long-term, 191–192, 194, 198,
199–200
past management, 203
patient Pollyanna, 197
sales cycle, 138–139, 152–157
selecting, 97–98
styles of management, 191–192,
201–202
See also managers
styles of sales management. *See* management; managers
subconscious/conscious communication, 104, 280
subconscious mind, 56, 280
successes, 298, 299
successful salespeople. *See* Heavy
Hitters/salespeople
Sun Tzu, 161
sustain strategy, 155
system engineers, 49

T
team players, 208–209
team sales, 50
technical fit of an account, 146
technical peer groups, 29
technical specification language, 28–
29, 265
Teflon management style, 196–197
telesales/telemarketing, 50
themes of sales cycle, 159–161
trances, 182, 288, 294

transparent persuasion, 35–36
triangulation, 48–55, 77, 142–143,
144
triangulation diamond, 51–55,
142–143
triggers, 74
trust, achieving mutual, 58–59
truth, 107–108
truthfulness, 94–98

U
unique events, 248
unpleasant images, 248–249

V
VAK. *See* representational systems
value of Heavy Hitters, 213
values, motivation and, 224–227
vignettes, 31, 33, 252–256
visual/auditory/kinesthetic (VAK).
See representational systems
visualization, 72–73
Visuals
adjusting communication to, 38
eye contact of, 89
eye movements of, 88
hand movements of, 110–111
handshakes of, 109
speaking characteristics of, 130–132
See also representational systems

W
Walsh, Bill, 78
win-win relationships, 8–9
wiring. *See* representational systems
word selection, 36–37

Y
yawning, 128

About the Author

THE PERENNIAL top sales producer at a billion-dollar software company, Steve Martin has over twenty years of sales experience. As vice president of sales for the past five years, he has successfully trained his salespeople in the principles of Heavy Hitter Selling.

He began his career programming computers as a teenager in the 1970s. Programming made him acutely aware of the preciseness and structure of language and the importance of models, the verbal descriptions and visual representations of how systems work and processes flow. Models enable repeatable and predictable experiences.

At this time, Steve was introduced to the concepts of neurolinguistics—the study of how the human brain uses and interprets language. When he made a career transition into sales, he quickly realized that the language his customers used was directly related to their behavior. He found he could build models to create successful relationships based upon a customer's language, personality, and thought process. Without any prior sales experience, he became the top salesperson at his software company for the following four years.

Today, Steve is still an avid student of neurolinguistics and human nature during the sales cycle. After working with hundreds of salespeople and meeting thousands of customers, he still enjoys the exhilaration and satisfaction of a successful sales call.